CONTESTED LANDS

T. G. FRASER is emeritus professor at Ulster University and the author of *Chaim Weizmann: The Zionist Dream* (2009) and, with Andrew Mango and Robert McNamara, *The Makers of the Modern Middle East* (2015).

Contested Lands

A History of the Middle East from
the First World War to the Present

T. G. FRASER

First published in 2021 by
Haus Publishing Ltd
4 Cinnamon Row
London SW11 3TW

This paperback edition published 2024

A CIP catalogue record for this book is available from the British Library

The moral rights of the author have been asserted

ISBN 978-1-914979-07-1

Typeset in Garamond by MacGuru Ltd

Cartography produced by ML Design and Rhys Davies
Maps contain OS data © Crown copyright and database right (2020)

Printed in the United Kingdom by Clays Ltd (Elcograf S.p.A.)

www.hauspublishing.com
@HausPublishing

For my grandchildren,
Adam, Aidan, and Grace

Contents

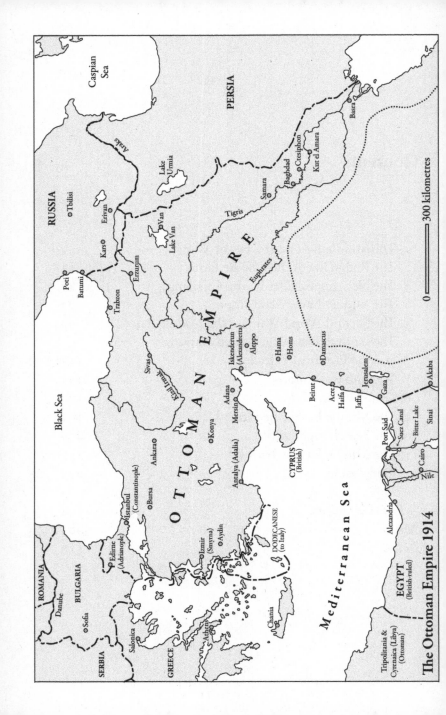

The Ottoman Empire 1914

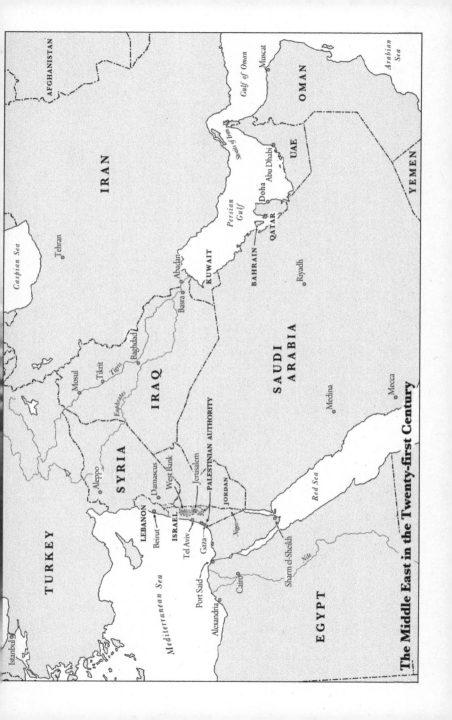

The Middle East in the Twenty-first Century

1

The Middle East on the Eve of War

The Middle East, as explored in this book, refers to the non-Turkish areas of the Ottoman Empire and their development in the century after the empire's collapse, together with the associated polities of the Arabian Peninsula and its coastal regions. In the summer of 1914, it is doubtful whether many people would have recognised the term Middle East; if they did, they would most likely have been unsure what part of the world it described. For most Europeans, especially those British who travelled to work, colonise, or garrison their eastern possessions, the region began and ended at Port Said, the northern point of entry into the Suez Canal. The term Far East was widely used, but that hardly applied to India, the 'jewel in England's crown'. From the late eighteenth century, the statesmen of Europe had been preoccupied with the Eastern Question, out of which emerged the term Near East, which was used in the United States to cover a swathe of countries from Morocco to Iran. In 1905, the distinguished Oxford archaeologist and sometime intelligence officer D. G. Hogarth entitled his study of the region *The Nearer East*, a concept which, he argued, included the Balkans, parts of which were still ruled from Istanbul and had some claims to an Islamic and Ottoman heritage.[1]

The region under discussion in this book possessed an enviable cultural heritage, had given rise to the world's three great Abrahamic religions, but in political terms in 1914 was subordinate to the rule of the Ottoman Turks, as it had been for four centuries. The First World War, with the defeat of Turkey, seemed to open up new possibilities for the peoples of the region; for a period, however, any political aspirations they might have held had to contend with the imperial ambitions of the victorious British and French who were working to their own agendas. As this chapter outlines, their uniliteral actions in carving out new political boundaries in the region were to have lasting consequences – even if their actual presence proved to be ephemeral.

The Ottoman Empire

The term Ottoman Empire, however, *was* generally recognised. In addition to the Turkish heartland of Anatolia, in 1914 the Ottoman Empire ruled, or claimed suzerainty, over extensive Arab lands from its capital in Istanbul as it had done for almost exactly four centuries. Until 1909, its head had been Sultan Abdülhamid II, who ruled from 1876 until he was overthrown by those discontented with his despotism. The empire was divided into vilayets, or provinces, each under an Ottoman governor-general and sub-divided into sanjaks. Four historic Arab cities of Aleppo, Baghdad, Cairo, and Damascus belonged, however nominally, to the empire, as did the holy cities of Islam – Mecca and Medina – and Jerusalem, which is sacred to the three great monotheistic faiths of Judaism, Christianity, and Islam. It was home, too, to the two holy cities of the Shi'a branch of Islam: Najaf and Karbala.[2] It was in the course of Britain's war with the Ottoman Empire in these areas that the term Middle East emerged in British usage, and since the British gained post-war hegemony in much of the region, albeit transiently, the descriptor Middle East gained favour. There have long been questions of inclusion or exclusion: do the terms Near East or Middle East take in North Africa, or Crete, or Iran, or Turkey? While relations with other regional powers, notably the Turkish republic, that emerged from the empire's ruins, and Iran, as Persia became in 1935, cannot be ignored, their affairs will only be treated when they impinge on the region under discussion.

By 1914, the Ottoman Empire had been shorn of its once extensive European territories – apart from a small enclave in Eastern Thrace, which enabled Istanbul to cling on as a European city, if only just. This long retreat had begun when the Turks failed in their siege of Vienna in 1683, continued as the Habsburg armies under their great general Prince Eugene expelled them from Hungary, and was completed with the rise of Balkan nationalism in the late nineteenth and early twentieth centuries. For the empire, the loss of these provinces enhanced the importance of its Middle Eastern lands, not least as a source of food.

The peoples of the empire

Of an estimated population of around twenty-seven million people, if Egypt is excluded, some seven million of the

Ottoman Empire's inhabitants were Arabs. If anything connected the Arabs to the Turks who had conquered them in the sixteenth century, it was the fact that the sultan was also the caliph, or successor, of the Prophet Muhammad. Like the Turks, most of the Arab population belonged to the Sunni or 'orthodox' form of Islam, this at a time when the empire seemed to be the last remaining political bulwark of the faith. This bond between rulers and ruled was less apparent among the Shi'a Muslim minorities, who formed much of the population in what was to become Iraq and had a significant presence in the future Lebanon and Syria. Meanwhile, the Turkish heartland's coastal regions of Anatolia were home to a large and thriving Greek Christian population. In the country's interior were the Christian Armenians and Sunni Muslim Kurds. The latter formed one of the largest minority communities in the empire, although their numbers were hard to judge since many were nomadic and they also had a substantial presence in Persia and, to a lesser extent, in Russia. Their post-war hopes for a Kurdish homeland were to be confounded.

Christians of various denominations could be found throughout the empire with some important enclaves, notably the Maronites around Mount Lebanon. The Maronites are a distinctive community. They have their own patriarch and rituals but also recognise the papacy and are in communion with the Roman Catholic Church. Maronite clergy were educated either in Rome or at the seminary of Saint-Sulpice in Paris, the latter reflecting their long-standing cultural links with France. There were also ancient Jewish communities, not just in the four holy cities of Jerusalem, Safed, Tiberias, and

Hebron but also in Baghdad, which had a long-established Jewish population of some 34,000. Smaller religious communities that had survived centuries of Sunni Muslim hegemony included the Alawites, Druze, and Yezidis. In short, this was a complex polity that required some skill in the art of government. An acknowledgement of this was the millet system, which devolved a certain level of autonomy to the minority monotheistic religions, including the Latin Catholic, Greek Orthodox, Armenian Catholic, Armenian Gregorian, Syrian and United Chaldean, Maronite, Protestant, and Jewish communities. The Ottoman Empire was not a theocratic state: despite the sultan's role as caliph, all religions and both genders enjoyed equality before the law.[3]

The economy

The region's population was united by their use of the Arabic language. Not only was it the language of the Holy Quran but it had long succeeded in supplanting its rivals as the means of universal communication. This was essentially a pre-industrial society in a region whose arid nature meant cultivable land was at a premium and fresh water was a precious commodity. The bedrock of the economy was subsistence agriculture, with the settled fellahin (peasants) growing wheat and barley, which had been the staples of life for millennia, in the winter and rice and millet in the summer. In addition to these customary staples, the region was famous for its olives and dates. Pastoral farming was almost entirely dependent on sheep and goats, equally prized for their meat, milk, and coats, and neither of which relied on abundant, lush pasture. The horse was a symbol of high social status, but it was the donkey that was used for travel and ploughing, while in the great desert areas, home to the nomadic Bedouin, all rested on the unique qualities of the camel. The Arab peasant farmers were passionately attached to their land but often their title to it was uncertain, little being owned outright. Much of it was common land, based on the *musha* system by which individual cultivators worked their holding under a two- or three-year grant. Such short-term tenancies did nothing to encourage farmers to make land improvements, although with economic life and educational opportunities largely the preserves of men, the woman's role was largely domestic and focused on the family.[4]

The empire's elites

Like other imperial rulers, the Turks were reliant on the cooperation of local elites whose power and influence rested upon the possession of urban and rural property, such as that attached to the *Waqf*, the Muslim charitable foundations devoted to religious purposes. These families were the *a'yam*, or notables, of Arab society, and included the Husseinis, Nashashibis, Khalidis, and Nusseibehs, who were subsequently to provide political and intellectual leadership to the Palestinians. By custom and tradition, the Husseinis held the influential office of mufti of Jerusalem, the chief Muslim Islamic legal religious authority. While in the not-too-distant past the Ottoman rulers had wished to curb the influence of such notable families, by the early twentieth century the *a'yam* had become a vital intermediary with the local populations and were made welcome in imperial circles in Istanbul.

In the overwhelmingly Shi'a vilayets of Baghdad and Basra, the leading families were Sunni. In what became Lebanon, powerful families among the Christian Maronites were the Gemayels and Frangiehs, while the Junblatts had emerged among the Druze. In the Hejaz region, the Hashemites enjoyed a category all their own. But interaction between such elite Arab families and the Turks was not confined to the local level; imperial Istanbul was a cosmopolitan city which attracted people from across the empire's diverse communities. At any one time, there were thousands of Arabs in the city, working in the bureaucracy, serving in the military, or conducting trade.

While these networks and linkages were significant in much of the empire's Arab heartland inland from the Mediterranean, they were much less so in the vilayets of Mosul, Baghdad, and Basra, which stretched along the Tigris and Euphrates rivers down to the Shatt al-Arab waterway at the head of the Gulf. Mosul in the north was predominantly Sunni and to that extent closer to Istanbul, but its population was divided between Kurds and Arabs. Baghdad, from where the Ottomans exercised military control of the region, was a sorry relic of what had in the Early Middle Ages been one of the richest and most cultivated cities in the world, rivalled only by Moorish Córdoba. The canals that had once provided water had fallen into disuse and, with no water-borne sewage system, the death rate was high, especially during the hot summer months. The governing elite was Sunni, but the mass of the population was Shi'a, so they did not look to the sultan as caliph of Islam but instead venerated their religious teachers in their holy cities of Najaf and Karbala.

European imperatives

Two developments threatened to bring even the relative backwater of Baghdad into the orbit of European imperial ambition. First, the realisation in the 1890s that there might be substantial oil reserves in south-west Persia led a British syndicate to petition the shah, who did not seem much interested, for a concession to exploit and export any oil that was found. Their activities proved so successful that they led to the establishment of the Anglo-Persian Oil Company in 1909 (it was later renamed British Petroleum). Soon after, the company constructed a great oil refinery at Abadan, which came into full production in 1913. In 1914, the British government, conscious of the need to have secure access to supplies for the Royal Navy's new oil-driven warships, acquired a majority shareholding in the company – but Abadan was perilously close to Ottoman territory, as events were to demonstrate.[5] The second development came in the wake of increasing German economic penetration of the Ottoman Empire. From 1893, this included the construction of a railway in Anatolia which, in 1899, a German-owned consortium requested to extend from Istanbul to the Gulf, the Baghdad Railway as it came to be known. The Germans emphasised that this was a purely commercial undertaking, but the British and French were not quite so sure. The railway, sanctioned by the Turks in 1903 but never completed, was little more than an additional piece of grit in Anglo-German relations, yet it signalled a growing relationship between Istanbul and Berlin.[6]

The position of the vilayet of Hejaz – with its headquarters at Taif, which lay along the Red Sea coast to the south of the Port of Aqaba – was even more peripheral and overwhelmingly barren. To its south was the vilayet of Yemen, whose tribes were in a state of semi-permanent revolt and whose inclusion within the empire was notional at best. The unique importance of the Hejaz lay in the fact that it contained the holy cities of Mecca and Medina, which are associated with the life of the Prophet Muhammad. The Ottoman writ rarely ran beyond the two cities. Indeed, it was in an attempt to link the territory more firmly to the rest of the empire and ease the problems of their garrisons that, in 1900, the authorities sanctioned the construction of the Hejaz Railway. But by 1908, its construction, which had reached as far as Medina, was brought to a halt. First among equals in the Hejaz were the Hashemites, whose head, Hussein bin Ali, born in 1853, was a descendant of the Prophet Muhammad. Well-versed in Islamic culture, he was appointed sherif, or guardian, of the Holy Places in 1908. This not only gave him an honoured place within the empire but provided him with a base should he ever wish to challenge the imperial rulers. As long as the sultan maintained the empire's Islamic character and his government was not too intrusive, Hussein bin Ali gave no obvious sign that he did.[7] But neither he nor the Ottomans exerted any authority in the Nejd in the peninsula's inhospitable interior where a young desert leader of political and military genius, Abdul Aziz ibn Saud, was steadily amassing the tribal support that would in time make him the founder of a country and a world figure.

A necklace of sheikhdoms around the rest of the peninsula's littoral formed a peripheral and unofficial part of the British imperial system. The exception was Aden, an important staging post on the route to India, which had been acquired in 1839 and was an outpost of the Indian Empire. Its strategic position at the entrance to the Red Sea assumed even greater importance with the opening of the Suez Canal. The sultanate of Muscat and Oman, with its long coastline on the Indian Ocean, had an ancient maritime trading tradition extending down the east African coast to Zanzibar. In an 1891 treaty, the sultan agreed not to cede any part of his territories to any other country than Britain, a pledge that seemed to satisfy the authorities in Calcutta and London.[8]

The sheikhdoms of the Gulf – of which Kuwait, Bahrain, and Qatar were the most significant – also retained their independence, but with one important difference. Under a series of treaties beginning in 1820 and ending with Kuwait in 1899 and Qatar in 1916, Britain progressively secured control of their foreign relations. By the early twentieth century, the Gulf and the Indian Ocean had thus clearly been marked as a British sphere of influence, important both strategically for the Royal Navy and for peaceful trading relations.

Egypt

Egypt merits special consideration, not least because in the late nineteenth century the balance of power over its affairs had shifted decisively from Istanbul to London. At the start of the nineteenth century, the country owed allegiance to the sultan, but over the course of the next 100 years this had become a fiction.

Key to understanding Egypt's unique role in world civilisation is the River Nile, which provides irrigation and carries rich alluvial soil from central Africa. On either side of the river lie the largely unproductive and seemingly unending Western and Eastern Deserts. But the fertility of the riverine strip itself and its delta underpinned the civilisation of the pharaohs; it made the country the so-called granary of the Roman Empire and, by the early twentieth century, the world's third-biggest cotton producer. By then, most of the country enjoyed a perennial irrigation system that freed it from dependence on annual inundation, enabling the production of three crops a year. Such a system, with its intricate networks of canals and sluices, relied upon the skill and hard work of the peasant farmer to operate and maintain it. The rice, wheat, barley, and millet they produced sustained a settled population estimated in the 1907 census at 11,189,978. Egypt was home, in addition, to some 97,381 nomadic Bedouin. With a population of 654,476, Cairo was the largest city in Africa, and its Al-Azhar University is the Islamic world's premier seat of learning. Though an overwhelmingly Sunni Muslim country, Egypt's population also contained 880,000 Coptic Christians. The second city, Alexandria, with 400,000 inhabitants, many of them Greek and Italian, had established itself as a major trading port. While the Nile remained the principal means of transport, the railway network linked Cairo with Alexandria and Port Said and reached southwards to Luxor with its incomparable monuments.[9]

But Egypt's position had long made it attractive to others. In 1517, the country had been conquered by the Turks, and it was not until the aftermath of Napoleon Bonaparte's brief Egyptian adventure in 1798–9 that the country had begun to free itself. The man who set out to transform and modernise the country was a former Ottoman officer of Balkan origin, Muhammad Ali, who dominated its affairs from 1805 until his death in 1849. Such were his achievements that in 1841 the sultan gave him the hereditary, although by no means unfettered, title of viceroy, thus establishing a dynasty that lasted until the 1952 revolution. Unfortunately, his immediate successors lacked his steel and proved unable to withstand the driving ambition of the Frenchman Ferdinand de Lesseps, whose vision and expertise were to transform Egypt's affairs.

The Suez Canal

De Lesseps's project in Egypt, the digging of a canal linking the Mediterranean to the Red Sea, was not new, but its excavation had been hampered by the belief that there were different water levels at each end, necessitating an expensive system of locks. But when this was shown in the 1830s not to be the case, the project could move forward unconstrained. Untrained as an engineer, de Lesseps proved to be a master of the art of negotiation, securing finance through the creation in 1858 of the Suez Canal Company, whose headquarters were in Paris, and the necessary concession from Viceroy Muhammad Said, who died in the course of the canal's construction. In 1866, Muhammad Said's successor, Ismail, was granted the coveted title of khedive by the sultan. The khedive's holding in the company was 176,602 out of 400,000 ordinary shares, safeguarding, it seemed, Egypt's position.

Opposition to the canal was to be expected, not least from the British, who were wary of French presence across their line of communication to India. Nevertheless, construction began in 1859. It initially used forced Egyptian labour, but this was ended in 1863 and replaced by modern mechanical methods, which accelerated construction. By 1869, the 120-mile-long waterway linking the two seas was ready. Its opening was marked by lavish ceremonies financed by Ismail, his guest of honour being a relative of de Lesseps: Empress Eugénie de Montijo of the French. On 17 November, the empress in her imperial yacht entered the northern entrance to the canal at Port Said at the head of a convoy of over forty vessels, followed by Emperor Franz Joseph of Austria with three Austro-Hungarian warships. Subsequent beneficiaries of the canal were to include the Habsburg port of Trieste and the Austrian Lloyd shipping line, which was able to develop services to India and the Far East. Two Prussian ships carried their crown prince, Frederick. The prince and princess of Holland were there, too, their country having a rich empire in the East Indies. More prosaically, however, Britain was represented by its ambassador.[10]

The khedive was anxious to put Egypt on the Western cultural map. The canal's opening was accompanied by the first performances at Cairo's new opera house where Giuseppe Verdi's *Rigoletto* was staged. Not content with this, Ismail contacted Verdi, one of the greatest composers of his time, with the proposal that he write an opera with an Egyptian theme. The result on 24 December 1871 was the first performance at the Cairo Opera House of one of the grandest of grand operas, *Aida*, with its spectacular evocation of pharaonic Egypt.[11] Ismail was opening up his country to the influences of Europe, but at a cost.

It was Egypt's fate that the completion of the canal came at the high point of European imperial expansion. It came, too, at a time when Ismail's spending was crippling the country's finances. Britain's initially tepid attitude towards the canal was changing, not least because it was soon clear that the bulk of the ships navigating it were British. Important as commercial considerations were, though, the key to Britain's interest was to be found in the so-called Great Game of empire, in which Britain constantly feared that its Indian empire was under threat of Russia's advance through central Asia towards the North-West Frontier. Should such a conflict develop, Britain could reinforce its Indian armies much more quickly via the Suez Canal than by the Cape Route. The same would hold true if Britain were to face a repeat of the Indian Rebellion of 1857, the memory of which was raw. By 1875, Ismail's only hope of financial survival was to sell his shares in the Suez Canal Company. Despite considerable misgivings in Britain the opportunity was grasped by Prime Minister Benjamin Disraeli, who bought the khedive's holdings for £4 million. While Disraeli does not seem to have intended a direct British interest in Egypt's affairs by doing so, before long that turned out to be the reality. selling the Suez Canal shares could not save Ismail, who was deposed in 1879, being succeeded by his son Tewfik.

British rule in Egypt

It was only to be expected that the European presence in the country, which had been steadily growing since Muhammad Ali's time, would provoke a reaction among Egyptians. In 1881–2, Colonel Ahmed Urabi led a military rising and became war minister. The dispatch of an Anglo-French naval force to Alexandria triggered serious rioting in the city and an Egyptian declaration of war. Tewfik's appeal to the British and French for assistance was the green light for them to act in his name, although only the former did, bombarding the city. In August 1882, British troops landed at the canal, defeating Urabi's army at the Battle of Tel al-Kebir in September and consigning him to exile in Ceylon, now Sri Lanka. Eventually allowed to return, Urabi died in Cairo in 1911, but the support he had mustered showed the strength of feeling among Egyptians that the country should not become a European possession; indeed, it did not become so until it was proclaimed a protectorate in 1914. Nevertheless, after the battle, its affairs were dominated by the British just the same. The popular contemporary slogan 'Cape to Cairo' told its own story of imperial ambition.

From the time of Sir Garnet Wolseley's victory over Urabi at Tel al-Kebir, no part of the British imperial system – for such was the reality – was more paradoxical than Egypt. Understandably reluctant to acquiesce in the loss of their richest province, the Ottomans clung to the principle, although not the reality, of suzerainty. Egypt still had its khedive, with elements of constitutional government. It also raised an army of some 18,000, albeit under British command. With remarkable candour, the secretary of state for foreign affairs, Lord

Granville, spelled out the new reality to his European counterparts on 3 January 1883: British troops were in Egypt but
would be withdrawn once the state of the country permitted;
Britain's role in Egypt was to give advice, or so it seemed. The
following year, Granville confirmed to the newly appointed
British agent and consul general, Sir Evelyn Baring (later
Lord Cromer), that he could dismiss any minister or governor who did not follow that advice. Baring, who held this
position from 1883 until 1907, was thus the real ruler of the
country, assisted by some 1,252 British officials and brooking
no opposition. The British encouraged various projects that
benefited Egyptian agriculture, especially the cultivation of
cotton as a cash crop, but perhaps the most dramatic of these
undertakings was the completion in 1902 of the barrage at
Aswan on the Nile, which it was hoped would help regu-
late the river's inundations. Egyptians, who had experienced increasing independence since Muhammad Ali's time,
resented this British tutelage, and a serious outbreak of discontent surfaced in 1893–4.

After the relatively brief period in office of Baring's successor, Sir Eldon Gorst, the post was given to General Lord
Kitchener of Khartoum in 1911, who held it until August
1914 when he was appointed secretary of state for war with
the rank of field marshal on the outbreak of the First World
War. Kitchener was the imperial soldier *sans pareil*, having
served for years in the region and commanded the Egyptian
Army at the decisive victory of Omdurman in the Sudan in
1898. He had also succeeded his fellow Anglo-Irishman Lord
Roberts as commander-in-chief during the South African
War, where he acquired a reputation for ruthlessness, and

then from 1902 to 1909 serving as commander-in-chief in India where he set in hand important army reforms. No less imperious than Cromer, his relationship with Khedive Abbas Hilmi II was abrasive. But with his long experience of Egypt and the Sudan and immense prestige at home, Kitchener was to prove an important intermediary between Britain and the Arabs as war threatened Europe in 1914.[12]

The Holy Land

So much of the post-1918 history of the Middle East was to be taken up with the affairs of Palestine that, like Egypt, it demands special attention. Administratively, no such place existed in the Ottoman Empire, the area falling partly under the vilayet of Beirut and the independent sanjak of Jerusalem. Still, the term Palestine was used widely in Europe and the United States, while to the Arabs it was Filastin. To the Jews it was Eretz Israel, the Land of Israel, and the homeland from which they had been expelled by the Romans. Also known as the Holy Land, Jews, Christians, and Muslims venerated the city of Jerusalem. Within the walled city was the Church of the Holy Sepulchre, for many Christians the traditional site of Christ's crucifixion and resurrection. Close by was what Jews call the Temple Mount and Muslims the Haram al-Sharif, or Noble Sanctuary. For the former, this was the site of the Temples of Solomon and Herod, where the Holy of Holies was located and which had been destroyed by the Romans, leaving standing only the Western Wall to remind them of their loss. For Muslims, it houses the sacred mosque of al-Aqsa and the Dome of the Rock as well as being the place from where they believe the Prophet Muhammad made his journey to heaven, having been transported there from Mecca.

The origins of Zionism

The population of this area was believed to be around 600,000, the vast majority of whom were Sunni Muslim Arabs but also with an Arab Christian and an old-established religious Jewish minority. From Roman times, the Jewish experience had been that of the diaspora or dispersion, both in the Middle East, where they generally were accorded a measure of tolerance, or in Europe, where they were not. The majority of the world's Jewish population lived within the boundaries of the Russian Empire, where they had long been confined to the Pale of Settlement region, characteristically living in small towns called *shtetls* and often subject to various forms of discrimination. Worse still were the periodic anti-Jewish riots, the pogroms. Although the position of the Jews in much of western and central Europe improved appreciably in the course of the nineteenth century, this was far from true of the Russian Empire. In 1881, Tsar Alexander II was assassinated in Saint Petersburg by a small group of revolutionaries, one of whom was a young Jewish woman. The murder triggered the anti-Jewish May Laws the following year, which placed Jews under even more severe restrictions. The result was a mass emigration of Jews to Austria-Hungary, Britain, and, overwhelmingly, to the United States.

But for a minority of Russian Jews there was a different path. Calling themselves Hibbat Zion, or the Love of Zion, they made their way to Palestine and established a group of agricultural settlements. The settlements struggled initially and might well have foundered but for the financial assistance of the French philanthropist Baron Edmond de Rothschild, with whose help and advice wine and citrus production were established. Their work proved to be the precursor of political Zionism, inspired in part by the Viennese journalist Theodor Herzl. Herzl had seen the growth of anti-Semitism both in the Austro-Hungarian capital Vienna with the rise of the anti-Semitic mayor Karl Lueger and in Paris at the time of the Dreyfus affair, which saw a Jewish officer falsely convicted of betraying military secrets. Despairing of the Jewish future in Europe, in 1896 Herzl published a pamphlet, *Der Judenstaat* (*The Jewish State*), in which he argued that the Jewish people needed their own nation state, either in Argentina or Palestine, and an organisation to bring it into being. His views were at variance with those of assimilationist Jews in western and central Europe, but they garnered vehement support from others, especially in the Russian Empire. The following year, Herzl convened the First Zionist Congress at Basle in Switzerland, the avowed purpose of which was the creation of a home for the Jewish people in Palestine. Although he died in 1904, other Jews were already taking up the work, fostering the use of the Hebrew language and purchasing land. Then, in 1909, the construction of a new city to the north of Jaffa began: Tel Aviv. How the Turks and Arabs would react to the growth of the Zionist venture was still a matter for conjecture in 1914.[13]

Arab politics and the Young Turks

The critical question on the eve of war was thus how the

relationship between the Turks and their Arab subjects would develop. Arab nationalism should not be seen through the lens of its European counterpart, although there were some elements in common. European nationalists were inspired by a pride in their nations' (sometimes invented) past; similarly, Arabs could look back on the centuries when their civilisation was at its zenith. But there was an evident need for modernisation in the Middle East. Arab nationalism had no one source, but the key ingredient seems to lie in the politicisation of small, elite, educated groups – both Muslim and Christian – in Damascus and Beirut. Their main demand was for increasing autonomy within the Ottoman Empire.[14] The need for change was also stirring among Turks. In 1908, there was an abrupt change in the politics of the empire, with the successful revolution of the Committee of Union and Progress (CUP), commonly known as the Young Turks. Its leaders – the Three Pashas – comprised two young army officers, Enver and Cemal, and a civilian, Talat. Under their leadership there was a drive to modernise the empire, not least its armed forces, with the Germans advising the army, the British the navy, and the French the gendarmerie. Alongside modernisation came 'Turkification', a manifestation of Turkish nationalism in which Arabs felt they were becoming second-class citizens. Although many Arabs, including journalists and politicians, voiced their opposition to the CUP's policies, there was as yet no strong evidence of a desire to break up the empire. Enver and his colleagues in the CUP remained firmly in control. Then, in the autumn of 1914, they would make a series of decisions that would change the Middle East forever as the Great Power rivalries of Europe found their echo in the region.

2

The Remaking of the Middle East

Enver's government had been edging steadily closer to Germany over the summer of 1914 as the crisis in Europe developed and war broke out. On 2 August 1914, the day after Germany opened hostilities with Russia, the two countries had concluded a secret treaty of alliance. This rather curious agreement was to come into operation in the event of Russian military intervention, which would give Germany a *casus foederis* with regard to Austria-Hungary and which would also apply to the Ottoman Empire. The Germans promised to make their military advisers available to the Ottoman Empire and to defend the empire's territory. The war that was unfolding sprang from rival European alliance systems and ethnic tensions that were of no concern to the non-Turkish peoples of the Ottoman Empire, but the effects of the conflict on their future were to be profound.

The Ottoman Empire and the war

Berlin and Istanbul were evidently on the same track by August, although the Ottoman Empire would not enter the war for another few months. Two events encouraged the relationship. Two Ottoman battleships, the *Reshadieh* and *Sultan Osman I*, which had been financed through public subscription and were being built in British shipyards, were requisitioned for the Royal Navy, arousing strong resentment throughout the Ottoman Empire. On 10 August, Germany's Mediterranean squadron, the powerful battlecruiser *Goeben* and the light cruiser *Breslau*, sailed into the Dardanelles, their commander, Admiral Wilhelm Souchon, having skillfully outfoxed his British pursuers. The two ships with their German crews were immediately acquired by the Ottomans, tangibly strengthening their link with Germany and offering fortuitous compensation for the two ships lost to the British. War was triggered in the Middle East on 29 October 1914 when the two Ottoman warships under the command of the German admiral Souchon – *Yavuz Sultan Selim* and *Midilli* as they had been renamed – bombarded the Russian Black Sea ports of Odessa, Sevastopol, Theodosia, and Novorossiysk. War with Russia's allies, Britain and France, followed on 5 November. Enver and his colleagues had committed the empire to the cause of Germany and Austria-Hungary.[1]

In aligning themselves with Berlin and Vienna, the CUP leaders had almost certainly been prompted by the long-standing Ottoman fear of Russian intentions. Beyond that, it is not clear what they were hoping to achieve. In reality, they had placed the empire's future at risk, staking everything on an Austro-German victory. That their future was now an Allied war aim became apparent as early as 9 November 1914 when, in a speech at London's Guildhall, Prime Minister H. H. Asquith raised the question of the empire's future, although the nature of Allied thinking emerged in piecemeal, and ultimately contradictory, ways.[2] Although the Ottoman soldiers were to prove formidable fighters, the empire's economic and technological infrastructure lagged far behind those of the other combatants. Both the Ottomans and the Allies moved quickly to consolidate their positions. On 14 November, the sultan issued a fatwa proclaiming jihad, or holy war, against Britain, France, and Russia. Among other things, the fatwa was intended to raise disaffection among the extensive Muslim populations in the three empires, but its effect was negligible. In India, the influential Muslim leader Nizam of Hyderabad issued a *firman* in favour of the Allies. Indeed, to have any real effect, the fatwa needed an endorsement from Mecca, but the sherif, Hussein bin Ali, refused to provide this, plausibly arguing that to do so would be an endorsement of an alliance with Christian Germany.

Egypt and the war

Anticipating a likely Ottoman attack on the Suez Canal, the British wasted no time in consolidating their position in Egypt with a series of unilateral actions that removed any flicker of doubt as to who ruled the country. On 18 December, Egypt's last residual link with Istanbul was broken: the nation was made a protectorate under the British Crown. Khedive Abbas Hilmi II, who had clearly resented the interference of Cromer and Kitchener, was immediately deposed in favour of the more pliant Hussein Kemal, the former khedive's uncle, who was elevated to the title of sultan. The title and role of agent and consul-general became what in reality it always had been: high commissioner. With thousands of imperial troops, mostly Indians, Australians, and New Zealanders as well as British, mustering in the country, Egyptians could only watch and wait.

The canal was an obvious objective for the Ottoman military governor and commander of the Fourth Army in Syria, Cemal Pasha. One of the original triumvirate of leading Young Turks, Cemal had as an adviser an able German officer, Colonel Friedrich Kress von Kressenstein, and believed that seizing the canal would lead to a general uprising against the British in the country. In January 1915, some 20,000 men of the Fourth Army, mainly Arab in composition, began their advance across the Sinai, their objective being to cross the canal and seize the key town of Ismailia on Lake Timsah. Defence of the canal was largely in the hands of Indian troops who had been held there on their way to reinforce the Western Front. Cemal's attack was launched on the night of 2–3 February but floundered and was immediately repulsed, leading to his retreat back across the Sinai. Britain's imperial lifeline for the passage of Indian, Australian, and New Zealand troops was thus secured. It was never again to be in serious danger from the Ottomans, although in the summer of 1916 Kressenstein made two other equally forlorn attempts. What's more, the Egyptian population had not rebelled – their discontent over Britain's unilateral actions notwithstanding – leaving the authorities free to develop the country as a major military base.[3]

Cemal's rule in Syria

If Cemal was denied military glory, he was soon to acquire a reputation of a very different kind. Back in Damascus, he faced an increasingly restive population. The Syrians were no more immune to the sense of war weariness than the Europeans: victory seemed elusive, and the war effort made increasing demands. Taxes on staples were increased, and much-needed animals were commandeered for the army. Egyptians were experiencing similar problems, but while their discontent could focus on the British, in Syria it was directed against the Ottomans. Cemal's consequent repression inevitably fell on those Arabs, including parliamentarians and journalists, who had emerged as critics of the CUP's policies before the war. His first eleven victims were hanged in Beirut on 20 August 1915. The following May, a further twenty-one executions were carried out in Beirut and Damascus, the latter in public. Condemned by Cemal as traitors, they quickly became martyrs in the eyes of their fellow Arabs, undermining for many of them any residual loyalty to the empire. The Jews were spared some of the worst of his intentions – partly because the Germans wanted to avoid alienating Jewish opinion – but even so Cemal expelled over 11,000. Most of them went to Egypt where they formed the Zion Mule Corps to assist the British, as they had during the Allies' disastrous Gallipoli offensive. Compounding the area's problems were famine, caused by the war's inevitable economic disruption, and the need to accommodate thousands of impoverished Armenians who fled there after the massacres of 1915.[4]

Allied war aims

In April 1915, Asquith directed a committee under the experienced diplomat Sir Maurice de Bunsen to explore possible British options in the event of a defeated Ottoman Empire. A broad pattern of official thinking began to emerge, although victory was a long way off and much was to change before it could be achieved. Britain's essential aim, it was thought, should be to secure its oil supplies by acquiring the whole of Mesopotamia from Basra to Mosul and with a corridor to Haifa on the Mediterranean coast. Russia would realise its longstanding ambition to acquire the straits of the Bosphorus and the Dardanelles, while French interests in the districts of Damascus and Beirut would be recognised. Gaining these areas had become the ambition of a pressure group, the Comité de l'Asie française, which had long fretted over the extent of Britain's imperial possessions. What's more, France had seen itself as a guarantor of the interests of the Catholic Church in the region. As the Comité saw it, the three Christian allies would share the protection of Protestant, Catholic, and Orthodox interests in Palestine – but, it would seem, not those of Muslims or Jews. While the British committee's deliberations, completed in July, had no immediate impact, they would surface in the work of one of its members, Sir Mark Sykes, the young Conservative MP for Central Hull, who had actually been to the Middle East.[5]

War with the Ottoman Empire undoubtedly posed a military problem for Britain in that it needed to secure major strategic interests in Egypt and Persia. In addition, as the war went on, the possibility of acquiring other imperial assets was opening up. But Britain, which had undertaken a land war in Europe for which it was almost culpably underprepared, was hard pressed to find the means of fighting the Ottomans as well. In August 1914, Germany attacked in Belgium and France with some 1.5 million men. The British Expeditionary Force of regular soldiers, in contrast, had an initial strength of 90,000 organised in four infantry divisions and one of cavalry. The sole home reserve was the Territorial Army, part-time volunteers who would only start reaching the front in the spring of 1915. The only available immediate reinforcements were the regular soldiers of the Indian Army, two infantry divisions, and a cavalry brigade who began to deploy in Europe just in time to help sustain their British comrades through the murderous Battle of Ypres in October and November. In brief, there was little to spare for a war in the Middle East.

Gallipoli and Mesopotamia

The hard military realities behind the Allies' position on the Western Front is an essential context for Britain's military and diplomatic actions in the Middle East in the years that followed. Attention has inevitably focused on the gallant but fatally flawed Gallipoli campaign. On 25 April 1915, Allied troops landed on the Gallipoli Peninsula, the immediate purpose being to dominate the straits of the Dardanelles and Bosphorus after a naval attempt had been called off following a considerable loss of warships. Control of the straits would have given the Allies an opportunity to capture Istanbul, possibly forcing the Ottoman Empire out of the war and taking pressure off the hard-pressed Russians. The combined

British, Australian, New Zealand, Indian, and French forces
– eventually numbering some 110,000 – fought heroically.
But so did the Ottomans. In January 1916, the last of the
expeditionary force was evacuated.[6] The costly Allied failure
at Gallipoli marked a major success for the Ottomans.

Britain's other military move against the Ottomans began
more successfully. As Ottoman intentions became increasingly uncertain in the autumn of 1914, on 10 October Brigadier-General W. S. Delamain was sent secret instructions
from the Indian city of Shimla to have his 16th (Poona)
Infantry Brigade of the 6th (Poona) Division ready to
protect British interests at the head of the Gulf. Having positioned itself in Bahrain, the Indo-British force landed at the
Shatt al-Arab waterway on 6 November, capturing the provincial capital of Basra on the 21st. With the arrival of the
two remaining brigades, the division was up to strength and
well able to thwart Ottoman counter-attacks. Accompanying Delamain's command as its chief political officer was Sir
Percy Cox, a veteran Indian administrator who had served as
political resident and consul-general in the Gulf from 1904
to 1913. So far this had been a limited operation that had succeeded in securing Britain's key oil installations at Abadan
just over the Persian border. In the spring of 1915, the arrival
of three further Indian infantry brigades permitted the creation of the 12th Indian Division which, together with the
6th Division, now constituted the II Indian Army Corps.

But the 12th was a hastily constructed formation, short
of essential equipment. Lack of adequate medical provision in a land of extreme temperatures and poor sanitation
meant that dysentery was widespread in the corps. These

shortcomings were compounded as the 12th advanced up the Tigris, reaching Kut al-Amara by September 1915. The decision was taken that, under the command of Major-General Charles Townshend, the 6th Division should take Baghdad. Victories were hard to come by, and capturing the city might help compensate for the defeat at Gallipoli. But, in reality, Baghdad had no strategic significance, and the logistical base for a successful campaign was totally inadequate: Basra was 500 miles away from the front; its port facilities were too underdeveloped to sustain a modern offensive. A lack of roads meant that supplies had to come along the Tigris, but there were not enough riverboats, meaning that of the 200 tons of the everyday supplies Townshend's division needed, only 150 tons arrived. On 22–25 November 1915, Townshend defeated the Turks at the Battle of Ctesiphon, but in doing so he lost 4,500 men. Forced to retreat to Kut, Townshend put his division in a state of siege. Costly relief attempts were defeated and, on 29 April 1916, he was forced to surrender with 13,309 Indian and British of his command, including over 3,000 Indian non-combatants, some 4,000 of whom were fated to die in captivity. Kut was the worst British military disaster since the retreat from Kabul in 1842, delivering a devastating blow to imperial prestige.[7]

Britain and the Hashemites

This catalogue of military failures forms the backdrop to other measures that Britain was undertaking against the Ottomans. Disaffected groups were widely exploited in the war – sometimes highly successfully, as Allied encouragement of the Czechs and some South Slavs was to demonstrate, and sometimes not, as the Germans discovered in their attempts to mobilise Indian revolution. If Arab discontent against the Ottomans was to be fomented, the obvious leader for the Allies to cultivate was the Hashemite Guardian of the Holy Places, Sherif Hussein, who for some time had been cannily inching towards the British.

While he had many claims to leadership, Sherif Hussein's appeal in the wider region was not universal: neither the Shi'as nor the Christians were likely to be attracted by his role within Sunni Islam, while the Egyptians had a sense of the superiority of their own civilisation over that of the desert. Crucially, however, Hussein had been edging away from the Ottomans. He seems to have been content with Sultan Abdülhamid II but, in common with Arabs elsewhere, he was increasingly uneasy at the policies of the CUP. Realising that the building of the Hejaz Railway meant the consolidation of Ottoman control, Hussein resolutely opposed its extension beyond Medina. The city had a strong military garrison, and the appointment of an assertive governor, Vehid Bey, in 1914 seemed a portent of Ottoman intentions towards the Hejaz, possibly including Hussein's deposition. It thus seems no coincidence that Hussein's second son, the Emir Abdullah, paid two exploratory visits to Cairo in February and April 1914. In light of the increasing Ottoman pressure, Abdullah explored in a somewhat oblique manner with Kitchener and his recently appointed oriental secretary Ronald Storrs what British attitudes might be towards his father, even suggesting, somewhat implausibly, making him a present of machine guns. This tentative Hashemite initiative was formally rebuffed, but an opening gambit had been offered, alerting Kitchener and Storrs to a possibility that might be developed in the event of war.

Although it diminished with time, the authority enjoyed by Kitchener in the early months of the war was surpassed by no other public figure: his picture became a national icon as tens of thousands of young men volunteered for what became known as Kitchener's Army. At the suggestion of Storrs, in September 1914, Kitchener sent a message to Abdullah to test what his family's attitude would be if war with the Ottoman Empire broke out. The response was that Hussein would not support the Ottomans if Britain gave an assurance that it would not interfere in the internal affairs of Arabia. This reply reached London after the outbreak of war. Kitchener replied, with government approval, giving such an assurance if what he called 'the Arab nation' came into the war, adding that the caliphate might come to Mecca or Medina. Hussein replied that he was not in a position to move for some time, but that he did intend to break with the Ottoman Empire. The possibility of Hashemite–British collaboration, however tentatively, had thus advanced one stage further. Until this could happen, the British were taking measures intended to foster Arab goodwill, signalling support for an Arab caliphate and their assistance in gaining independence.

The McMahon–Hussein correspondence

In December 1914, Sir Henry McMahon was appointed as the first British high commissioner in Egypt. McMahon's entire service had been in India where, in 1913–14, he had been instrumental in demarcating its border with Tibet, the McMahon Line as it was known. But he was unversed in the intricacies of the Middle East, and he was about to engage in one of the most crucial negotiations in its modern history. Fortunately, experienced hands were available for him to draw on: Storrs, who was still oriental secretary in Cairo, had been the principal conduit between the British authorities and the Hashemites, and the newly appointed director of intelligence, Captain Gilbert Clayton, was an artilleryman by training; he had seen action at the Battle of Omdurman before transferring to the Egyptian Army.

This ambitious group was soon joined by other young men, including the archaeologist T. E. Lawrence, who had excavated on a number of sites in Ottoman territory prior to the war under the guidance of the leading Middle East scholar D. G. Hogarth, keeper of the Ashmolean Museum in Oxford. An amateur soldier, Lawrence was to achieve undying fame as Lawrence of Arabia for his exploits in the Arab revolt. In 1915, the group was joined by the veteran Hogarth, now a lieutenant-commander in the Royal Naval Volunteer Reserve, who became head of the newly created Arab Bureau. Working under Clayton's overall ambit, Hogarth's bureau was to serve both as a source of pro-Allied propaganda and a means of monitoring Arab sentiment. It was at Hogarth's recommendation that, in December 1915, Gertrude Bell came to Cairo. Bell had an intimate knowledge of Arabia, her travels there being recognised in 1918 by the Founder's Medal of the Royal Geographical Society. After working in Cairo, Bell went to Basra in the Mesopotamian theatre of operations where she was to remain for the rest of the war and beyond. A well-informed team, devoted to the British Empire but engaged with the Arab world, their legacy for the Middle East was to be far reaching.

Their immediate task was to translate into action the promising feelers that had been exchanged with Hussein. The sherif was too old to lead a military campaign, while Abdullah, pivotal to the contacts so far, was a diplomat rather than a soldier. The potential military role fell to Hussein's third son, Emir Feisal. Feisal, too, had to act warily, and he visited Istanbul for assurance that the government had not been planning his father's deposition. stopping in Damascus on his return journey, he made contact with Syrian nationalists. The protocol that came out of this meeting made support for the British and a revolt contingent upon independence of all the Arab areas in the empire. With Syria firmly in Cemal's grip, the document lacked substance – but it offered a clue about nationalist hopes and intentions. The mission also signalled Feisal's increasing prominence.

By the summer of 1915, the British were forced to come to terms with their floundering campaign in Gallipoli. Judging that the time had come to make his move, Hussein wrote to McMahon on 14 July. In essence, his letter asserted his claim for an independent nation uniting the whole Arab area, with the exception of Aden, and the creation of an Arab caliphate. Replying on 30 August, McMahon temporised, confirming Britain's support for Arab independence as given by Kitchener but refusing to be drawn on the question of borders. Then, on 24 October 1915, assisted by Clayton and in consultation with Sir Edward Grey, secretary of state for foreign affairs, McMahon appeared to give Hussein the substance of what he wanted: the central assurance was that, subject to certain modifications, 'Great Britain is prepared to recognise and support the independence of the Arabs in all regions within the limits demanded by the Sherif of Mecca'.[8] The modifications were the exclusion of Mersina and Alexandretta and the recognition of Britain's need to secure its defensive and economic interests in the vilayets of Baghdad and Basra. Hussein was willing to concede the former and negotiate over the latter. Much more contentious, at the time and later, was McMahon's assertion that 'portions of Syria lying to the west of the districts of Damascus, Homs, Hama and Aleppo cannot be said to be purely Arab and should be excluded from the limits demanded'.[9] Hussein's view was that these were Arab areas in which Muslims and Christians had a common heritage and would be treated equally.

McMahon's letter of 24 October had thus served its purpose in opening the way for the subsequent Arab Revolt, but it was to cause controversy. Part of this controversy turned on the meaning of 'independence', which the Arabs interpreted as a pledge of support for an independent Arab kingdom, a promise that had real significance in their society. Then there was the question of Palestine, which had not yet been mentioned but would soon come to the fore. Both McMahon and Clayton subsequently claimed that they had intended to exclude Palestine from the proposed Arab kingdom, but they were arguing post hoc, and at the time the Arabs saw no reason to question its inclusion. While McMahon's letter of 24 October was not an actual treaty, it did set out in broad terms how Britain saw the region's future at that time.[10]

The Sykes–Picot Agreement

As these contacts were maturing, discussions of a very different nature were taking place in another forum, and they were to influence the way the Middle East would emerge. What was at stake was nothing less than how essential British and French interests could be reconciled and safeguarded once victory had been achieved. The negotiations were conducted by two men, both of whom had claims to knowledge of the region. France's ambitions were in the hands of François Georges-Picot, a partisan of the pro-colonial lobbying group Comité de l'Asie française and the son of an eminent historian. Prior to the war, he had briefly been consul-general in Beirut in 1914 before joining the London embassy. In his hasty departure from Beirut, Georges-Picot had entrusted his US colleague with secret papers relating to his Syrian contacts. When these documents were discovered by Cemal, they led to a number of executions of Syrian activists.

His British counterpart was Mark Sykes, who had travelled widely in the region and had written three books about the Ottoman Empire. Negotiations between the pair began in November 1915. Georges-Picot was adamant over French claims to Syria, while Sykes's priority was Mesopotamia. They agreed that Britain should control the districts of Baghdad and Basra but not Mosul, while France would have the coastal areas of what became Syria and Lebanon. In addition, Britain and France were to recognise an independent Arab state or states, as set out in a map, in which they would have their own direct or indirect administration. Palestine was to have an international administration, while Arabia was not mentioned. The Sykes–Picot Agreement, as it came to be known, was conveyed by Edward Grey to the French ambassador on 16 May 1916. It was, in essence, a blueprint for partition and, for the time being, a secret.[11]

Feisal, Lawrence, and the Arab Revolt

Ever prudent, Hussein did not launch his revolt until 5 June 1916. But, given the British defeats at Gallipoli and Kut, perhaps the time was not exactly auspicious. It also did not help that Hussein's cause was not widely supported outside his immediate territory. Cemal's ruthlessness precluded any rising in Syria. There was no mass desertion from the Arab units of the Ottoman Army. Instead, under the command of the three brothers, Abdullah, Ali, and Feisal, was a force of several thousand Arab irregulars, brave fighters but untrained in modern warfare, who were opposed by an Ottoman army that had already shown its military qualities. An early attack on Medina was beaten off by its strong Ottoman garrison. The man who had done so much to promote the revolt did not live to see fruits of his work: the day of the revolt, Kitchener drowned when HMs *Hampshire* taking him to Russia hit a mine off the Orkney Islands.

In an attempt to gauge the strength of the revolt, Storrs and Lawrence travelled to the Hejaz in October to meet the Hashemites. Having met Abdullah and Ali, Lawrence was in no doubt that the future of the rising lay with Feisal, later recording that he immediately identified that this man would be the leader of the Arab Revolt. He also saw the Arab forces for himself, realising that they were essentially a collection of individual fighters under tribal leaders who could not be welded into an organised army. While Lawrence did not believe that the Arabs could prevail against entrenched Ottoman troops, he recognised other important qualities: their mobility and skilled musketry made them ideal for a guerrilla campaign. These perceptions were to form the basis of the strategy and tactics that Feisal and Lawrence would pursue. The meeting between the two men also laid the foundations of the subsequent relationship they were to form. Lawrence's autobiographical account of what followed, *Seven Pillars of Wisdom*, may be ranked with the *Anabasis* as a classic of its kind.

Clayton evidently realised the value of the encounter. Overriding Lawrence's protests that he was not a soldier, in November 1916 Clayton ordered him to return to Feisal in the somewhat ill-defined role of liaison officer. Hussein had already acquiesced in the arrival of a British military mission, realising that his men needed to learn modern military skills. The mission included Major H. G. Garland, an explosives expert. It was immediately clear that the bond between Feisal and Lawrence had been renewed. At Feisal's suggestion, Lawrence adopted the Arab dress that would become his trademark, the emir having persuaded him that his men identified military uniform with Ottoman officers. With his headdress, flowing white robe, and the golden hooked *jambiya* (dagger) in his belt, Lawrence was marked out as a man of standing.

The Arab army, now some ten thousand strong, began the campaign that was to see Feisal in Damascus at the head of his victorious fighters. Lawrence also took the political decision – essential, he believed, given the trust that they had between them – to make Feisal aware of the Sykes–Picot Agreement. It was a bold course of action, but it proved to be fully justified once the Bolsheviks made the terms of the agreement public. The answer to the powerful Ottoman force at Medina proved to be simple: they were blockaded for the rest of the war. Ottoman military and supply operations in the region were disrupted by blowing up sections of the Hejaz Railway and derailing trains, a technique taught by Garland and widely adopted by Lawrence and the Arabs. Lawrence realised the potential of the little port of Aqaba which was captured on 6 July 1917. It was then developed into a major supply base for equipment for Feisal's army. Feisal could now prepare to move his forces northwards in support of a planned British offensive from Egypt.[12]

Weizmann and the Zionist campaign

Just as Britain's alliance with the Hashemites developed over time, so, too, did its alliance with the Zionist movement, partly because of the obvious difficulty that its headquarters were in Berlin. Nevertheless, Zionism had a following among the British Jewish community, one of its leaders being a Russian-born scientist at the University of Manchester, Dr Chaim Weizmann.

Born in 1874 into a relatively prosperous middle-class family, Weizmann was reared in the shtetl of Motol, where he was taught Jewish law and scripture. He specialised in chemistry during his secondary education in nearby Pinsk, after which his studies took him to Germany and Switzerland where he earned his doctorate. In 1904, he took up an appointment at the University of Manchester. In addition to being a trained scientist, Weizmann had been active in Zionism almost from the start. His work in Manchester put him in touch with two leading politicians, the young, then-Liberal Winston Churchill and Arthur James Balfour, the Conservative former prime minister, each of whom was to prove instrumental in the Zionists' quest for a national home. Weizmann and Balfour met in Manchester in 1906, and while there was no immediate follow-up, the encounter seems to have made its mark on the veteran politician. Although Weizmann could not have predicted what was to follow, he was helping to foster an invaluable network of contacts in British politics.

An important ally of Weizmann's was the editor of the *Manchester Guardian*, C. P. Scott, whom he met immediately after the outbreak of war. Scott pointed out to Weizmann that there was a Jew, Herbert Samuel, in the cabinet and also said that he could make contact with the influential chancellor of the exchequer, David Lloyd George. Asquith's Guildhall speech prompted Samuel, the first practising Jew to make cabinet rank, to propose to Grey that they consider a Jewish state in Palestine should Turkey be defeated, sentiments that Samuel repeated when Weizmann met him at Scott's suggestion. At his meeting with Lloyd George, Weizmann was warned of the likely opposition he would find in the assimilationist sections of the British Jewish community. These contacts matured during 1915, with both Samuel and Weizmann arguing that Palestine should become a British protectorate.

Weizmann had attracted the attention of British political

leaders through his enlistment into war service to work on the mass production of acetone, the propellant for cartridges and shells, the latter having been in scandalously short supply. His success marked him out in the mind of the newly appointed minister of munitions, Lloyd George, who in December 1916 became prime minister of a coalition government in which Balfour was foreign secretary. The support of both the new premier and foreign secretary for Zionism was to be critical. The year 1917 saw Allied fortunes touch their nadir: both Jutland and the Somme in 1916 had failed to deliver the hoped-for decisive victories, and French and British offensives in 1917 proved to be no better. The Austro-Hungarians and Germans almost drove Italy out of the war with their victory at Caporetto. What's more, the overthrow of the tsar in March, followed by the Bolshevik Revolution, heralded the collapse of the Eastern Front. There also seemed to be no immediate answer to Germany's unrestricted U-boat campaign, although it was instrumental in influencing the one positive development: the US declaration of war on 6 April. But key groups in the United States had no reason to like the Allies, among them Jews who had fled persecution in Russia. This dismal scenario was played out as the British explored the possibility of an understanding with the Zionists in 1917.[13]

The Balfour Declaration

The idea of Jewish settlement in Palestine was initially sparked in January 1917 by Sykes, who had become increasingly involved with its future in the course of his negotiations with the French. Sykes had asked Weizmann for a clear statement of what the Zionists wanted. The subsequent memorandum, drafted by Weizmann and his close colleague Nahum Sokolow, a noted literary figure, proposed that Palestine be recognised as the Jewish national home. It should come under an unnamed suzerain government, clearly intended to be Britain, which would ensure that the Jewish nation had civic, national, and political rights and would encourage Jewish immigration. This document became the foundation of the Zionist cause, all the more so when Weizmann was elected president of the English Zionist Federation. Once he was made aware of the Sykes–Picot Agreement, Weizmann had to work hard to ensure that the new state would be some kind of British protectorate rather than any possible alternative such as internationalisation or a form of Anglo-French condominium. At what proved to be a key meeting between Weizmann and Balfour on 19 June, the foreign secretary agreed that a declaration of support for Zionism should be issued by Britain. A month later, Balfour was given a Zionist draft that would have committed the government to reconstituting Palestine as the national home of the Jewish people.

On 3 September 1917, in the absence of Lloyd George and Balfour, the matter came before the War Cabinet. As Lloyd George had predicted, strong opposition had already been voiced by the country's Jewish elite, who argued that what Jews had achieved at home would be undermined by arguing for Palestine as a Jewish homeland. These sentiments surfaced strongly in the cabinet contribution by the secretary of state for India, Edwin Montagu, who castigated the prospect of a Jewish national home as undermining him as a Jewish

Englishman. At a subsequent cabinet meeting, criticism also came from the former viceroy of India, Lord Curzon, who had visited Palestine and raised the future of what he called the country's Muslim inhabitants. Balfour was determined to press ahead nevertheless, and, at a cabinet meeting on 31 October, he turned to the pro-Allied propaganda that could be conducted in Russia and United States, where Zionism had the backing of the Jews. Montagu had already left for India, while Curzon's argument was countered by alluding to the country's ability to sustain a larger population. Even so, their reservations did find their way into the final declaration, which was issued in Balfour's name on 2 November:

> His Majesty's Government view with favour the establishment in Palestine of a national home for the Jewish people, and will use their best endeavours to facilitate the achievement of this object, it being clearly understood that nothing shall be done which may prejudice the civil and religious rights of existing non-Jewish communities in Palestine, or the rights and political status enjoyed by Jews in any other country.[14]

Maude, Allenby, and British victory

As the First World War began its final year, Britain had entered into a series of engagements with the Hashemites, the French, and the Zionists. In doing so, it aroused expectations that would always be difficult to fulfil, let alone reconcile. The war against the Ottoman Empire remained overwhelmingly a British affair. France contributed some colonial troops, but its main argument for a future voice in the Middle East rested upon the enormous sacrifices of its army in Europe. Italy entertained some hopes, having been promised Ottoman territory in the 1915 Treaty of London, but it had problems enough trying to survive; the United States, meanwhile, had never been at war with the Ottoman Empire. Under two highly able commanders, Maude and Allenby, British military prospects in the Middle Eastern front in Mesopotamia and Palestine were at last looking promising.

It was a truly imperial force that Britain mustered in its two final victorious campaigns against the Ottomans. Reorganised by General Sir Stanley Maude as the I and III Indian Corps, British imperial forces had defeated the Ottomans at Baghdad under his leadership on 9–10 March 1917, entering the city the following day. His was a welcome victory at a low point in Allied fortunes. But the campaign proved to be a serious drain on Indian manpower resources, which were already badly stretched: seventy-three of Maude's eighty-six infantry battalions and forty-one of his forty-three cavalry squadrons were from India. It was, above all, an enervating campaign during which some 12,000 Indian and British soldiers died of disease, including Maude from cholera in November 1917.

Percy Cox, now civil commissioner, had the responsibility of setting up an administration for the three vilayets of Baghdad, Basra, and Mosul. His deputy was Arnold T. Wilson of the Indian Army who had served in south-west Persia before the war. These two men, together with Gertrude Bell, were fated to preside over the emergence of Iraq.

General Allenby's entry into Jerusalem, 11 December 1917.
(Pictorial Press Ltd/Alamy Stock Photo)

There were few signs that the British presence was welcome. In the spring of 1918, the overall manpower crisis saw two Indian divisions transferred to the Palestine command, which had lost troops to the European theatre. Although Maude's successor, General Sir William Marshall, advanced as far as Kirkuk and the outskirts of Mosul in 1918, the worst of the fighting in what had been an especially fraught campaign was over.[15]

During the first years of the war, the British had accumulated a large Egyptian Expeditionary Force of British, Australian, New Zealand, and Indian troops with the initial purpose of safeguarding the Suez Canal; but at the end of 1916, the troops' commander, Sir Archibald Murray, was pressed to take the offensive. In March 1917, Murray's campaign was rebuffed at the Battle of Gaza, leading to his replacement in June by General Sir Edmund Allenby, the successful commander of the Third Army in France. A cavalry officer, Allenby was the ideal choice for the kind of mobile warfare suited both to the terrain and to his Australian, New Zealand, and Indian horsemen. On his right flank was Feisal's Arab army, now some 25,000 strong and highly mobile. The first phase of the campaign climaxed with the capture of Jerusalem on 11 December.

In the spring of 1918, the Egyptian Expeditionary Force was weakened when most of its British units had to be rushed to France to help counter the great German spring Offensive. Their replacements were fifty-four Indian infantry battalions and thirteen cavalry squadrons. Hastily trained, the replacements were brigaded with more experienced troops. By the time Allenby was ready to renew the offensive in September, only one of his eleven divisions was predominantly British. With this force he achieved a great victory at the Battle of Megiddo fought between 19 and 25 September, which destroyed two Ottoman armies. Also, on 25 September, in one of the last great cavalry operations in history, the troopers of the Jodhpur and Mysore Lancers and the Sherwood Foresters Yeomanry captured the key port of Haifa. The victories at Megiddo and Haifa opened the way to Damascus.[16] With the concurrence of Allenby and the local commander, the Australian General Henry Chauvel, Feisal's men entered the city on 1 October; the British followed the next day. On his arrival, Feisal was greeted warmly, and Hussein was proclaimed king of the Arabs. Lawrence's own moment of triumph was briefly delayed when, still in Arab dress, he was held captive by a patrol of over-zealous Indian cavalry. Lawrence remained in Damascus for only three days, having completed his military task when the two allies, Allenby and Feisal, met at last. Already something of a legend, Lawrence left for home almost immediately, never to see Syria again.[17] Refusing to accept the honours and decorations that his exploits had earned, he served briefly in the Colonial Office with Churchill before enlisting as an ordinary serviceman in the Royal Air Force. He died on 19 May 1935 as the result of a motorcycle accident.

With the defeat of their armies in Mesopotamia and Syria, and their allies in Germany and Austria-Hungary close to collapse, the Ottomans had no alternative but to seek an armistice. This was signed on 30 October 1918 on board the battleship HMS *Agamemnon*, which was anchored in Mudros Bay off the island of Lemnos. The formal fighting in the Middle East was over, and the region's future was seemingly in the hands of the victorious British. But as events were to show, the task of reconstituting the Middle East had barely begun.

3

The New Imperialists Under Challenge

The British and French proconsuls working to establish the Anglo-French imperium in the Middle East in the aftermath of the war were doing so in a world very different from the one that had gone to war in 1914. Three great empires – Russian, Austro-Hungarian, and Ottoman – had collapsed, while three dynasties – the Hohenzollerns, Habsburgs, and Romanovs – had abdicated, fled, or been murdered. The Ottoman dynasty was soon to follow. The new Bolshevik regime in Russia was preaching revolution, which had echoes in cities as far apart as Glasgow, Munich, and Budapest. President Woodrow Wilson of the United States had articulated the concept of self-determination, and although Wilson had intended this concept to be applied in Europe, it was soon being articulated in the colonial empires – and the victorious British Empire was not immune. The year 1919 was to see the start of the Irish War of Independence with the proclamation of independence by Dáil Éireann and the murder of two unarmed men of the Royal Irish Constabulary in County Tipperary in January. Later that year saw widespread disturbance in India, culminating in the tragedy of the Amritsar Massacre on 13 April when troops under the command of Brigadier General Reginald Dyer opened fire on an unarmed crowd killing at least 379 people and injuring hundreds more. The peoples of the Middle East did not exist in a vacuum, nor did their aspirations develop in one.

The Paris Peace Conference: Feisal and the Zionists

On 18 January 1919, the peace conference convened in Paris.[1] The future of the Middle East was far from a priority. Of the five major powers, the Italians had little interest in the region beyond their unrealistic hopes for a presence in Anatolia, an aspiration that had been stoked by the Treaty of London in 1915; the Japanese had none at all. Wilson was prepared to intervene, as was his secretary of state, Robert Lansing, but since the United States had not been at war with Turkey and had no obvious Middle Eastern agenda to pursue, the Americans were not particularly engaged on this issue. Rather, central to Wilson's agenda was the proposal for a League of Nations, and this would prove a useful device for settling the Middle East. As for the French, the overriding priority for their premier, Georges Clemenceau, was to ensure that the German settlement safeguarded his country's security. He seemingly hoped to engage British sympathies when he conceded prior to the conference that Mosul, allocated to France under the Sykes–Picot Agreement, should join Baghdad and Basra under British control. For their part, Lloyd George and Balfour were strong advocates of the Balfour Declaration, and, despite French opposition, they also insisted that Feisal's case for Arab independence be heard.

With Allenby's troops dominating the region, Feisal's position in Damascus seemed strong, especially since well-informed British voices saw no reason to accede to French demands in the region. On 15 November 1918, Hogarth recorded his view that no part of Syria would willingly accept a settlement with the French; Clayton, meanwhile, attacked the Sykes–Picot concept of two administrative areas, arguing that Britain should have the trusteeship for Palestine and act as adviser to an independent Arab state with its capital at Damascus. His view was that French trusteeship should be confined to Lebanon and Armenia. But the French were not to be gainsaid. On 6 November 1918, Georges-Picot landed at Beirut, claiming Syria for France. The French foreign minister, Stephen Pichon, was similarly unyielding on the Sykes–Picot Agreement, justifying his position on what he argued were his country's responsibilities towards the Syrians. It was, however, becoming apparent that the former Ottoman territories and German colonial possessions would not be treated as colonies but rather held in trust through a system of League of Nations mandates that served as a convenient mask for imperial ambitions.

When Feisal and his colleagues arrived in Europe for the conference, they received a tepid welcome from the French, who treated them as guests rather than as delegates. Designated plenipotentiary by his father, Feisal brought with him as an adviser Nuri al-Said, a young Iraqi who had taken part in the revolt and was joined by Lawrence as his interpreter. Nuri was to be a key pillar of the Hashemite cause until his brutal murder in the 1958 revolution. With his quiet dignity, Feisal was treated with courtesy by the delegates, even though it was clear that his mission for the Arabs was peripheral to the main work of the conference.

The Zionists, too, were preparing for the conference. Feisal and Weizmann had met once before when the latter visited the Middle East in the spring of 1918. The Zionist leader's hope was that, if he could enlist Feisal's support, Arab opposition (which he had already sensed on his way through Jerusalem) could be marginalised. In return, Weizmann offered the prospect of technical and economic assistance. The two leaders met in London on 11 December 1918, with Lawrence as interpreter. Each rejected the Sykes–Picot Agreement. Weizmann was quite open in stating the Zionist case: essentially, that the forthcoming conference and Feisal should recognise the rights of the Jews in Palestine, which would come under British trusteeship. Four to five million Jews would be settled, and the Arab peasantry would be safeguarded. Feisal replied that he would assure the conference that their two positions were in harmony. Their discussion was embodied in a document that they both signed on 3 January 1919. Under the Feisal–Weizmann Agreement, as it was called, close cooperation between the Arab state and Palestine was to be promoted, the boundaries of which were to be agreed subsequently. The Balfour Declaration was to be implemented, including large-scale Jewish immigration, while the rights of Arab farmers would be protected. The Zionist Organisation would send experts to investigate how the Arab state could be developed.

Feisal did, however, enter the important qualification that he would not be answerable for failing to carry out the agreement if the establishment of the Arabs translated differently

Emir Feisal and T. E. Lawrence, Paris Peace Conference, 1919.
(Alamy)

to what was expected. In any case, the subsequent collapse of Feisal's position in Syria was to render the agreement void.

Accompanied by Lawrence as translator, Feisal presented his case on 6 February, having previously submitted his main points in a memorandum. Wilson, Lloyd George, and Clemenceau were there to hear him. The core of Feisal's message did not differ substantially from what Hussein had argued in his letters to McMahon during the war, with the added elements that the Arabs had contributed to the Allied victory and that the area in question was suitable for self-determination. The independent Arab state should embrace all the regions south of Alexandretta, since the inhabitants spoke Arabic and were of common stock. In addition, Feisal reminded them, the Allies had promised the Arabs their independence at the end of the war. The French had prepared a counter-attack in the form of a Lebanese–Christian delegation whose members castigated the idea of putting the people of Syria under Bedouin leadership. But Wilson, it seems, was much taken with Feisal.[2]

Before the Zionists could make their case, Sykes, who had championed the Zionist cause and had just returned from a hectic factfinding tour of Syria and Palestine, died on 16 February in Paris of the worldwide influenza epidemic. The five-man Zionist mission appeared before the Supreme Council on 27 February. Hearing them were the five foreign ministers and, for a brief period it seems, Clemenceau. Balfour's sympathy was a given. Weizmann's colleague Sokolow opened by claiming the historic rights of the Jews to Palestine, demanding that these rights be recognised by a national home there, that sovereignty should be given to the proposed League of Nations with its mandate given to Britain, and that the country be governed so as to secure the national home. Sokolow argued that this would lead to an autonomous commonwealth which would respect the rights of the non-Jewish population and the status of Jews elsewhere. Weizmann focused on practicalities, especially how the country could absorb the one million Jews whom he claimed were waiting to come. Although there were some 600,000 to 700,000 existing inhabitants in Palestine, he argued that there was enough capacity to absorb between four and five million immigrants without adverse effect on their rights.

Sokolow and Weizmann's submissions, followed by their colleagues Menachem Ussishkin, representing Russian Jews, and the French Zionist André Spire, were then almost totally rebutted by the Frenchman Sylvain Lévi, who opened by stating that he was not a Zionist. Conceding that the Zionists had created the foundations for development in Palestine, he argued that the country could not provide a European standard of living for the Jews who might go there. As a French Jew, he was afraid of the concept of dual citizenship. Finally, he turned to the principles of equality embodied in the French Revolution, which could not justify the Jews having an exceptional position in Palestine. It fell to Weizmann to rescue the situation. Lansing posed the key question to him: did the national home mean an autonomous Jewish government? In a reply that was to help define Zionism in the years ahead, Weizmann said that under a mandatory power, Jewish institutions would be built up so that Palestine would become as Jewish as America was American or England was English. After the meeting, Balfour's secretary came to congratulate Weizmann.[3] While there was no immediate follow up in Paris, the Zionist delegation had, in fact, mapped out almost exactly the course that Palestine was soon to take. Although Feisal's reaction seemed generally supportive, there were already signs of discontent among the Palestinian Arabs.

In Paris, discussions between Lloyd George and Clemenceau over the future of Syria became increasingly acrid, with the former arguing for revision of the Sykes–Picot Agreement while the French premier, having already ceded Mosul, insisted on its continued implementation. On 20 March, Pichon made his bid. On the basis of the agreement, he insisted that Syria be treated as a region with France as the League of Nations mandatory power. Lloyd George retorted that the Syrian campaign had cost the British Empire 125,000 men and scorned the French contribution. He further argued that from 1917 it had been the British Army that had taken the brunt of the casualties in Europe. The two men then quarrelled over the status of Britain's pledge to Hussein: Pichon argued that France had no agreement with him, while Lloyd George quoted McMahon's 24 October letter to the effect that it was only the strip of land to the west of the districts of Damascus, Homs, Hama, and Aleppo that had been excluded from the promise of support for Arab independence. On that basis, Hussein had significantly contributed to the Allied victory.

Wilson clearly felt that the quarrel had gone on long enough. The only question for the Americans was whether the Syrians would accept France. If the question were to come before the conference, he felt that they would need to find out the wishes of the population. Neither Lloyd George nor Clemenceau was enthusiastic, but a commission was established under Dr Henry C. King, president of Oberlin College in Ohio, and Charles R. Crane, a Chicago manufacturer.[4] Before they could set to work, the British would come to experience the full measure of discontent in the Arab world.

The Egyptian Revolution

Britain's success against Turkey had depended in no small measure on its control of Egypt as a base with ultimately some one million troops drawn from Britain, Australia, New Zealand, and India forming the Egyptian Expeditionary Force under Allenby's command. The troops inevitably placed great strain on Egyptian infrastructure, with food and animals being requisitioned and an inevitable rise in prices. Thousands of men were recruited into the Egyptian Labour and Transport Corps. Thanks to decent pay, recruitment initially went well, but its appeal faded as the realities of military life became clearer, and neither the military nor local agents were always fastidious in their recruitment methods. There also were racial tensions, notably with the Australian and New Zealand troops. In April 1915, Australian soldiers caused considerable destruction in Cairo's Haret el-Wasser brothel district. Coupled with resentment over Britain's unilateral actions in 1914, Egypt had no shortage of grievances. But while they were fully engaged in the war, the British failed to sense what was happening.

In 1919, these grievances compounded into what rapidly became a truly revolutionary national movement. Its leader, Saad Zaghlul Pasha, had devoted his life to the country's welfare, even within the framework of British control. Born to a village headman in the Nile Delta around 1857–60, Zaghlul had supported Urabi's challenge to the British as a young man. studying at the Al-Azhar University, he became successively a judge, minister of education, and minister of justice during a career that culminated in the role of vice-president of the Legislative Assembly before it was prorogued at the start of the war. Although his policies were staunchly Egyptianisation, he was thought of as an able administrator rather than a politician. During the war, Zaghlul and his colleagues, many of whom had governmental experience, worked unobtrusively to build up a politically active network that could be triggered when the opportunity arose.

They did not wait long. Two days after the armistice with Germany, Zaghlul led a delegation to meet Sir Reginald Wingate, who had succeeded McMahon in 1916, demanding an end to the protectorate. Although he was privately in favour of making concessions, Wingate could not concede this point, nor would the delegation be permitted to present their case in London. On the same day, Zaghlul moved to give the delegation a permanent basis as the Egyptian Delegation or Al-Wafd al-Misri – Wafd in short. A memorandum was sent to the peace conference, arguing that the protectorate was a wartime measure and that the British had always said their presence was temporary. The Hejaz, an undeveloped desert country, had been admitted to the conference, but Egypt, by comparison an advanced country, was entitled to its independence. The most that the British would concede was that the prime minister, Rushdi Pasha, could go to London, but when his request that Zaghlul could join him was refused, his government resigned.

As the crisis developed, the key figures on the British side, Wingate and Allenby, were both absent either in London or at the peace conference, leaving General Sir Edward Bulfin in charge. Wingate's pleas for concessions found no echo in a Foreign Office led by the staunch imperialist and former Indian viceroy Lord Curzon. Instead, on 6 March 1919, the military authorities warned Zaghlul that they would act against him if his activities resulted in disorder. He and his supporters protested, and two days later he and three others were exiled to Malta. Lawyers and government officials then went on strike, quickly followed by disturbances in Cairo, Alexandria, and the countryside. Fourteen people were killed and fifty wounded in a confrontation at Tanta in the Nile Delta. On 14 March, worshippers attacked an army convoy after Friday prayers at Cairo's Al-Azhar Mosque, thirteen of whom were killed by the soldiers. Egyptians were also killed at Alexandria and at Damanhur in the Nile Delta. In an attack on the Luxor–Cairo train, seven soldiers and a prison inspector were killed, for which twenty-eight people were executed. Cairo was shut down, with no tram or rail transport. Telegraph and telephone lines were severed by protestors. It was a national movement, from the delta to Upper Egypt, Cairo, and Alexandria, and it was joined by Copts as well as Muslims. On 16 March, an unprecedented event took place in Cairo, when over 300 women staged a demonstration. They were led by Huda Shaarawi who had been born in 1879 into one of Egypt's leading families and whose husband was active in the Wafd.

Although the police made every effort to contain their demonstration, the sight of these veiled women openly protesting caught the public imagination in Egypt and abroad.[5]

In one sense the Egyptian Revolution, for such it was, was poorly timed: the British were in the process of demobilisation and so still had an enormous military force in the country. steadily the military gained control, but in view of the situation the government decided that Wingate should be replaced by the more experienced Allenby, who was given supreme authority in all civil and military matters. If the government thought that he would largely confine himself

Women addressing a crowd in Cairo, 1919.
(© Bettmann/CORBIS)

to the latter, they were soon to be disabused. Indeed, he had earlier expressed views similar to those of Wingate. On 26 March, the day after Allenby's arrival in Cairo, he outlined his priorities to an assembly of Egyptian leaders, assuring them that he would bring the disturbances to an end, that he would conduct an inquiry into the causes of discontent, and that he would redress grievances. On the 31st, he telegraphed London recommending that Zaghlul and his colleagues be released and allowed to travel to Europe. This is not quite what many in government expected, but Allenby had his way, announcing on 7 April that the four men could travel where they wanted. His measure was celebrated by large crowds at Zaghlul's house. But his dramatic reversal of policy did not bring an immediate end to the protests. By early May, Allenby reported that the revolution had cost around 1,000 Egyptian lives, as well as seventy-five British, plus a number of Indian, Greek, and Armenian casualties.[6]

On Lloyd George's suggestion, the government in London decided that a commission under Lord Alfred Milner should investigate the protectorate. Milner had impressive credentials, having made his name as high commissioner in South Africa. More pertinently, Milner's early service had been in Egypt, where he had become under-secretary for finance and, in 1892, had published *England in Egypt*, which ran to several editions. His colleagues represented various shades of opinion: General Sir John Maxwell, who had served in Egypt but was better known for presiding over the courts martial and execution of leaders of the 1916 Easter Rising in Dublin; former ambassador Sir Rennell Rodd; the Labour MP General Sir Owen Thomas; the Liberal journalist J. A. Spender; and C. J. B. Hurst, legal adviser to the Foreign Office. Imperial statesman though he was, Milner soon caught the mood of Egypt. His overriding purpose was to reach a settlement that would safeguard Britain's strategic interests, even if that meant negotiating with Zaghlul and sacrificing the protectorate. Negotiations were not straightforward, and following a breakdown of trust, on 23 December 1920, Allenby ordered the deportation of Zaghlul and five colleagues, initially to Aden and then to Seychelles.

Aware that the structures through which Britain had controlled Egyptian affairs had broken down, Allenby was convinced that the protectorate had to end. Through his staff, he

was able to identify a number of politicians who were prepared to form a government under the right conditions. By
this stage, even his political masters in London could see that
the protectorate had to go, but they felt that British imperial communications through the Suez Canal had to be safeguarded by binding agreements. The latter was a step too far
for the Egyptians. Allenby's preferred formula was that the
protectorate be abolished and independence granted, but
with Britain retaining liberty of action if needs demanded.
The real guarantees of Britain's position in the country were
the strength of the Mediterranean Fleet and the British garrisons, he believed.

Curzon and the British government still needed to be
convinced. Many Conservatives in Lloyd George's coalition government had been incensed at the signing of the
Anglo-Irish Treaty on 6 December 1921, which had set up
the Irish Free State for most of the country, castigating it as
a surrender to violence. Allenby was to fare no better at their
hands. With negotiations between Cairo and London at
something of an impasse, on 3 February 1922 Allenby left for
home, having already told Curzon that if his advice were to
be rejected then he would resign. Accused by Lloyd George
of proposing to abandon the entire British position in the
country without guarantees, Allenby confirmed that he
would resign, at which point the prime minister conceded.

On 28 February 1922, Allenby's Declaration of the Independence of Egypt was unveiled. Egypt was declared to be an
independent sovereign state, and the protectorate was abolished. The country was to have its own foreign policy, but
it would be conducted in conformity with that of Britain.

Britain's strategic concerns were secured by the fact that her military, naval, and air force presence was untouched. On 15 March, Egypt formally declared its independence with Sultan Ahmad Fuad as King Fuad I. On one level, Allenby's policy was one of real statesmanship: it set Egypt on its own course not tied to the British Empire. On another, he was perhaps over-optimistic, since Britain retained a powerful presence in the country and too much had happened since 1919 for the two sides to really trust each other's good faith. Zaghlul and the Wafd in particular denounced what had been a unilateral announcement, just as in 1914. Egypt was about to make its mark for a quite different reason. Before 1922 ended, on 4 November the Valley of the Kings was the scene of the most famous archaeological discovery of the century when a team of excavators led by Howard Carter uncovered the tomb of the Pharaoh Tutankhamun, its incomparable treasures displayed in time in Cairo's Egyptian Museum. The world was reminded of Egypt's unique contribution to world civilisation.[7]

With a constitution in place, Zaghlul was released in March 1923. Elections in January 1924 saw his Wafd party gain a decisive majority, enabling him to form a government. Always a champion of education, he established free schooling and reformed higher education at Fuad I University, while Cairo flourished as a cultural centre. But Zaghlul was still distrusted by the British, and this came to a head with the murder in Cairo on 19 November 1924 of Major-General Sir Lee Stack, governor of the Sudan and commander of the Egyptian Army. Zaghlul and his ministers attended the funeral, but an irate Allenby presented the Egyptian government with a demand for a large indemnity. Under severe pressure, Zaghlul's government complied but resigned. In May 1926, the Wafd won new elections, but Zaghlul did not return as prime minister. He died in 1927, mourned as an uncompromising Egyptian patriot.

The King–Crane Commission and Arab politics

At the same time that the British were having to confront the challenge of the Egyptian revolution, clear signs were emerging of discontent in Palestine, now under military administration as Occupied Enemy Territory Administration (South), generally known as OETA (South), with Major-General Sir Arthur Money as its military governor. The Syrian coastal plain was designated OETA (North), while the interior under Feisal was OETA (East), all French and Arab troops being under Allenby's overall command. As early as 1 April 1919, Balfour warned Weizmann that Zionist activities in Palestine were creating tensions there. Weizmann confirmed that they were committed to the terms of the Balfour Declaration with its promised safeguards for the non-Jewish population, but he confessed concern at the attitudes of British officers in Palestine. There was some substance to this.

On 5 May, Clayton forwarded a report from Money in which the general emphasised the degree of Arab opposition to the programme that the Zionists had presented to the conference, to the extent that a US or French mandate would be preferable to that of the British. Clayton added his appreciation that the Arabs' fear of Zionist aims was growing daily. It was true that the Arabs of Palestine were finding a voice. This was the thrust of a report called 'The Arab Move-ment and Zionism' sent to Curzon on 12 August by Major J. N. Camp, the assistant political officer in Jerusalem. Dis-missing the 1919 Feisal–Weizmann Agreement as worth-less, Camp focused on al-Nadi al-Arabi (the Arab Club), which was led by the Husseini family, as being opposed to Zionism, although he concluded that all important Muslims and Christians were opposed to Zionism. He believed that trouble could be avoided by peaceful Jewish penetration.

On 10 June 1919, the King–Crane Commission arrived in Palestine, spending some six weeks there and in Syria. The commission had by then become an all-American affair, the British and French having withdrawn. Feisal and his sup-porters in the Syrian elite made every effort to convince its members that the country was ready for independence. On his return from Paris, Feisal had sought to reinforce his and Syria's credentials by calling an assembly that proclaimed itself the national congress. On 2 July, the assembly declared for complete independence as a constitutional monarchy. It voiced total hostility to any form of French mandate, but, if such a thing were inevitable, the United States was the pre-ferred option. Those who might have supported the French, notably the Maronite Christians, were not heard, although the commissioners did visit over forty towns taking evi-dence. Their report was presented to the peace conference on 28 August 1919. By then, however, the report's progeni-tor, President Wilson, had already left, and it was put to one side, the principal recommendation for a US mandate being ignored. The work of the commission thus became an irrel-evant by-product of the conference, but its conclusions form an interesting commentary on the political temper of the area. They had concluded that only a small fraction in Syria supported a French mandate, while in Palestine 90 per cent of the population was opposed to Zionism.[8]

Throughout this period, Feisal had played to what strengths he had. He had the support of many Syrians who preferred him over the prospect of a French mandate. He had McMahon's pledge to Hussein on the basis of which he had led the successful Arab Revolt. But Lawrence had early on made Feisal aware of the Sykes–Picot Agreement with its clear implications for the future of Syria, and even before the armistice he had indicated to Allenby his distrust of French intentions. But the British had broader considerations than their dispute with the French over Syria. There was a pressing need for imperial demobilisation and retrenchment at a time when they were facing military pressures in Ireland, India, and elsewhere in the Middle East. Anglo-French relations needed to be sustained, especially since US intentions for the post-war world were unclear. Where Britain's priorities would fall soon emerged. On 9–11 September 1919, Lloyd George and Allenby met at Deauville, agreeing that British troops would evacuate OETA (North) and that Feisal's subsidy would be halved, with France making up the remainder. When Lloyd George and Feisal met in London, the latter warned that this could result in bloodshed.

The San Remo Conference and the mandates

Feisal's position weakened during the winter of 1919–20. Domestically, he had to rely on the support of nationalist groups opposed to any kind of compromise with the French. On 8 March 1920, he was proclaimed king of Syria. In France, Clemenceau – never a totally committed colonialist – had been replaced as prime minister by Alexandre Millerand, who was. A portent of French intentions was the arrival in Beirut of General Henri Gouraud as high commissioner and commander-in-chief, a veteran colonial soldier who had lost an arm at Gallipoli. The conference that was to settle the affairs of the Arab areas of the former Ottoman Empire (to the satisfaction of the victorious powers at least) convened at San Remo in Italy in April 1920. Before it could commence, the febrile nature of Arab politics had been exposed. Feisal's proclamation as king attracted demonstrations of support in Palestine, which were banned by the British. During the feast of Nabi Musa on 4 April, the mayor of Jerusalem, Musa Kasim al-Husseini, along with Haj Amin al-Husseini and the newspaper editor Arif al-Arif organised a pro-Feisal demonstration in the city. Serious violence resulted in which five Jews were killed and some 200 injured, while four Arabs were killed and twenty-one injured.

When the future of Palestine came before the conference, Curzon and the French quarrelled over the Balfour Declaration, the latter questioning the extent to which it had been accepted by the Allied powers. What really concerned the French was their traditional role as protector of Catholic interests, although they seemed to have been reassured. Lloyd George agreed that the northern boundary of Palestine should not extend to the Litani river. This concession opened the way for agreement that Britain should have the mandate for Palestine and Iraq, and France for Syria. The

Palestine Mandatory was charged with implementing the Balfour Declaration. The clear winners at the conference were the Zionists, who had achieved their aim, consistently pursued by Weizmann, of a British mandate that incorporated the Balfour Declaration, and the French who now had a free hand in Syria. The mandates were held to have a higher purpose under the League of Nations than crude colonial annexation. Contrary to their aspirations for independence, with a few exceptions, the Arabs saw mandates very differently.[9] As Lawrence pointed out in a letter to *The Times* on 23 July, the Arabs had fought the Turks to win their independence, not to change masters.

The San Remo Conference was followed on 10 August 1920 by the Treaty of Sèvres, which was intended to put an end to the war with Turkey. Its severity was such that the Turks, now ably led by the nationalist general Mustafa Kemal, could not accept it and, although signed, it never came into force. The treaty did provide for Kurdish autonomy with the possibility of independence, but when it was subsequently superseded by the Treaty of Lausanne in July 1923, this suggestion had disappeared. From then on, the Kurds were divided among the emergent Turkish Republic, Syria, Iraq, and Persia.

The end of Hashemite Syria

For his part, the Frenchman Gouraud wasted no time in building up his forces to include tanks, heavy artillery, and aircraft, none of which could be matched by Feisal's army. After a period of negotiation, on 20 July 1920 Gouraud proclaimed that Feisal had not acceded to French demands, and he attacked towards Damascus. On 24 July, Feisal's outnumbered and outgunned forces were overwhelmed at the Battle of Maysalun. Their commander, Yusuf al-Azmah, a former Ottoman officer, was among those killed and, as a result, became a Syrian martyr. Feisal fled to British-controlled Haifa. Keen to assert France's control, on 1 September, Gouraud proclaimed the separation from Syria of a Greater Lebanon with its capital at Beirut, including the areas of Mount Lebanon, Tripoli to the north, Tyre to the south, and inland to the Biqaa Valley. Although the Lebanese Christians had lobbied for such an outcome, Greater Lebanon also embraced Sunni and Shi'a Muslims as well as the Druze, the consequences of which were to emerge through time.[10]

The creation of Iraq

The three former vilayets of Baghdad, Basra, and Mosul were quiescent in the immediate aftermath of the armistice with Turkey. While there was some political activity, the former Ottoman administrative cadres had left with the empire's collapse, leaving the running of the country in British hands. In April 1918, the civil commissioner Sir Percy Cox went on leave, and Arnold Wilson was appointed acting commissioner, a post that he was to hold until October 1920. Unconvinced by the mandate systems, which he contemptuously dismissed as a subterfuge, and still less by the prospect of independence, Wilson believed that what the country needed was authority. Its history of decay, the collapse of its administrative system, its inability to compete economically, the absence of a nationalist movement outside a small group, and its lack of homogeneity, had led him to this conclusion. Curzon's suspicion that he was administering the country like an Indian province was not wide of the mark, while the India Office counselled him that the idea of making it some kind of protectorate had been overtaken by events.

Such strictures did not deflect Wilson from the course that he was pursuing, but with little sign of any political initiative the country became increasingly restive. His one major attempt, a constitutional committee chaired by Sir Edgar Bonham-Carter, offered nothing more than a British-dominated council of state with limited Arab participation. Even so, nationalist groups were active, notably the Shi'a-based Haras al-Istiqlal, or Independence Guard. The announcement of the mandate that had been sanctioned at San Remo provoked disturbances involving both Shi'as and Sunnis in Baghdad. Attempts by Wilson to placate opinion proved ineffectual, and at the end of June 1920 an armed rebellion broke out that soon covered much of the territory and involved large-scale deployment of British and Indian troops. When it ended in October, some 8,450 insurgents had been killed, as well as 426 British and Indian soldiers. By then, Wilson's period in office had ended. On 11 October, Cox returned as high commissioner of Iraq, as Mesopotamia was called from the time of the San Remo conference. Cox's first actions were to create a provisional government with a council of state. Feisal was the obvious candidate to become head of state, and he indicated his interest in taking it on, provided provision could be made for his brother Abdullah. Such a mechanism to accommodate the dynasty's ambitions was in the making.[11]

The Cairo Conference

In January 1921, responsibility for Middle Eastern affairs passed to Winston Churchill with his appointment as colonial secretary. As secretary of state for war, he had been much exercised about the military costs that Britain was facing as the result of the situation in Iraq, Palestine, and Egypt, and he was determined to address this. On Iraq, Churchill had to be briefed on the tentative overtures that were being explored with Feisal. On 12 March, he presided over the Cairo Conference, which brought together Britain's military and political paladins in the region, including Samuel, Cox, Lawrence, and Bell as well as army and air force chiefs. While much of the discussion inevitably focused on how to reduce military costs, including how the Royal Air Force could be used to control the territory, the real purpose of the conference was to be found in its political decisions. Feisal was to be offered the throne in Iraq while, east of the Jordan, Palestine was to become a new entity, Transjordan, ruled by Abdullah. On the conclusion of the conference, Churchill travelled to Jerusalem for consultations with Abdullah. He also met Palestinian and Jewish delegations. To the demand of the former that the principle of the Jewish national home be abandoned, Churchill replied that the Balfour Declaration was settled British and Allied policy, although this rather tepid attitude to the declaration unsettled the Zionists.

The Cairo Conference had two immediate and far-reaching consequences. Iraq was going to be a difficult inheritance for Feisal, who was scarcely known in the country and had to guard against the accusation that he was a British appointee. He would also be a Sunni Arab head of state of a country in which Sunni Arabs were in a minority. He did, however, have support as an Arab leader, and a council in Baghdad declared him king. On 23 August 1921, the ceremony duly took place. After a transition period, Britain also recognised a government in Amman under the Emir Abdullah. The next step was to separate the fledgling Transjordan from the Palestine Mandate. Once this move had been sanctioned by the League of Nations, Britain formally recognised the independence of Transjordan under Abdullah in May 1923. Britain now had Hashemite allies in two Arab capitals, but at a time when the future of their homeland in the Hejaz was proving problematic.[12]

Defining the Palestine Mandate

The previous pro-Feisal disturbances in 1920 had signalled the fragility of the Palestine Mandate, but the Cairo Conference was scarcely over when they were eclipsed in ferocity. What began as a quarrel between communist and non-communist Jews in Jaffa on 1 May 1921 somehow escalated into Arab attacks there and elsewhere in which forty-seven Jews were killed and 146 wounded. The security forces killed forty-eight Arabs and wounded seventy-three. The chief justice, Sir Thomas Haycraft, whose report on the violence was published in October, identified hostility towards the Jews, especially the Arabs' fear that increasing Jewish immigration would erode their political and economic position. Haycraft also felt that the lifestyle of the young immigrants contrasted with that of the Arabs. Lloyd George's choice as the first high commissioner for Palestine was his old political ally, Herbert Samuel. Although he was worried that his policies might be not be universally accepted because they were coming from a Jew, he accepted the appointment. In fact, Samuel moved to accommodate Arab fears, even if in doing so he aroused them among the Jews. Faced with the disturbances, for example, he put a temporary halt on Jewish immigration. Then, on 3 June 1921, Samuel gave a royal birthday speech in Jerusalem in which he made it clear that Britain would not support the creation of a Jewish government over the non-Jewish majority. He also insisted that immigration policy be linked to the country's ability to absorb.[13]

These events coincided with the emergence of a young man who would dominate Palestinian Arab politics in the years ahead. Born in 1895, Haj Amin al-Husseini belonged to one of the great *a'yam* families of Jerusalem, claiming descent from the Prophet Muhammad. Deeply religious, he studied Islamic theology and law at Al-Azhar University in Cairo before making the haj to Mecca. Haj Amin became an Ottoman officer on the outbreak of war, but he subsequently joined Feisal's revolt. Alienated by the Balfour Declaration, he became active in the political organisation al-Nadi al'Arabi and was one of the organisers of the 1920 demonstration. His moment came in March 1921 when the office of Grand Mufti, as it had recently been renamed by the British, became vacant with the death of Haj Amin's half-brother. Assuring Samuel of his good faith, Haj Amin campaigned for the succession. The disturbances that wracked the country after the Jaffa affray in May stood in the way temporarily, but Samuel confirmed Haj Amin's appointment once they were over. This move was to have major consequences for the politics of

Palestine with decades of leadership until his death in Beirut in 1974.[14]

During the winter of 1921–2, a Palestinian delegation led by Musa Kasim al-Husseini and Shibly al-Jamal campaigned for independence, the end of Jewish immigration, and revocation of the Balfour Declaration. While their lobbying failed, coinciding as it did with the publication of Haycraft's report, they managed to convey the strength of Arab opposition to mandatory policy. The best that they secured was an assurance from the Colonial Office in April 1922 that while the Balfour Declaration was government policy, it would ensure that the section dealing with non-Jewish inhabitants was implemented.

Indeed, with the mandate due to be ratified by the league in July 1922, the British government felt it necessary to spell out its position. On 3 June, the 'Statement of British Policy on Palestine', known as the Churchill white paper, was released. Weizmann's response to Lansing at Paris had long been a hostage to fortune; the government had no such aim as to make Palestine 'as Jewish as England was English'. There had never been any intention of subordinating the Arabs, but the Balfour Declaration had said that the Jewish national home was to be created 'in' Palestine. The statement went on to confirm that the declaration was not negotiable and that the Jews were in Palestine as of right. The national home was defined as the development of the existing Jewish community to become a centre in which Jews could take 'an interest and a pride'. While this definition of the national home was far from welcome to the Jewish leadership, just as unsettling was the principle that immigration would depend on the country's absorptive capacity.[15] In short, the white paper seemed to have moved far from the hopes for British policy that Weizmann and his colleagues had entertained in November 1917.

Abdul Aziz ibn Saud and the collapse of Hashemite Hejaz

Abdul Aziz ibn Saud, with his base in the Nejd, had hardly featured in any of these proceedings. In the years before the outbreak of war, he had been preoccupied with sustaining his position in the Nejd against the Turks and tribal rivals. The key to his eventual success lay in his support for the doctrines of the eighteenth-century religious teacher Muhammad ibn Abd Al-Wahhab, who taught a 'pure' form of Islam. After a defeat in 1912, Ibn Saud formed an elite Bedouin force, the Ikhwan, or Brothers, who shared his values – at least initially. Despite receiving a British subsidy, he took no part in the Arab revolt, his eyes clearly focused on sustaining his base in the Nejd. The decisions of the San Remo and Cairo conferences meant that he now had three rival Hashemite-ruled states to contend with – the Hejaz, Iraq, and Transjordan – but what seems to have spurred him into action in August 1924 was Hussein's proclamation of the Caliphate when it had been abolished by the Turks. Hussein's troops were no match for the Ikhwan who quickly took Taif and Mecca, forcing Hussein to abdicate and be succeeded by his son, Ali. The fall of Jeddah the following year forced Ali to abdicate, too. With the Hashemite cause in the Hejaz in ruins, Ibn Saud was proclaimed king in January 1926.[16] Hussein, a pivotal figure for so much of the period, died in Amman in 1931. The new Saudi Arabia was formally recognised by Britain in 1927, and its ruler could proceed with welding the various elements of his kingdom into a single polity.

4

The Middle East in Transition

By the mid-1920s, much of the Middle East was under mandates: British in Iraq and Palestine, French in Syria and Lebanon. These countries were not colonies but had rather been awarded to Britain and France as Class A mandates under the provisions of Article XXII of the Covenant of the League of Nations, to which body the mandatory powers were ultimately responsible. These mandates followed a broadly similar pattern, the principal exception being Palestine, where Britain was charged with facilitating the creation of a Jewish national home. Reflecting the Wilsonian high-mindedness that had helped conjure them into being, the mandates were to provide administrative advice and assistance to enable the countries concerned to become independent members of the league, although for Palestine that referred merely to self-governing institutions.[1]

French rule in Syria and Lebanon

The French attitude to its new mandatory territories was essentially colonial; Gouraud's two successors as high commissioner were also generals from the French colonies. From the start, they showed their distrust of Syria's Sunni majority by drawing their administrators largely from the minority communities. This discrimination was especially marked in their local troops, where Alawites and Druze were favoured in recruitment. (These two communities were designated semi-autonomous areas of their own: the Alawites in Latakia on the coast and the Druze in Hawran in the south.) As elsewhere in the empire, the French stamped their identity on the education system with an emphasis on the study of French history, culture, and language. The fiscal and economic policies adopted were also closely aligned to France, while French interests controlled much of the infrastructure. The budget was dominated by expenditure on the military. French control rested ultimately on their access to airpower, Senegalese troops of their colonial army, and the Troupes Spéciales du Levant. Recruited from the Syrian minority communities, the Troupes Spéciales provided a model for later armed forces. This policy of what was, in effect, *francisation*, ignored the potential of Syrian nationalism which was not far below the surface.

In 1925, the veteran politician Dr Abdul Rahman Shahbandar, a survivor of Cemal's persecutions, was permitted to form the Hizb Al-Sha-ab, or People's Party in Syria, which found a following in the commercial and professional middle classes. Its programme stood for national independence, the defence of native industries, and the country's reunification (with the exception of the Maronite areas of Mount Lebanon). Indeed, when trouble broke out, it did so not in Damascus or the Sunni heartlands but in the Druze area of Hawran that the French had created. The Druze, led by Sultan Pasha al-Atrash, seemed to have concluded that what the French were offering was a sham, a feeling reinforced by high-handed attempts at land reform and compulsory labour for road building. They were soon joined in revolt by Shahbandar, who proclaimed a provisional government with al-Atrash as president on 9 September. As uprisings spread across the country, Fawzi al-Qawuqji, an Arab captain in the French forces and former officer in the Ottoman Army, and his troops rose at Hama. The fighting was widespread and bitter, marked by atrocities on both sides. In October, it seemed possible that the rebels might take Damascus, much of which they controlled, but French power began to prevail. Not only were they able to bring in reinforcements from their colonial troops but they made devastating use of air power against which the rebels had no answer. When the fighting ended in 1927, much of Damascus and other cities were in ruins. The revolt was ultimately suppressed, its leaders in exile and the People's Party banned, but it showed the French that there had to be a different way to govern the country under the mandate. In the aftermath, a new move-ment – al-Kutlah al-Wataniyya, or National Bloc, once again drawn from the country's elite – moved to fill the political vacuum.[2]

Although the Alawite enclave remained quiescent during the revolt, it was apparent that France's only active support in the region was from the Lebanese Maronites. The Greater Lebanon that Gouraud created contained Shi'as and Sunnis in the Biqaa Valley and elsewhere who would almost cer-tainly have preferred rule from Damascus rather than Beirut.

In 1926, the French awarded Lebanon a constitution in which the principal governmental tasks were to be allocated across the various religious communities, but it proved to be a recipe for bitter in-fighting. This was followed in 1932 by a census, the last of the century, that listed the population at 861,399, with Christians having a majority over all other religious groups in a ratio of six to five. Census figures are never static and, with a high Muslim birth rate and Western-educated Christians able to seek opportunities abroad, an erosion of the Christian majority seemed possible. Nevertheless, the 1932 census results were to have a far-reaching impact on the country's future.[3]

Arabs and Jews under the Palestine Mandate

Relations between the two communities in Palestine, while never cordial, were largely quiet from the 1921 disturbances until 1928 when violence broke out once more. At a time of worldwide economic depression from which Palestine had no immunity, Jewish immigration continued at a steady pace. In 1922, the Jewish population of Palestine, known as the Yishuv, accounted for 83,790 in a total population of 752,048; in 1929, they were 156,481 in a population of 992,558, the overall population increase reflecting a high Arab birth rate.[4]

The mandate also carried certain responsibilities. Under Article 4, the British were charged with recognising a Jewish agency that would cooperate with the administration in economic and social matters affecting the establishment of the national home. This agency would be permitted to develop natural resources as well as public works, services, and utilities. The Zionist organisation was to be recognised as such an agency. The key body here was the World Zionist Organisation (WZO).

Weizmann was elected president of the WZO at the International Zionist Congress in London in July 1920 – but his leadership was not unquestioned. In particular, he quarrelled with the leading US Zionist, Justice Louis D. Brandeis, and the dispute was resolved only by making the latter honorary president of the WZO. An essential part of Weizmann's political philosophy and strategy was his faith in British good intentions, but his Anglophile credo was not always shared by his colleagues. Another critic who surfaced at the congress asserted that the Jews had fared better under the Turks than under the British. He was the then relatively unknown David Ben-Gurion.

Ben-Gurion, who galvanised Zionist endeavours on the ground, was in most respects the polar opposite of Weizmann. Born David Grün in the small town of Plonsk in Russian Poland in 1886, Ben Gurion acquired his Zionism at an early age through his father, a member of the Hibbat Zion movement. In 1906, he arrived in Palestine, living initially at what was then the small settlement of Petah Tikvah. Hebraicising his name to Ben-Gurion, he soon immersed himself in politics, which became the abiding passion of his life. In common with many of colleagues, his Zionism was combined with socialism. Educational opportunities in Palestine were few. In contrast to Weizmann's sophisticated scientific training in central Europe, Ben-Gurion managed a brief spell at the University of Istanbul before this was interrupted by the outbreak of war. Expelled by Cemal, he spent part of the war in the United States, finally joining the British-sponsored Jewish Legion but saw no active service through illness.

The operation of the mandate, with its encouragement of Jewish institutions, provided the platform for Ben-Gurion's entry into public life. With his socialist convictions, he became the leading figure in the Histadrut, the General Federation of Jewish Labour, which was founded in 1920. Ben-Gurion and the Histadrut embodied the practical thrust combined with socialist idealism that lay behind Jewish activity in Palestine for much of the 1920s and which was to build the foundations of the national home.[5] Closely aligned with the Histadrut, both ideologically and in terms of its leading personalities, was Mapai, the Palestine Jewish Labour Party. As its name suggests, Mapai was a socialist party, and it dominated the Yishuv and the State of Israel politically in its formative years.

The British administration was, in effect, shadowed by a Jewish counterpart. Under a general assembly – the Va'ad Leumi, or National Council – the work for the national home went forward. The Jewish National Fund, sustained by contributions from Jews around the word, enabled them to purchase land, mostly in the coastal plain and the Jezreel Valley. A distinctive feature of Jewish settlement was the establishment of the kibbutzim, the first of which dated from 1921. These were self-sufficient communal villages, predominantly agricultural. Once the security situation in Palestine deteriorated, some also acquired a defensive role.

Tel Aviv, Haifa, and the Jewish areas of Jerusalem such as Rehavia expanded. Important infrastructural projects were started, notably the Palestine Electric Company, and in 1925 a long-held dream of Weizmann's was realised in the opening by Balfour of the Hebrew University on Jerusalem's Mount Scopus. The Yishuv also had its secret defence force, the Haganah, whose primary purpose was the defence of Jewish settlements from possible Arab attacks. In short, under the aegis of the mandate, the Zionist leaders were steadily building an embryonic state.

The leadership of Weizmann and Ben-Gurion was not unchallenged. In 1925, the Odessa-born journalist Ze'ev Jabotinsky seceded from the WZO to found a rival right-wing revisionist Zionist movement, which ten years later morphed into the New Zionist Movement with himself as leader. Unlike the more cautious leaders of the WZO, at the heart of the revisionist agenda was the vision of a Jewish state in Palestine on both sides of the River Jordan. Jabotinsky's initiative proved to be the origin of a fundamental left–right split within Zionism, which over time was to have profound political consequences. Another challenge was emerging. While Zionism in this period was essentially secular in character and belief, the organisation also contained within it the supporters of the Mizrachi movement, which had its origins in the pre-war period. The movement's aim was to represent within Zionism the ideal of orthodox religious belief which they held was compatible with its political ambitions. Although the Mizrachi worked within the overall organisation of Zionism, the post-war period was to see the rise of Orthodox political parties that were able to exercise considerable political power.[6]

Arab institutions in the 1920s did not mirror the breadth

of those of the Jews. While the terms of the mandate laid out in broad detail what Britain's responsibilities were in relation to the development of the Jewish national home, there was no similar *vade mecum* for the Arabs beyond a repetition of the Balfour Declaration's assurance of the civil and religious rights of the existing non-Jewish communities. In 1921, however, the supreme Muslim Council was established. It was charged with the administration of the Waqf funds and the sharia courts. As mufti of Jerusalem, Haj Amin became its president, marking him out as religious leader of the Arabs and giving him authority over the distribution of the Waqf funds. For political purposes the British also recognised the Arab Executive Committee, led by Musa Kasim al-Husseini, the former mayor of Jerusalem who died in 1934. But, like that of Weizmann and Ben-Gurion, the dominance of the Husseini family did not go unchallenged. Opposition came from one of the other leading Jerusalem families, the Nashashibis, who formed the rival, but ultimately ineffective, National Defence Party in 1934. But neither of these bodies carried the political and economic weight of their well-organised Jewish counterparts.[7]

Palestine in crisis

The comparative peace in Palestine owed much to the prudent policies of Samuel and Field Marshal Herbert Plumer, Viscount of Messines who succeeded him as high commissioner in 1925. Both men were content to see to the business of administration while ensuring law and order. The latter was maintained by the Palestine Gendarmerie, a paramilitary force created by Churchill in 1922, which provided a convenient home for former members of the Royal Irish Constabulary and its auxiliaries, who had been the backbone of the Crown forces during the Irish War of Independence but were being stood down. Such was the peaceful state of the country that in 1926 Plumer disbanded it. Its replacement was the Palestine Police, drawn from local communities and including a small British contingent. But the lack of a paramilitary gendarmerie left the authorities ill-prepared when violence recurred, with only two armoured-car squadrons to cover both Palestine and Transjordan.

The Arabs were aware that constitutional and political changes were taking place in Egypt and elsewhere in the region, whereas there was no sign of any comparable political progress in Palestine. When trouble came, it did so over the most sensitive place in Jerusalem, the Western Wall, as well as what was then the narrow passageway to it, situated at the foot of the Haram al-Sharif/Temple Mount. Jews had been allowed access to it for centuries under a series of agreements and conventions, with the provision that nothing should be erected on the pavement. British policy was to uphold these conventions. But on 24 September 1928, Yom Kippur, Judaism's holiest day, some Jews put up a screen to separate men from women, and the police took it down. This incident proved to be the disturbing prelude to a tragic series of events the following year. On 15 August 1929, Jews processed to the Western Wall, followed the next day by Arabs. This triggered widespread attacks on Jews, 133 of whom were killed and 339 wounded, while 116 Arabs were killed and 232 wounded, mostly in security operations. Attacks were also made on the holy cities of Safed and Hebron where sixty Jews were killed.[8]

Faced with the sudden end of the relative calm of the 1920s, the government appointed a commission of inquiry chaired by Sir Walter Shaw, which reported on 31 March 1930. Essentially, Shaw concluded that the outbreak was the result of Arab fears about Jewish immigration, which he felt was excessive, and the amount of land purchased. Weizmann, who had been made president of an expanded Jewish Agency the previous year, realising the danger to Zionist hopes that was being threatened, began to lobby in London. The result was that the Labour prime minister, Ramsay MacDonald, made a statement to parliament in which he confirmed Britain's commitment to the national home. MacDonald was supported by Stanley Baldwin for the Conservatives and Lloyd George for the Liberals, but, even so, the government appointed a commission chaired by Sir John Hope Simpson to chart a way forward on the crucial areas of land settlement and immigration. His report, published on 20 October 1930, threatened to undermine the main thrust of progress on the national home so far: it advised that if Arab living standards were to be maintained, there was no room for more immigrants on the land unless there was further development of Jewish land and better cultivation of Arab land. His conclusions were endorsed in an accompanying white paper. Bitter at the apparent failure of his pro-British policies, Weizmann resigned as president of the WZO and the Jewish Agency but worked to secure political support in London. On 13 February 1931, MacDonald wrote to him. He did not rescind the white paper, but he did offer reassurance on the key

Zionist concerns of immigration and land purchase, neither of which would be ended. Throughout the ebb and flow of British policy, Weizmann's undoubted gift for diplomacy had again been deployed. There the matter came to rest, but the real challenges were not far distant.[9]

Iraq: From mandate to independent kingdom

Feisal's accession to the throne of Iraq was always problematic, as both he and the British were uneasily aware. He was an outsider to the country and a Sunni Arab in a country where they were in the minority. Above all, if Feisal were to carry the necessary authority as the country's sovereign, he could not afford to be seen as Britain's placeman. Clearly, too, as the events of 1920 had demonstrated, the mandate was deeply resented by his subjects. The Anglo-Iraqi Treaty of 1922, which was to last for twenty years, was an initial attempt to finesse relations between the two countries, combining the mandate with Iraqi sovereignty, but the latter was clearly constrained by continuing British control of foreign policy, finance, and security. In a further refinement of the mandate, the British also agreed to the creation of a constituent assembly, which immediately gave rise to the formation of two political parties opposed to the treaty. Cox's response was one of repression, which simply underscored the reality of continuing British power. The treaty was signed in October, but such was the strength of opposition to it that the British soon made modifications. The period of twenty years' duration was now changed to the date of Iraq's admission to the League of Nations or four years after the treaty of peace with Turkey. Two issues remained to be resolved. The new Turkish Republic led by Mustafa Kemal had ambitions towards the former Ottoman vilayet of Mosul with its substantial Kurdish population. The discovery of oil made it more attractive to the British, and the matter was resolved in the latter's favour in the Treaty of Ankara concluded between Britain, Turkey, and Iraq in 1926. The second area of contention was the proposal for conscription, which the ruling elite in Baghdad saw as essential for their control of the country. The proposal aroused a fierce reaction in the Shi'a majority. Such was the strength of their opposition that the British made it clear that they could not support it.

The man who had emerged as the Hashemite monarchy's strongest supporter was Nuri al-Said, Feisal's colleague in the Arab Revolt and at the Paris Peace Conference. In 1930, he negotiated a new treaty that gave Iraq control over defence and security. For its part, Britain retained a military presence and two air bases, one at Habbaniya and the other at Shu'aiba. Nuri was also able to chart Iraq's move into full independence by applying to the League of Nations for membership. In October 1932, Iraq's membership was approved by the league, ending the mandate and making the country an independent kingdom. As events were to show, this did not end Britain's role in the country. What's more, Feisal was not destined to see how his newly independent kingdom would develop. In failing health, he died, still a comparatively young man, the following year.[10]

Egypt from treaty to treaty

In Egypt, the decade from the mid-1920s to the mid-1930s was one in which a variety of competing interests jostled for power and influence. Lord Lloyd, who succeeded Allenby as high commissioner in 1925, was an imperialist who saw his purpose as defending British interests. King Fuad, who distrusted the Wafd, was intent on asserting the prerogatives of the palace. And, while the Wafd, led by Mustafa al-Nahhas after Zaghlul's death in 1927, remained a powerful force, it was not the only political party. There were those of a secular persuasion who looked with admiration on the republic that Mustafa Kemal was creating in Turkey. But those who advocated constitutional politics faced several major hurdles. The most obvious of these was the incomplete nature of the country's independence. Its economy was also badly affected by the worldwide depression at a time when it was trying to provide for a rapidly rising population, and there was an unease felt by religious groups over policies of a secular nature.

Although Western education still had only a fledgling presence in the country, it had existed for some time. US Protestant missionaries had been active in the Christian communities of the nearby Levant in the mid-nineteenth century, their principal legacy being the opening in 1866 of the American Protestant College in Beirut, which in 1920 became the American University of Beirut. Egypt, too, became the focus of mission work, notably the mission of the United Presbyterian Church of North America, which was founded in 1858 and led by Andrew Watson, a Scottish-born immigrant to the United States, who with his wife worked in Egypt for some fifty years. Their son, Charles, was born in Egypt in 1871 and studied in the United States before returning to Cairo. Charles Watson's long held vision was of a university similar to that in Beirut, but the path was not straightforward. The project needed money, and the British, while not totally obstructive, had their own educational plans and were not anxious to see the creation of a rival. By 1919, Watson had raised significant capital from a range of US donors and had his sights trained on a possible location in the city centre owned by a Greek tobacco magnate, Nestor Gianaclis, but the price was still beyond him. The project was rescued by the outbreak of the revolution in spring 1919, which caused a crash in property values and thus enabled Watson to purchase the property. The necessary educational credentials were secured by a charter from the Board of Education of the District of Columbia. An important endorsement for the fledgling institution came in 1924 when Prime Minister Zaghlul along with five colleagues attended the graduation, or commencement, ceremonies. From its formal inception in 1919 to his retirement in 1945, Watson served as president of the American University in Cairo, which admitted its first female student in 1928.[11]

The cause of Egyptian women was taken up by Huda Shaarawi, who had come into prominence for her role in the 1919 revolution. After her husband's death in 1922, she turned increasingly to social concerns, especially the position of women. The following year, she became chair of the newly formed Egyptian Feminist Union, a key moment coming in 1923 when, after attending a women's congress in Rome, she and a colleague appeared at Cairo railway station unveiled and were immediately joined by other women who were there to welcome them.[12]

Discontent with the existing order could be found amongst religious groups, too. Muslim unease found its focus with the formation in 1928 by Hassan al-Banna of al-Ikhwan al-Muslimun (the Muslim Brotherhood). Originally concerned with religious teaching, the movement soon dedicated itself to the creation of a state that would be guided and permeated by Islamic principles. In the 1930s, it attracted into its ranks many Egyptians who were alienated by the way their country seemed to be Westernising, condemning Western values and advocating sharia law. It also found support in other areas of the Middle East, and its beliefs proved to have an enduring appeal. However, the Muslim Brotherhood was regarded with deep suspicion by those who believed in a secular Arab nationalism.[13]

The restless ambition of the Italian dictator Benito Mussolini brought the affairs of Egypt back into sharp focus. On 3 October 1935, the Italian Army invaded Abyssinia, as Ethiopia was then called. The unequal struggle had immense implications for Egypt. The plight of the Abyssinians in the face of aggression provoked sympathy among Egyptians. To the west of Egypt was the Italian colony of Libya, which the Italians had wrested from the Ottomans in 1911–12. Conquest of Abyssinia now placed the Italians on another flank. The British, although confining themselves to diplomatic methods, were well aware of the potential danger to their communications through the Red Sea. Were Anglo–Italian relations to worsen, Egypt would inevitably become a war zone. The consequent strengthening of the British garrison with the dispatch of an infantry brigade, armoured units, and a mechanised artillery brigade, together with the reinforcing of the Mediterranean fleet at Alexandria all seemed to put a question mark against the reality of independence. Egyptian politicians, regardless of party, insisted on a new treaty that would clarify relations between the two countries. Negotiations between Prime Minister al-Nahhas and the powerful British high commissioner, Sir Miles Lampson, resulted in an agreement signed on 26 August 1936. In the course of the negotiations, King Fuad died, to be succeeded by his young son, Farouk. The agreement secured the right for Britain to retain troops at Alexandria for eight years, with retention of military assets in the Western Desert and along the Canal. Critically, as events were soon to confirm, in the event of war Britain was to be afforded all the country's facilities.[14]

The Palestine Mandate under review

Ultimately, Mussolini's Italy was not an existential threat to Britain. Adolf Hitler's Germany was. Once Hitler – in open defiance of the Treaty of Versailles – announced rearmament in March 1935, followed by the remilitarisation of the Rhineland twelve months later, British defence planners had to consider the possibility of another war with Germany. When, in December 1937, Mussolini joined the Anti-Comintern Pact that Germany and Japan had concluded the previous year, the danger signals were clear. These developments helped set the context for British policy in the Middle East. There was, of course, a further dimension to National Socialist Germany, which was Hitler's obsessive hatred of the Jews.

Immediately after Hitler gained power in January 1933, Jews were systematically excluded from key areas of national life. In 1935, the Nuremberg Laws divided the population into two categories: the *Reichsbürger*, defined as those of so-called German blood, were to have the benefits of full citizenship, while the *Staatsangehörige*, those of Jewish ancestry, were not. In such a climate of fear and discrimination, large numbers of Jews were moved to emigrate, but with the US Immigration Act of 1924 preventing mass movement to the United States, Palestine was the obvious option. By 1936, the Jewish population stood at 370,483 out of a Palestinian population of 1,336,518. Not only was there a surge in the population of the Yishuv but these new immigrants wished to recreate the urban lifestyles of central Europe. Emblematic of this cultural life was the arrival of one of the world's leading conductors, Arturo Toscanini, to conduct a series of six concerts by the Palestine Symphony Orchestra.

Faced with what they saw as the transformation of their way of life in Palestine, the Arabs reacted in a variety of ways. Their rising temper was revealed in November 1935 when the radical religious leader Sheikh Izz ad-Din al-Qassam led a group of armed followers into the Galilee hills. He was soon killed by the police, but his funeral in Haifa was the occasion of a great Arab demonstration. His name was to inspire a later generation. On 15 April 1936, the Arab Revolt in Palestine began with the murder of a Jew near Nablus. This was quickly followed by a general strike of Arab labourers, shopkeepers, and transport workers. The supreme Arab Committee, later termed the Arab Higher Committee, was formed under Haj Amin. The committee's immediate demand was an end to Jewish immigration, but it was also seeking to establish a government.

The British response to the Arab campaign was partly military and partly political. Military units were brought in from Egypt and Malta, and under Sir Charles Tegart, formerly of the Indian Police, a barrier was constructed along the northern border in an attempt to starve the rebels of men and supplies. In addition to their own security forces, the British turned a Nelsonian eye on the activities of the illegal Jewish defence force, the Haganah, comprising some 20,000 young men and women, which had been formed in 1920 to defend Jewish settlements from Arab attacks.[15] Even so, pressure was being put on British resources just as the international situation was causing mounting concern.

In an attempt to reach a political way forward, in August 1936 the government appointed a royal commission chaired by Lord Peel. The commission's dominant voice turned out to be that of Professor Reginald Coupland, Beit Professor of Colonial History at the University of Oxford. Coupland had made a particular study of nationality questions in South Africa and Canada, and he was also well versed in the details of the Irish settlement. Once in Palestine, Coupland quickly concluded that a radical move was needed. On 23 December 1936, he first suggested to Weizmann the possibility of having two big areas, and on 8 January 1937 he followed this up with the suggestion of a partition leading to two independent states. Weizmann realised that the idea could lead to the early achievement of a Jewish state, albeit in only part of the country. A few weeks later at a meeting at Nahalal, the two men came to the unofficial understanding that they would argue for the proposal. At a series of meetings at Helwan in Egypt, Coupland convinced his colleagues that they could recommend such a division but left the details to be worked out. When the commission's report was signed on 22 June 1937, largely drafted by Coupland, it followed his line of reasoning that there were two distinct communities in Palestine. From his premise that there was an Arab community that was Asian in character and culture while that of the Jews was European, Coupland concluded that there was no sense of a common citizenship. It therefore followed, he argued, that since neither side could rule all of Palestine, each should have part of it: in short, partition. A rough plan of partition was sketched with the Jewish area comprising much of the coastal plain and Galilee. Jerusalem, with a corridor to the coast, was to remain a British enclave. Conceding that the proposed Jewish state would have an Arab community of at least 225,000, Coupland proposed a possible population transfer, possibly by compulsion.[16]

The report's key recommendation of partition did not have an easy passage in London where influential pro-Zionist speakers such as Lloyd George, Samuel, and Churchill bitterly attacked the proposal in both houses of parliament, the essence of their case being that partition would negate the Balfour Declaration. The cabinet, on the other hand, endorsed partition on the grounds that it offered each of the two protagonists national independence, although worries were expressed about certain aspects, particularly its effect on Indian Muslims who were so vital to the strength of the British Indian Army. Key to success would, of course, rest with the Jews and the Arabs. The reaction of the former came at the Twentieth Zionist Congress in Zurich in August 1937. Weizmann continued his strong support for partition and Ben-Gurion was broadly in favour, although he had concerns over population transfer. The leaders of US Zionism, Louis Brandeis and Stephen Wise, were unhappy but agreed to a compromise in which the Zionist Congress rejected the partition proposal as it stood but authorised the leadership to negotiate with the government.[17] When the Arab Higher Committee and an Arab National Conference met at Bloudan in Syria on 11 September, partition was rejected. The British government thus had to reckon with a lukewarm Zionist response to partition and an Arab determination to fight it because it would require them to give up part of their land.

In British governmental circles, opposition to partition had its focus in the Foreign Office and its diplomats in the Middle East, concerned as they were with oil supplies, the Suez Canal, and imperial lines of communication. Their opposition was fuelled by moves that were being made by Mussolini's Italy. In July 1937, it was reported that the Italians were reinforcing their army in Libya with two divisions, producing a motorised army of 60,000 that would threaten the British position in Egypt. Italy's propaganda machine, notably its powerful radio transmitter at Bari, was directed at winning Arab support. Mussolini was portrayed as the Protector of Islam, having been presented with the 'Sword of Islam' during a visit to his Libyan colony in March. Three British cabinet meetings in late 1937 signalled an about-turn on the question of partition. At the second, on 8 December, members were presented with a paper from the foreign secretary, Anthony Eden, that accepted the Arab position. It was immediately clear that he had the support of the prime minister, Neville Chamberlain, who concluded that, while no policy could please everyone, partition would not give the Jews much satisfaction and it would still antagonise the Arabs. The new proposed commission to examine partition was to preclude any forcible transfer of Arabs. The brief was to delineate two states that were as homogenous as possible and should be self-supporting. It was allowed to conclude that it could find no workable scheme. In case the chair of the commission, Sir John Woodhead, was in any doubt, he was sent a confidential letter to the effect that he would be at liberty to pronounce against partition.[18] When the commission eventually reported on 9 November 1938, three possible partition scenarios were presented, each one judged to be unworkable.[19] Even before Woodhead reported, on 24 October a committee chaired by Chamberlain pronounced partition to be dead and that a conference would be convened in London.

By then, of course, Britain's international position had deteriorated alarmingly – and not just with respect to Italy. Not only had Hitler annexed Austria and the Sudetenland but Japan's aggression in China opened up the prospect of a war against three antagonists. In a war that seemed increasingly inevitable, Britain needed a stable Middle East with its key communications and its oil. The Middle East conference opened in London on 7 February 1939, but it proved to be a pointless affair since it was clear that, as war threatened, strategic considerations were driving British policy. At a meeting of the cabinet committee on Palestine on 20 April,

Chamberlain could not have made this any clearer, concluding that since Britain needed to have the Muslim world on
its side it would be necessary to offend the Jews and not the
Arabs. On 17 May, the colonial secretary, Malcolm Mac-
Donald, set out British plans for Palestine in a white paper.
Palestine was to become independent in ten years' time as
a united country. Further Jewish immigration would be
limited to 75,000 over the next five years, any more needing
Arab consent, leaving the Jews as a minority of one-third in
the country and thus ending Britain's commitment to the
national home. As a wartime measure, it was to prove invaluable in helping Britain's Arab friends keep the Middle East
quiet in the Allied interest.[20] For the Palestinians, the Arab
Higher Committee was divided: the National Defence Party
led by Ragheb Bey Nashashibi accepted that the statement
went far to meet their case, but Haj Amin, then in exile in
Lebanon, did not. The Arab Revolt had by then been suppressed at the cost over 3,000 lives, but in political terms its
impact had been marked.

Jewish reaction to the white paper was a mixture of
outrage and despair. The winter of 1938–9 witnessed a dramatic deterioration in the position of the Jews in Germany,
which now included Austria and the Sudetenland. In early
November, a pogrom was unleashed, known as *Kristallnacht*,
in which some 100 Jews were killed with thousands more
sent to concentration camps, while synagogues and Jewish
businesses were destroyed. Then, on 30 January 1939 came
Hitler's Reichstag speech in which he chillingly referred to
the destruction of the Jews of Europe in the event of war. By
August 1939, it was clear that war was imminent. When the

Zionist Congress met in Geneva from 16–24 August, during which time the Nazi–Soviet Pact was concluded, the circumstances could not have been bleaker. It fell to Ben-Gurion to define Jewish policy in a war that was now only days away: namely, that they would assist the British as if there were no white paper and they would fight the white paper as if there were no war.[21] Relations between the Zionists and the British were never really to recover from the white paper. On 1 September, the anticipated German invasion of Poland took place. Two days later, Britain and France declared war on Germany. For the second time, the peoples of the Middle East were to be embroiled in a war not of their making, while for the Jews of Europe the reality that lay behind Hitler's threat was to become all too apparent.

5

The Second World War and the Middle East

The period between the outbreak of hostilities and the German invasion of Norway and Denmark on 9 April 1940 became known as the Phoney War, at the end of which, on 10 May, as the German armed forces surged across the Netherlands, Belgium, Luxembourg, and France, Churchill replaced Chamberlain as prime minister.[1] For the two million Jews of recently conquered Poland, however, this period was anything but a phoney war: throughout the winter of 1939–40, the SS under Heinrich Himmler waged a ruthless campaign against them, forcing them into ghettoes in Warsaw and other major cities such as Lodz and Cracow, sealed off from outside society.[2] During this period, the balance of power in the Middle East seemed to rest firmly with Britain and France. Essentially a central European in outlook, Hitler did not seem to have the region on his agenda; Mussolini, who did entertain ambitions as the 'Protector of Islam', had not rushed to join his German partner in declaring war. Both the Egyptian and Iraqi governments moved prudently, breaking off diplomatic relations with Germany but making it clear that their only military obligation to Britain was to act in self-defence.

The expanding conflict

Two events in the summer of 1940 marked the end of this period of watching and waiting in the Middle East. First, on 22 June, France signed an armistice with Germany. Under its terms, France was to retain a government headed by the venerable Marshal Philippe Pétain with its headquarters at the spa town of Vichy. On 24 October, Hitler met Pétain at Montoire where the latter accepted the principle of collaboration between their countries. Although collaboration was an ambiguous term that could, and did, take many forms, it had serious implications for British security in the Middle East where Syria and Lebanon could no longer be regarded as friendly territory. Some, few at first but growing in numbers as the war progressed, joined the Free French of General Charles de Gaulle. The bitter split between the supporters of Vichy and the Free French was to have considerable impact in the Levant.

The second of these events came on 10 June when Mussolini declared war, the potential Rome–Berlin Axis now a reality. His decision posed an immediate threat to the British position in Egypt. The newly appointed governor and commander-in-chief in neighbouring Libya was Marshal Rodolfo Graziani, who could deploy the Fifth and Tenth Armies. But his army was rather less formidable than it appeared on paper: it was deficient in armour and motorised transport, and it was September before he felt that it was ready to cross the border into Egypt. It then halted to re-equip, giving the British time to respond. Instead of reinforcing his army in North Africa, on 28 October 1940 Mussolini launched an ill-fated invasion of Greece. Back in Egypt, Britain's commander-in-chief Middle East was General Sir Archibald Wavell, an officer of fine talent and impeccable credentials, whose outnumbered Western Desert Force, commanded by Lieutenant-General Richard O'Connor, consisted of just two divisions, the 7th Armoured and the 4th Indian. With Britain itself under threat of invasion and starved of military materiel, Churchill's government took the brave decision to send an armoured brigade around the Cape to reinforce Wavell. His counter-offensive routed the Italian Army, which retreated into Libya having sustained enormous casualties. The Italian threat to Egypt was apparently over, but a greater one was soon to emerge.

These events in Egypt turned Hitler's attention to the Mediterranean theatre where his naval commander, Admiral Erich Raeder, was recommending some assistance to the Italians. Seemingly unconvinced by the leisurely pace of Graziani's advance into Egypt, on 12 November 1940 Hitler ordered that an armoured division be put on standby depending on how the Italian forces were faring in Egypt. Had German armoured troops indeed been deployed at that time, they might well have overwhelmed Wavell's command and taken Egypt. But Mussolini was not ready for German assistance.

It was not until 11 January 1941, with his allies in full retreat, that Hitler issued Directive Number 22 ordering support for the defence of Libya against British armoured forces in what was soon designated Operation Sonnenblume (sunflower), initially by the Fliegerkorps X flying from bases in Sicily.[3] This dramatic intervention, for that is what it was, was agreed at a meeting with Mussolini on 19 and 20 January.

The chosen German commander was Major-General Erwin Rommel, who had led his armoured division with skill and daring during the invasion of France, capturing most of the 51st Highland Division at Saint-Valery. In late February, the German 5th Light Division began deploying in Libya, followed by the 15th Panzer Division, forming the Deutsches Afrikakorps (German Africa Corps).

Determined to maintain the momentum that they had gained against the Italians, Wavell and O'Connor continued their offensive into Libya, but their hopes for final victory were dashed when the government decided to send a force of some 60,000 men from the Middle East in a fruitless attempt to assist the Greeks at a time when Rommel was ready to make his own initial moves in the desert. It was the turn of the Western Desert Force to be pushed back, O'Connor being taken prisoner. Pressed by Churchill to resume the offensive, in June Wavell mounted Operation Battleaxe, but the balance of advantage was now held by Rommel, and it failed. Egypt once again lay under threat.

The crises in Iraq and Syria

Germany's active engagement in the war in the Middle East dramatically changed the situation, but it was not the only problem that Britain faced in the spring of 1941. Hitler's dramatic string of victories convinced many that his was going to be the winning side.

In Iraq, Feisal's death in 1933 was followed by a period of instability in which the army grew in power and influence with many officers chafing at the country's continuing dependence on Britain. At the heart of the army was a group of nationalist officers known as the Golden Square. The head of the German legation in Iraq, the highly experienced Dr Fritz Grobba, was assiduously spreading his country's message, especially among army officers. This instability was compounded with the death of King Ghazi in April 1939 after a car crash. As his son, King Feisal II, was only a four-year-old child, power lay with the king's uncle, Abd al-Ilah, as regent. Both the regent and Nuri al-Said, his prime minister for much of the time, maintained a pro-British position, which put them at odds with the Golden Square, whose sympathies were turning increasingly to those of the Axis. Shortly after the outbreak of war, the Golden Square invited the exiled Haj Amin to Baghdad where he reinforced anti-British sentiment.

During the first phase of the war, Nuri's position was increasingly challenged by a young lawyer of strong nationalist convictions, Rashid Ali al-Gaylani, who joined forces with the officers of the Golden Square. In March 1940, Rashid Ali became prime minister, holding the office until the following January when clashes with the regent forced his resignation. The initiative now rested with the military of the Golden Square, who seized control of the government on 1 April 1941, forcing the regent to take refuge in the British air base at Habbaniya. A government of national defence was then formed under Rashid Ali. Faced with this challenge, Wavell's Middle East Command seemed poorly positioned to respond, faced as he was with the loss of troops to the Balkan campaign and with Rommel's desert offensive. On the initiative of the viceroy, Lord Linlithgow, and his commander-in-chief, Sir Claude Auchinleck, troops were rushed from India to Basra, enabling the British to gain the upper hand by early May. Their action came just in time since, on 23 May, Hitler, who had been preoccupied with his imminent invasion of the Soviet Union, signed a directive on the Middle East authorising an operation in Iraq. From the premise that the Arab Freedom Movement was Germany's natural ally in the region, Hitler had decided to assist Iraq by forming a military mission under Luftwaffe general Hellmuth Felmy. By agreement with the French, arms were to be supplied from bases in Syria. He was too late. Some German aircraft had already crossed Syria to reach Iraq, but the Luftwaffe was too embroiled in its operations in Crete for this to have any effect. On 30 May, as British forces approached Baghdad, Rashid Ali, Haj Amin, and some supporters took refuge in Turkey and Iran, while the principal officers of the Golden Square were executed. Iraq and its oil had been saved for the Allied cause, but the ability of the army to stage a coup was to prove an uneasy precedent for the Hashemites.[4]

After the French armistice in 1940, the British and French in the Levant did not go out of their way to provoke each other, although German and Italian personnel were active in Syria and Lebanon. In January 1941, the German profile was raised with the arrival as minister plenipotentiary of Otto von Hentig, who lost no time in emphasising his country's goodwill towards the Arab and Muslim worlds. The French high commissioner in the Levant was General Henri Fernand Dentz, who was completely loyal to Vichy. The passage through Syria of German aircraft and munitions for the Iraqi rebels convinced the British of the need for action. On 8 June

1941, the British announced that Free French and imperial troops, mostly Australian and Indian, had crossed the border into Lebanon. The Vichy troops defended themselves tenaciously, inflicting a serious reverse on the invading forces at the Litani River. There was also fratricidal fighting between French soldiers loyal to Vichy and those supporting the Free French. On 14 July, Dentz agreed to an armistice. With the end of the campaign and the Free French now in control, the British no longer had to factor in any hostile activity by collaborationist governments in Damascus and Beirut.[5]

The new delegate general and commander-in-chief Levant was General Georges Catroux, a leading Free French supporter who had been de Gaulle's representative in the Middle East. Catroux issued proclamations declaring the independence of Syria on 27 September and Lebanon on 26 November 1941, adding that France would not allow her interests in the Levant to be handed over to the enemy and that she would retain control of the army, security forces, and much of the infrastructure. In practice, however, the Gaullist authorities showed little urgency in implementing independence. Clashes between protestors and the French authorities and troops occurred in both Lebanon and Syria, effectively ending any possibility that France might retain some of the special presence in the Levant that colonial partisans had so coveted. Britain had recognised Catroux's declarations of independence in 1941, while the United States and the Soviet Union followed suit in 1944. Even so, the path to real independence was precarious. In the summer of 1943, elections were held in Lebanon for a chamber of deputies with the Maronite Bishara al-Khuri becoming president, choosing as his prime minister the Sunni Riyadh al-Sulh. Out of this arrangement came the unofficial National Pact that was to govern the country's affairs henceforth, whereby the president would be a Maronite, the prime minister a Sunni, the speaker a Shi'a, and the commander-in-chief of the army a Maronite with a Druze as chief of staff. Parliament and the administration were to represent Christians and Muslims in the proportion six to five, reflecting the result of the 1932 census.[6]

When, in November 1943, the government demanded a final end to the French mandate, the French arrested al-Khuri and most of his ministers. But the time for such action had long passed. Massive demonstrations involving both Christians and Muslims forced their release. Although the French retained some military presence, Lebanon had become a free country. Elections were also held in Syria in July 1943 with Shukri al-Quwatli coming to power. Although powers were steadily transferred from Paris to Beirut and Damascus in 1944, the French presence in Syria ended much as it had begun. In May 1945, both countries saw demonstrations against the continuing presence of French troops, who responded by bombarding and shelling Damascus for three days with a high number of casualties on both sides. After an appeal by al-Quwatli, British troops still garrisoned in the country intervened to calm the situation. In April 1946, French troops finally left Syria, followed by Lebanon in December.[7]

The battles for Egypt

With the failure of his Operation Battleaxe, Wavell, who had shouldered enormous burdens over the previous year, including the conquest of Italian East Africa, was transferred to the India command in June 1941. His replacement was Auchinleck, whose swift response to the Iraqi crisis had convinced Churchill of his ability to bring renewed vigour to the Middle East. Auchinleck was not a British Army officer, but he had served in the Indian Army in various capacities since 1903, seeing action in Egypt and Mesopotamia in the previous war. Conscious of the deficiencies experienced in the Mesopotamia campaign, he waited until 17 November before launching his offensive, Operation Crusader. His striking force was the newly formed Eighth Army, consisting of two corps. On the opposing side, however, Rommel had at his disposal a well-balanced force of three German divisions, with the conversion of the 5th Light Division into the 21st Panzer Division and the formation of the 90th Light Division, as well as the Italian XXI Corps, his whole command now called Panzer Group Africa. Also deployed was the Italian mobile XX Corps, which included the Ariete Armoured Division.

The resulting battles were fierce and at times confused, but British pressure steadily prevailed, and by 7 December Rommel had decided to retreat. Once it had time to reorganise and re-equip, the Eighth Army seemed to be in a position to move to the final defeat of the Axis Army. On that day, however, the entire complexion of the war changed with the Japanese attack on Pearl Harbor and British possessions in the east.

The sequence of disasters facing the British in South-East Asia had immediate and lasting consequences for Auchinleck's command. The 18th Division, which was on its way to join him, was diverted to Malaya where its men were captured, while the 17th Indian Division was held back in India. Many Australian and New Zealand troops were sent home to prepare their defences. By contrast, on 5 January 1942 a supply convoy reached Libya from Italy with fifty-five tanks, armoured cars, and anti-tank guns. By the end of the month, a complete Italian division had also landed, enabling Rommel to return to the offensive, regaining Libyan territory he had lost in the Crusader battles. As the two armies geared up for the coming battles, February 1942 saw a major crisis in Anglo-Egyptian relations. For most of the war under its pro-British prime minister Hussein Sirri, Egypt had abided by the provisions of the 1936 treaty, allowing the British a free run of her facilities. Inevitably, however, there were those in the country who believed an Axis victory was likely and wished to prepare for the day when Rommel's forces would enter Cairo.

On 1 February 1942, unrest led to Sirri's resignation. The British could not contemplate a change in Egyptian policy at such a critical time. Ambassador Lampson visited the royal palace insisting to the young King Farouk that he appoint a government of the Wafd led by al-Nahhas, with whom he had negotiated the treaty. Farouk was given only until the following day to comply. When his advisers sought to temporise, three British tanks with infantry entered the grounds of the royal palace. Accompanied by the commander of British troops in Egypt, Lampson insisted to the king that al-Nahhas be appointed. The ensuing appointment of al-Nahhas's government ensured that Auchinleck and his successors could fight their critical battles with a secure country to rely on, but Lampson's imperious action became known to Egyptians as the Great Humiliation.[8]

Both sides were preparing a renewed offensive, but on 26 May 1942 Rommel moved first. Over the next month, he completely outmanoeuvred the Eighth Army, now commanded by Lieutenant-General Neil Ritchie, in the Battle of Gazala, capturing the port of Tobruk with its garrison of over 30,000 on 20 June before advancing into Egypt. The scale of Rommel's victory seemed confirmation of Axis supremacy in the North African theatre, he himself being awarded his field marshal's baton. Certain that final victory was imminent, Mussolini came to North Africa with a large retinue to prepare for his triumphal entry into Alexandria and Cairo. Direct command of the retreating Eighth Army was assumed by Auchinleck who halted its retreat at what proved to be the fine defensive position of El Alamein a mere sixty miles west of Alexandria. Such was the apparent threat to the port that the fleet left for Haifa and Port Said, while preparations were made to render its base facilities unusable. Such measures, while prudent, proved to be unnecessary, since El Alamein was well placed to thwart a further Axis advance.

What became the First Battle of El Alamein began on 1 July 1942 when Rommel unsuccessfully attempted to breach the British line. Over the following weeks, Auchinleck repeatedly foiled every thrust Rommel made until on 27 July each side was exhausted. Mussolini had returned to Rome, his dream of an Egyptian triumph in ashes. Churchill came to Egypt in early August. Deciding on a change of command, he replaced Auchinleck as commander-in-chief Middle East by General Sir Harold Alexander, while Lieutenant-General Bernard Montgomery took command of the Eighth Army. The latter steadily amassed his strength before launching his decisive offensive at the Second Battle of El Alamein on 23 October. Twelve days later, Rommel began his retreat from Egypt, never to see it again. From Graziani's initial invasion to Montgomery's victory, what might be described as the Battle for Egypt had lasted just over two years.

The Holocaust

Although the Holocaust rightly belongs to the history of Europe, its consequences for the Middle East were so profound that any modern history of the region must take full account of it.[9] German policy before the war was to encourage Jewish emigration from Europe, albeit for those who could afford to pay, but with the conquest of Poland and the creation of ghettoes this changed. On 22 June 1941, the war entered an entirely new dimension with the invasion of the Soviet Union aimed at creating *Lebensraum* for Germany and the destruction of communism, believed by Hitler to be 'Judeo-Marxism'. Early successes in the campaign brought a further four million Jews into Hitler's ambit. When the precise orders for the extermination of Europe's Jews was given is not known, but on 31 July 1941 a directive from Hermann Göring to Reinhard Heydrich of the SS charged the latter with a 'final solution of the Jewish question'. There was no doubt that Hitler was behind the order and policy. Propaganda minister Dr Joseph Goebbels came to the fore in supporting him. The consequences quickly followed. In the autumn, the remaining German Jews were transported to the east, where they were murdered in Riga and Kaunas in November. At the rear of the

Eastern Front, four *Einsatzgruppen* (death squads) of the SS carried out mass executions. In November, Odilo Globocnik, the Austrian former Gauleiter of Vienna and now head of the police and SS in Lublin, began the construction of gassing facilities.

In what seems to have been an attempt to coordinate what was happening, on 20 January 1942 Heydrich chaired a conference of government representatives at the Berlin suburb of Wannsee. Confirming that the measures against the Jews would be pursued across occupied Europe, Jews were to be divided into those fit enough to be worked to death in forced-labour camps and those judged unfit who would be killed. This policy was dubbed Operation Reinhard after its author's assassination in Prague in May. The camps at Chelmno, Belzec, Sobibor, and Treblinka existed for the sole purpose of extermination, while the complexes at Majdanek at Lublin and Auschwitz-Birkenau near Cracow were both work and death camps, with new arrivals selected by SS doctors either to be worked to death or immediate dispatch to the gas chambers. Almost one million Jews were killed at Auschwitz-Birkenau alone. The exact number of Jews who were murdered remains unknown but was between 5.6 and 6 million. The fact is that by 1945 Jewish life in much of Europe had perished. So, too, by their own hands, had at least some of the principal instigators – Hitler, Göring, Goebbels, Himmler, and Globocnik – while others, such as Rudolf Höss, commandant at Auschwitz-Birkenau, met their fate at the hands of the victors. One of the main instigators of the Holocaust, Adolf Eichmann, seemed to have evaded justice by fleeing to Argentina where he was eventually traced and captured by Israeli agents. Brought to Israel, he was put on trial in Jerusalem and executed in 1962.

Palestine in the war

British policy in Palestine throughout the war continued to be based on the 1939 white paper. This included strict control over what was classed as illegal immigration, with many refugees being deported. In November 1940, the SS *Patria*, with 1,700 deportees bound for Mauritius, was sabotaged by the Haganah in Haifa harbour in an attempt to prevent it sailing, but it sank drowning over 250 passengers. The *Struma*, carrying 769 Jewish refugees, arrived at Istanbul in December 1941. Refused entry into Turkey and forbidden by the British to sail for Palestine, in February 1942 the vessel had to leave harbour for the Black Sea where it sank as the result of a mysterious explosion, only one of its passengers and crew surviving. Despite these tragedies, many in the Yishuv still believed that British policy would change after the war.

German successes in North Africa and then advances into the Caucasus created a fear among the Jews that Palestine might be conquered. With the Axis seemingly unstoppable in 1941, the Jewish Agency decided that elements of the Haganah should be mobilised as an elite force, the Palmach, or assault companies. Early recruits were the future generals Yitzhak Rabin and Moshe Dayan, and men of the Palmach took an active part in the invasion of Vichyite Syria.[10] In addition some 26,000 Jews, including 4,000 women, enlisted in the British forces. Meanwhile, encouraged by Axis propaganda, many Arabs looked to Berlin and Rome. With the suppression of the Palestinian Arab Revolt in 1939, Palestinian Arab politics were largely suspended for the duration of the war. Haj Amin left his temporary exile in Iran for Europe where he had an initial meeting with Mussolini before travelling to Berlin where he met Hitler on 28 November 1941. In the end, neither side did very much to aid the other. The mufti's main activity was involvement in the recruitment of Bosnian Muslims into the Waffen SS Handschar division. Photographs of him reviewing them did little to aid the Palestinian Arab cause after the war.[11]

The end of the Axis threat to Egypt in November 1942 saw the start of a shift in attitude in sections of the Jewish population, and this coincided with news in the course of 1942 of what was being perpetrated in Europe. Overt opposition to the British came chiefly from the Irgun Zvai Leumi (National Military Organisation) that had broken away from the Haganah at the time of the Arab Revolt and attracted supporters from Jabotinsky's Revisionists. Jabotinsky had died in 1940, and his heir was a young lawyer, Menachem Begin. Born in 1913 into a religious family in Brest-Litovsk, Begin's political allegiance to the Revisionists came in 1929 when he heard Jabotinsky speak. On the outbreak of war, since Brest-Litovsk initially fell within Soviet-occupied Poland, he was able to make his way to Palestine, but his father, mother, and brothers were killed in a massacre of Jews during the subsequent German invasion of the Soviet Union. In October 1943, he became commander of the Irgun, announcing early in 1944 a declaration of war against the British.[12] The Irgun mounted a number of attacks on British facilities throughout 1944, but, although the organisation lacked the capacity to mount a serious campaign, its activities demonstrated a new tone among some young Jews that set them apart from the more cautious approach of Ben-Gurion and the established leadership. An even more immediately dangerous threat to the British came from Lohamei Herut Israel (Fighters for the Freedom of Israel), commonly known by its acronym Lehi, which was formed in 1940 by the fiercely anti-British Avraham Stern who had broken away from the Irgun. An erudite graduate of the Hebrew University, Stern was a determined revolutionary who wished to take the fight to the British Empire and did so.[13] He was killed by the police in Tel Aviv in 1942, but the leadership was taken up by Nathan Yellin-Mor. Although few in numbers, Lehi was an unrelenting enemy of the British mandate. The organisation struck at the heart of the British presence in the region. On 6 November 1944, Lord Moyne – the British minister in the Middle East, a member of the Guinness brewing family and a close friend of Churchill – was assassinated in Cairo by two Lehi members who were caught and executed.[14]

The United States and the Middle East

By the time of the United States' entry into the war in December 1941, the number of Jews in the USA was almost five million and had long since outgrown its early status as a relatively poor immigrant population. It was well established and organised, and it felt the fate of European Jews keenly. At a Zionist Conference that convened at the Biltmore Hotel on 9–11 May 1942, Zionist policy took a dramatic new turn, resolving that Palestine be established as a

Jewish commonwealth. This became known as the Biltmore Program. This move was partly a response to the tragedy that was unfolding in Europe and partly a riposte to Britain's 1939 white paper, which looked set to make the Jews a perpetual minority in Palestine. While it was not a solely American–Jewish initiative – since both Weizmann, president of the WZO, and Ben-Gurion, chair of the Zionist Executive, were present – it was a clear indication that the focus of Zionist work would henceforth be in the United States.[15] The anguished reaction of the Jewish community to events in Europe was demonstrated by a rally of 20,000 in New York's Madison Square Garden on 21 July at which both the state governor and the city's mayor spoke, with messages of support coming from Churchill and President Franklin D. Roosevelt, who promised to bring the perpetrators to account.[16] Political support for the Biltmore Program was taken forward by the American Zionist Emergency Council (AZEC) headed by Rabbi Stephen Wise and Rabbi Abba Hillel Silver. They attracted bipartisan political support, with resolutions introduced into both houses of Congress demanding the Biltmore Program's implementation. The sponsors in the Senate were Robert Wagner (Democrat, New York) and Robert A. Taft (Republican, Ohio). With the approach of the 1944 presidential election, in which Roosevelt was running for an unprecedented fourth term, both the Democratic and Republican platforms endorsed the Biltmore Program. Roosevelt assured Wagner that were he to be re-elected he would bring about its earliest realisation.[17]

Beyond the crucial supply of material to the British and the Soviet Union, the United States left the conduct of the war in the Middle East to the British, but the Americans had one area of immediate concern. In 1933, the Standard Oil Company of California had secured an oil concession from Ibn Saud's government in Saudi Arabia. This holding was expanded in 1936 when it was joined by the Texas Oil Company to form the California Arabian standard Oil Company, which by the eve of war was producing oil in commercial quantities. The US war effort, spanning as it did the European and Pacific theatres, was beyond all precedent in its degree of mechanisation and hence demand for oil. While the United States had its own domestic oil fields and could draw on others in the western hemisphere, the scale of the war effort was threatening to result in a dangerous depletion of domestic oil reserves and potential. This fear led to a major expansion in Saudi Arabia with the company being renamed the Arabian American Oil Company (Aramco) in 1944.[18]

Saudi Arabia had thus come to be a significant factor in US foreign policy, with Roosevelt assuring Ibn Saud in May 1943 that there would be no change in the basic position of Palestine unless the Arabs and the Jews were fully consulted. On 13–14 February 1945, on his return from the Yalta Conference, Roosevelt arranged to meet Ibn Saud on board the cruiser USS *Quincy* moored in Egypt's Great Bitter Lake on the Suez Canal. Learning at first hand of the Saudi King's opposition to Zionism, Roosevelt subsequently had a letter sent on 5 April assuring him that he would not assist the Jews against the Arabs nor make any move hostile to the Arab people.[19] This was to be one of his last actions, as he died on 12 April. How Roosevelt would have reconciled these different promises in the post-war world is impossible to speculate.

6

The United States, the United Nations, and the Future of Palestine

By the spring of 1945, Egypt, Iraq, Lebanon, Saudi Arabia, and Syria had declared war on Germany, numbering them among the forty-six allied nations whose representatives were assembling for a historic conference in San Francisco. The purpose of the conference was to take forward Roosevelt's vision of a world organisation that would continue into the post-war era the wartime collaboration of the ad hoc collection of countries fighting against Germany and Japan. The hope was that the new international organisation would succeed where the League of Nations had palpably failed. That the five Arab countries signed the Charter of the United Nations Organization (UNO) on 26 June 1945 marked a decisive moment in their evolution as free and independent states. Not since the Ottoman conquests had the Arab world been able to do such a thing.

However, the UNO failed to match up to Roosevelt's ideal. By 1947, its two most powerful members, the United States and the Soviet Union, were locking themselves into the Cold War, which was to permeate the international system until the collapse of the latter in 1991. With its strategic position and increasingly valuable oil resources, the Middle East inevitably became a key factor in this new conflict. As in both world wars, the peoples of the Middle East were to be affected by international events in which they had little direct interest and over which they certainly had no control.

The status of Palestine was quite unlike that of the five independent Arab states, since it remained under the mandatory rule of Britain. Jewish Agency leaders had hoped for representation at the San Francisco Conference and that the future of Palestine would be discussed, but neither was permitted. Clearly, the creation of the new world body and the imminent demise of the League of Nations under which the mandate operated made clarification of its position essential. At the final session of the League Assembly in April 1946, Britain announced its intention to govern Palestine according to the principles of the mandate until an alternative was found. On 18 April, the assembly confirmed that with the termination of the league the system of mandates would end, but it noted that the principles of Article 22 of the League Covenant were embodied in Chapters XI, XII, and XIII of the United Nations Charter dealing with non-self-governing territories and trusteeship.[1] Chapter XII, Article 77, of the charter allowed for trusteeship agreements for territories currently under mandate, a possibility that was to surface over the coming period.[2]

Post-war Arab politics

As the Second World War drew to an end, proposals began to emerge – floated by Egypt's al-Nahhas and Iraq's Nuri among others – for some kind of supranational body that would give greater cohesion to the Arab world. On 12 July 1944, the Egyptians invited Iraq, Syria, Lebanon, Transjordan, Saudi Arabia, and Yemen to a conference to explore the matter. This obviously raised the question of Palestinian representation. Not only was Palestine not an independent country but the fragmented nature of its politics made it difficult to find agreement on a representative, attempts to revive the defunct Arab Higher Committee having failed. In the end it was a non-party Arab, Musa al-Alami, who represented the Palestinians when the conference convened in Alexandria. On 7 October, the conference agreed a protocol for the formation of a League of Arab states with its membership open to all independent Arab countries. Decisions would only be binding on the states that accepted them; no state would pursue a foreign policy prejudicial to that of the league or its members; and the league's council would mediate in any dispute likely to lead to war between members. It also came out in support of the rights of the Palestinian Arabs, distinguishing between the suffering of the Jews in Europe and Zionism, which it opposed. The Alexandria Protocol was formally agreed at a meeting in Cairo of a General Arab Congress on 22 March 1945. The Arab League, initially consisting of Egypt, Iraq, Lebanon, Saudi Arabia, Syria, and Transjordan, with Yemen joining shortly after, was set up with its headquarters in Cairo and an Egyptian secretary-general.[3] Full independence was granted to

Transjordan the following March, when Abdullah became king.

A new dimension to Arab nationalist politics in the postwar era was provided by the Ba'ath (Renaissance) Party. Its founder was Michel Aflaq, an intellectual born into a prosperous Christian family in Damascus in 1910. Education at the Sorbonne brought him into contact with French left-wing circles, and he was for a brief period a communist. The party that he founded in 1943 espoused both socialist principles and the pursuit of Arab unity.[4] Over time, the Ba'athists came to have a considerable role to play in the political development of Syria and Iraq. Of greater significance at the time, however, was the growing power of the Muslim Brotherhood, notably in Egypt. Faced with rising violence, in December 1948 Prime Minister Mustafa al-Nuqrashi outlawed the organisation – only to be murdered. His death was followed by the assassination of Hassan al-Banna in February, but the movement had the capacity to survive the death of its founder.

Palestinian Arab politics remained in limbo for most of the war, with the Arab Higher Committee in suspension, its leaders in exile or deported to the Seychelles. In the light of Haj Amin's wartime activities, there was no prospect of the British permitting him to return to Palestine, nor did all Palestinians trust his judgement. On the collapse of Germany, he had made his way to France and then reached Cairo where King Farouk gave him sanctuary. The other Arab parties, of which Nashashibi's National Defence Party was the most important, could neither attract mass support nor agree on unity. It took the sustained efforts of the newly created Arab

League to get agreement on a new Arab Higher Committee on 23 November 1945, under the acting chair of Tewfik al-Husseini. Jamal Bey Husseini, who had been detained in Southern Rhodesia after the failure of the Iraqi revolt, became the committee's main spokesperson on his release.[5]

The Jewish Revolt

In one sense, nothing in Palestine seemed to have changed. Britain – with its high commissioner General Sir Alan Cunningham, and its army, police, and administration – was still running the country. several things had changed, however. The war had exhausted the British Treasury, forcing a request to the United States for a loan to keep the country fiscally afloat and thereby making American opinion matter more than ever. If a straitened Britain were to revive economically, it would need to have access to cheap fuel – and that meant Middle East oil. It needed access not only to the oil fields but to the pipelines that crossed Arab territories to the terminal at Haifa.

In 1945, Britain elected a new Labour government led by Clement Attlee. The Labour Party, which had long shared the social democratic ideals of Zionism, voted at its 1944 annual conference to support the principle of a Jewish Palestine. The minister responsible for Palestine was the foreign secretary, Ernest Bevin, a redoubtable former trade union leader who had been a pillar of the wartime coalition government. His principal adviser on Palestine was Harold Beeley, an academic historian who had written on Palestine before the war and who joined the Foreign Office in 1946 having been involved with the San Francisco Conference. Bevin's view was that Britain's interests in the Middle East demanded a pro-Arab policy: in short that it would adhere to the 1939 white paper, at least until a more permanent way forward could be found.[6]

Bevin's policy effectively marked the end of the cooperation with the British that Ben-Gurion and the Jewish Agency leaders had been following since the start of the war, making some kind of clash inevitable. For the members of the Irgun and Lehi this simply meant a continuation of the campaigns that they had waged during the war, even though their resources could not match those of the British, but the Haganah, with a membership in the tens of thousands, was a very different proposition. Its leader was Dr Moshe Sneh, a medical doctor who had served in the Polish Army before reaching Palestine. The British had never given the Haganah any official recognition, but neither had they felt the need to suppress it. Armed resistance carried obvious dangers for Ben-Gurion and the leaders of the Jewish Agency, which was a legal organisation, but on 7 October 1945 Sneh was sent a carefully worded letter sanctioning a campaign involving sabotage. Realising the need for cooperation among the three groups, Sneh brought together Begin and Yellin-Mor to form the Hebrew Resistance Movement.[7]

Their joint campaign began on the night of 31 October 1945 with a range of symbolic targets being attacked. The Haganah targeted the instruments used by the British against illegal immigration, sinking two police patrol boats at Haifa and one at Jaffa. Members also staged 500 explosions across the rail network. The railway was also the target for the Irgun, which destroyed a locomotive and damaged six others in an attack at Lydda. Lehi made an unsuccessful attempt to sabotage the oil storage tanks of the Consolidated Refineries at Haifa, in the course of which one member died in a premature explosion. The British military response was to increase their police and army presence to 100,000 men, including the 6th Airborne Division, which had arrived in September. But this was not a financial burden that they could long sustain. Backed by virtually the entire Yishuv, the Hebrew Resistance Movement was impervious to penetration, while in view of what had happened in Europe the security forces had to be constrained in their actions.[8] The combined campaign continued throughout the winter of 1945–6. On 25 February, an attack on three airfields destroyed many aircraft. On 25 April, Lehi killed seven paratroopers in Tel Aviv. The climax came on the night of 16–17 June when a joint operation destroyed ten of the eleven road and rail bridges into Palestine, while Lehi targeted the railway workshops, during which operation eleven of its members were killed.

These strikes provoked a strong British security reaction. Since the Haganah was not a legal organisation, the Jewish Agency bore the brunt of the backlash. In Operation Agatha, or Black Sabbath to the Jews, some 17,000 troops were deployed on 29 June, sealing off Tel Aviv and the Jewish neighbourhoods in Jerusalem and Haifa. Many leaders were detained, some being deported to Africa. Ben-Gurion, however, was in Paris at the time. Sneh and other leaders of the resistance evaded arrest, while Weizmann was left alone. The leaders of the rather depleted Hebrew Resistance Movement planned a joint riposte, including an Irgun bomb attack on the seat of government in Jerusalem's King David Hotel that it had been incubating for quite some time, but counsels were divided. Weizmann helped convince the Jewish Agency to call off the joint action. Anxious, it would seem, to keep the Irgun part of the overall campaign, Sneh asked Begin to postpone the attack on the hotel. Nevertheless, it went ahead on 22 July 1946, demolishing an entire wing of the building and causing ninety-one British, Arab, and Jewish deaths. The King David Hotel explosion was caught on film, confirming British impotence.[9] The attack's immediate result was Sneh's resignation as head of the Haganah and the suspension of its armed operations, concentrating instead on bringing in illegal immigrants. The Hebrew Resistance Movement was formally called off by the Jewish Agency in August, although the operations of the Irgun and Lehi continued. A legacy of bitterness between the Haganah and the Irgun continued long after they were dissolved.

President Truman and Palestine

From the time of the Biltmore Conference in 1942, American-Jewish leaders realised that the path to a favourable political outcome would run through Washington and, once the location of the new world body was confirmed, New York. The Nazis' genocide of European Jewry meant that the two loci of Jewish religious, communal, and political life were Palestine and the United States; the achievement of a Jewish state was thus to be brought about, in effect, as the result of an alliance between the two. Few presidents had a more inauspicious start than Harry S. Truman. Unconsulted as vice-president by Roosevelt, self-educated, and, apart from military service in France in the First World War, largely untravelled, Truman had to decide on the use of atomic weapons against Japan within his first months as president and presided over the collapse of relations with the Soviet Union in the years after. Initially, he had no particular stance on Palestine, but he did have friends in the Jewish community, notably Eddie Jacobson with whom he had gone into business in Kansas City. Two of Truman's valued advisers had decided views. One was David Niles who came from a poor Boston Jewish family. Deeply moved by the survivors of the death camps, Niles argued that something had to be done for them. The other, Clark Clifford, had a close eye on the 1948 presidential campaign; he believed that the Jews were entitled to their country and that Truman should not give the Republicans any political advantage. That political factors were partly behind the decisions Truman ultimately took need not be doubted, but they do not show the complete picture. Like his fellow citizens who saw the newsreel footage of the liberation of the survivors, Truman was shocked by what he learned of the fate of European Jews.

The pro-Zionist sympathies of Niles and Clifford were matched on the other side by influential voices in the Department of State, notably the head of the Division of Near Eastern and African Affairs, Loy W. Henderson. Son of a Methodist minister, Henderson's first posting was as vice-consul in Dublin in 1922 when the fledgling Irish Free state was tearing itself apart in civil war. His determinedly anti-communist views unfashionable in wartime, in 1943 he was appointed ambassador to Iraq where he became aware of the extent of Arab opposition to Zionism. He concluded that a Jewish state could only come about through violence and that Arab hostility meant that the Jews would end up having exchanged the European ghettoes for a large one in the Middle East.[10] Henderson's views were reinforced by those of the highly influential under-secretary at the Department of State, Dean Acheson, who did not share Jewish aspirations over Palestine.

Truman's immediate instinct was to help the Jewish survivors in Europe in some way, sending Earl G. Harrison of the University of Pennsylvania to report on their condition. The policy of General Dwight D. Eisenhower's military administration, which was governing in the immediate aftermath of the war, was that the 'displaced persons' should return to their home countries, but Harrison quickly concluded that the desire of the Jews was to go to Palestine. On the suggestion of the Jewish Agency, he recommended that 100,000 Jews should be admitted, and on 31 August 1945 Truman, citing the horrors of the camps, asked Britain to issue 100,000 immigration certificates. To do this, however, would be in breach of the white paper limit of 75,000, and Britain refused, with the egregious comment that the Jews should not be at the head of the queue. Irked by Truman's intervention, Bevin sought a more direct American involvement in Palestine, proposing a joint committee to investigate the linked issues of displaced persons and Palestine. The Anglo-American Committee of Inquiry, announced on 13 November 1945, was composed of six US and six British members. As their *vade mecum* they had *A Survey of*

Palestine, a remarkable two-volume compilation of facts and figures compiled by the government of Palestine. Running as the *Survey* did to 1,139 pages, committee members could hardly plead ignorance.[11]

The committee heard evidence in Washington and London, visited camps in Europe, and travelled to Palestine where they met the mandatory government, the Jewish Agency, and the Arab Higher Committee. When they reported in April 1946, the Jewish Agency had secured one concession, that of the 100,000 immigrants, but on the critical matter of statehood things had not gone their way. Two US members who were broadly sympathetic to Zionism, James G. McDonald and Bartley C. Crum, advocated Jewish statehood through partition, as did the British Labour MP Richard Crossman. Their colleagues believed that the country should be neither a Jewish nor an Arab state but should continue under some form of trusteeship. Grasping at the prospect of the 100,000 immigration certificates, Truman gave the report an initial welcome, but the British, the Jewish Agency, and the Arab Higher Committee were opposed.[12] A refinement attempted by Truman also failed. He sent Henry F. Grady to London to negotiate, but the result – which would have seen continuing trusteeship with autonomous Arab and Jewish provinces – still fell far short of Jewish hopes of statehood. On 7 August, Truman rejected the proposals.[13]

In September 1946, the British launched their Palestine Conference, which turned out to be yet another sterile exercise. There were, however, important developments maturing. At a meeting of the Jewish Agency Executive in Paris in

August, there was divided counsel on how best to proceed, but the initiative was seized by the Lithuanian-born Nahum Goldmann who had long seen partition as the only realistic way to statehood. He also had indications, probably from Niles, that Truman might be about to make a major move on Palestine. The result, backed by Ben-Gurion and by Sneh, was a majority agreement to secretly abandon the Biltmore Program and to work instead for partition on the basis of 'the establishment of a viable Jewish State in an adequate area of Palestine'. This was the proposal that Goldmann immediately took to Washington. Truman, meanwhile, was under considerable political pressure, facing midterm congressional and gubernatorial elections at a time when he could show no progress on the 100,000 immigration certificates. Truman chose Yom Kippur, the holiest day for Jews, on 4 October 1946 to issue a statement of his administration's policy. Reiterating that he would continue to work for the immigration certificates before those in the camps had to face another winter, he then endorsed the Jewish Agency Executive's still-secret decision on partition that Goldmann had confided in him. Truman's Yom Kippur Declaration marked a decisive stage in the evolution of US policy towards Palestine and in the Middle East more generally. Roosevelt's assurances to the Arabs were consigned to the past and, while the State Department did not give up on its pro-Arab stance, it was in the context of a White House now set on support for Jewish statehood through partition.[14]

The Palestine question at the United Nations

By the start of 1947, the British were ready to admit defeat. The winter of 1946–7 was proving to be one of the harshest on record, while the future of India – the core of their colonial empire – was the main priority. The Palestinians, led by Jamal Bey Husseini, maintained their adamant opposition to partition, while the British and Ben-Gurion could not agree on what might constitute an 'adequate' area for a Jewish state. On 7 February 1947, the government presented the two protagonists with its final proposals. When these were promptly rejected, the future of Palestine was laid before the secretary-general of the United Nations Organization, Trygve Lie, on 2 April 1947. Since it was hoped that the new world body would be more effective than its predecessor, the matter was taken seriously, a special session of the General Assembly being called for May. An early boost for the Jewish case came on 14 May when the Soviet Union's Andrei Gromyko announced support for Jewish statehood. The following day the United Nations Special Committee on Palestine (UNSCOP) was formed, its brief being to consider all questions relevant to Palestine, taking into account the special interests of Judaism, Christianity, and Islam. It was to report back to the General Assembly by 1 September. Arab countries and the major powers would not be included in its membership. Latin America was represented by Guatemala, Uruguay, and Peru, the British Commonwealth by Australia and Canada, Eastern Europe by Czechoslovakia and Yugoslavia, Asia by Iran and India, and Western Europe by the Netherlands and Sweden, whose Emil Sandström was to be chair.[15]

The two protagonists responded to the creation of UNSCOP very differently. The Arab Higher Committee decided on a boycott, despite a direct appeal from UNSCOP. Jamal Bey Husseini later justified this decision on the grounds that previous commissions had given them nothing. The Zionists, by contrast, viewed UNSCOP as the vehicle by which they could achieve their aim of statehood through partition. Their first target was to undermine the credibility of the British mandate, which might preclude any suggestion of continuing trusteeship. They achieved this through the well-publicised drama of the *Exodus 1947*, a former US ferry that the Haganah was using to convey some 4,500 illegal immigrants. Intercepted by the Royal Navy, its passengers were landed at Haifa where their emotional arrival was witnessed by Sandström and one of his colleagues. Instead of interning the passengers in Cyprus, as had hitherto been the case, they were returned to two camps in Germany, with all the collateral damage to Britain's reputation that this action caused.[16] In addition, the Irgun maintained its campaign, hanging two British sergeants as a reprisal for the execution of three of its members. UNSCOP decided that it could not interfere with the judicial administration of Palestine.[17]

Partition presented more of a challenge, not least since the Jewish Agency was still publicly committed to the Biltmore Program. But Ben-Gurion and the head of the Jewish Agency's Political Department, Moshe Shertok (later Sharett) charged two liaison officers, David Horowitz and Abba Eban, with the task of ensuring that the committee members were kept aware that partition was the goal.[18] Indeed, when it came to the public hearings in Jerusalem, it became clear that the Jewish Agency's aim was partition, not the Biltmore Program. On 8 July 1947, Weizmann admitted to the committee that they realised that they could not have the whole of Palestine, but, unlike the 1937 British scheme, partition would have to include the Negev desert in the Jewish state. He was followed by Ben-Gurion, who confirmed that they would consider a Jewish state in an area less than the whole of Palestine. Partition was now clearly in the public domain. Ben-Gurion privately conveyed to committee members that this was his position. To hear the Arab case, the committee travelled to Beirut to meet the foreign ministers of Egypt, Iraq, Lebanon, Saudi Arabia, Syria, and Lebanon. They heard the Lebanese foreign minister, Hamid Frangieh, denounce partition as unworkable and reiterate the Arab demand that Palestine be a unitary state with a Jewish minority that would have equal rights of citizenship. He was really too late.[19]

The *Report to the General Assembly by the United Nations Special Committee on Palestine* was signed off in Geneva on 31 August 1947. Referring to the *Exodus 1947* affair and the ongoing efforts to bring in illegal immigrants, the report noted the rift that existed between the administration and the Jewish community. On one issue the committee was unanimous. The British government had finally conceded defeat, informing the committee that the mandate was unworkable and that the promises made to the Arabs and Jews were irreconcilable. UNSCOP recommended the termination of the mandate and that Palestine should become independent.

On the future structure of Palestine there was, however, no unanimity. In a minority submission, the members from

India, Iran, and Yugoslavia supported the creation of an independent federal state of Palestine, while the Australian member could not support any proposal. The majority recommended a 'plan of partition with economic union'. The justification for partition did not differ in essence from that set out by Coupland in the Royal Commission report ten years earlier. It worked from the premise that while the Arabs and Jews each had a valid case, these were irreconcilable, and that partition could meet the national aspirations of both, albeit partially. There was a basic conflict between 650,000 Jews and 1.2 million Arabs who had different ways of living that precluded cooperation between them. Recognising the limited geographical area of Palestine, the independent Arab state and the independent Jewish state should enter into a treaty of economic union, preserving common currency, customs, transport system, postal and telephone links, as well as the ports of Haifa and Jaffa. Sacred as it was to the three Abrahamic religions, the city of Jerusalem, including Bethlehem, was to be placed under an international trusteeship with the United Nations as the administering authority.

The proposed boundaries for the two states were complex. The Arab state was to be in three parts: western Galilee, the interior region of Judea and Samaria, excluding Jerusalem, and the coastal plain some five miles wide from Ashdod to the Egyptian border. Its Jewish counterpart was to take in eastern Galilee, the Plain of Esdraelon, most of the coastal plain, including Haifa, Tel Aviv, and Jaffa, and the Negev desert. The demographics of these proposed boundaries would, it was believed, result in an Arab state of 725,000 Arabs and 10,000 Jews, the Jerusalem enclave with 100,000

Jews and 105,000 Arabs, while the Jewish state would have 498,000 Jews and 407,000 Arabs, with the possible addition of some 90,000 Bedouin. Part of the large Arab population in the Jewish state was accounted for by the 70,000 Arabs of Jaffa, but the committee did not wish to separate it from Tel Aviv with which it was contiguous.[20]

The United Nations Partition Resolution

The report now had to be placed before the body that had commissioned it, the General Assembly of the United Nations, where a two-thirds majority would be required for its proposals to become recommendations. Since these proposals were highly complex and members were queuing up to discuss them, the General Assembly converted itself into the Ad Hoc Committee on the Palestinian Question. Everything now turned on how the members would decide to vote. Neither of the two parties concerned had a vote, but both the Arab Higher Committee and the Jewish Agency were allowed to present their respective cases, their views coming early on in the discussions. Jamal Bey Husseini's speech dismissed the UNSCOP proposals as a basis for discussion. Instead of a forensic examination of the details of the partition plan, he denounced the right of the United Nations to interfere with the Palestinians' national aspirations as well as the Jewish claims. His statement was based on the past ten years of Arab policy, and, while the Arab Higher Committee had no vote, he was supported by the Arab members. The Jewish Agency's spokesman, Rabbi Abba Hillel Silver, portrayed partition as a sacrifice for the Jews, who, he claimed, had by implication been promised the whole of Palestine, including Transjordan, in the Balfour Declaration. Despite this, he conceded that they would work with partition, subject to certain modifications, chief among which was Jewish West Jerusalem.

The British response to UNSCOP came at a cabinet meeting on 20 September 1947. Bevin and his officials were agreed that the Middle East was an area of key strategic interest. His cabinet colleagues concurred in the view that as the partition plan was unfair to the Arabs, Britain could not support it, nor any partition plan, nor the minority proposals. Furthermore, in the light of this decision, Britain would not assist with the implementation of partition but would proceed to an early withdrawal from the country. The British spokesperson made it clear in the Ad Hoc Committee that the General Assembly would have to find a mechanism for implementation that did not involve the mandatory administration.[21] By contrast, the Soviet Union came out strongly behind the UNSCOP partition plan, an important commitment given that the Soviets could cast three votes in the General Assembly and the fact that the countries of Eastern Europe were by 1947 mostly firmly in Moscow's camp.

The key response to the UNSCOP proposals would inevitably be that of the United States, which, on Truman's instructions, had held back from intervening in its deliberations. With feelings in the administration divided over the merits of partition, it took some time for a clear declaration to emerge. American-Jewish leaders, realising that statehood was within reach but that there were countervailing voices in the Department of State, orchestrated a sustained lobbying campaign involving leading Democrats, state governors, and trade union leaders to ensure that Truman backed partition. In a key position was General of the Army George Catlett Marshall, secretary of state since January 1947, a public servant cast in the mould of Cincinnatus. As chief of staff of the army throughout the war, Marshall was the indispensable military adviser to Roosevelt, as well as one of the rocks on which the Anglo-American military alliance was grounded. The US delegation to the UN was divided on the merits of partition. Realising that this was the case, when Marshall spoke to the General Assembly on 17 September, he temporised, confining himself to saying that the United States gave 'great weight' to the UNSCOP proposals.

Ranged against the proposals were Henderson, who believed that partition could only be implemented through force, and James Forrestal, secretary of the newly created Department of Defense, who opposed any policy that might alienate the oil-producing Arab states. US strategy was thrashed out at a meeting between Marshall and the delegation on 24 September. At an appropriate time, the United States would declare support for a workable plan of partition. Should this fail to attract the necessary two-thirds support, they would have to decide either on an alternative or a vote to show lack of support for the UNSCOP plan. The merit of this strategy was that it upheld the integrity of the United Nations. On 9 October, Truman issued instructions to the Department of State to support the partition plan. This is what Herschel Johnson announced the following day, but with the qualification that modifications would be sought to reduce the number of Arabs in the Jewish state.[22]

On 21 October 1947, the Ad Hoc Committee appointed two subcommittees to formulate detailed proposals based on the UNSCOP minority and majority recommendations. Subcommittee 2, composed of Colombia and Arab and Islamic states, was tasked with taking forward the minority plan for a unitary Palestinian state, while Subcommittee 1, which included both the United States and the Soviet Union, had responsibility for partition with economic union. As Johnson's speech had already signalled, a principal American aim was to make the Jewish state more homogeneous, which was no easy task given the intermingling of settlements. The only two possibilities for reducing the Arab population were the city of Jaffa and the Negev desert. The Zionists, and Weizmann especially, viewed the Negev with its mineral resources and access to the Gulf of Aqaba as vital for the progress of the future Jewish state. Once again, the veteran Weizmann's talent for diplomacy was mobilised. On 19 November, at a meeting in the White House, he convinced Truman to instruct his delegation that the Negev was not to be touched. The Americans were also deeply concerned about the need for an implementation mechanism were partition to have any prospect of success. At an early meeting, Britain's Sir Alexander Cadogan merely proffered his personal view that the British would not hinder a peaceful transfer of authority. On that somewhat intangible basis, on 19 November the subcommittee submitted its plan whereby the mandate was to end by 1 August 1948 with the partition with economic union in place by 1 October. During the period of British withdrawal, a five-member United Nations Commission would be charged with setting up the two administrations, settling their frontiers and those of the Jerusalem enclave. The Jaffa enclave, but not the Negev, was to be included in the Arab state. The following day, Cadogan publicly confirmed that Britain would neither cooperate with the proposed commission nor would it acquiesce in the establishment of the two administrations. Confounded, the Americans could only hope – vainly as it turned out – that the British might reconsider.[23] Subcommittee 2's report attacked both the legality and practicality of partition, recommending that Palestine become independent as a unitary state, with minority guarantees.

Events in New York now moved swiftly to their climax as the Ad Hoc Committee considered the two subcommittee submissions. Subcommittee 2's submission had scant hope of support beyond its own members. For the Palestinians, Jamal Bey Husseini warned of the violent consequences of partition. Once again, Cadogan repeated Britain's policy of non-cooperation, forcing the Americans to strengthen the implementation provisions. In regretting the British stance, Johnson expressed the hope that the boundaries between the two states would be as friendly as that between Canada and the United States. When the Ad Hoc Committee voted on Subcommittee 1's proposals on 25 November, they were endorsed by twenty-five votes in favour, thirteen against, with seventeen abstentions and two absentees. This vote was scheduled to be confirmed in the General Assembly but was short of the two-thirds majority needed for its adoption. Faced with this setback, an intense lobbying campaign was launched by the Jewish Agency and the Americans to persuade the necessary small group of states to endorse the plan.

The Jewish Agency's one success came when Weizmann convinced the veteran French statesman Léon Blum to vote in favour, but the real initiatives were coming from the Americans, whose UN delegates were told to operate without restraint. Interventions were also made in foreign capitals.

In the General Assembly on 29 November 1947, the partition plan was passed by thirty-three votes to thirteen with ten abstentions.[24] Of the states that had abstained or been absent on the Ad Hoc Committee vote on 25 November, France, Belgium, the Netherlands, Luxembourg, New Zealand, Haiti, Liberia, Paraguay, and the Philippines voted in favour, while Thailand, which had been opposed, was absent; Chile, which had been in favour, abstained; and Greece, which had abstained, voted against. The vote was historic. While resolutions of the General Assembly are recommendations, US officials believed that on this occasion, as the successor to the League of Nations, the General Assembly was legislating. The resolution was cited by the Israelis in their subsequent independence declaration. While the partition resolution was welcomed with relief and rejoicing throughout the Jewish areas of Palestine as opening the way to imminent statehood, there was an important dissenting voice. Loyal to the teaching of Jabotinsky and the revisionists, the Irgun repudiated partition, condemning it as illegal, vowing that it would never be recognised, that Jerusalem was the capital, and that the whole of Israel would be eternally restored.

Partition in the balance

The plan itself was never implemented, at least in the way that its authors had intended. The United Nations Palestine Commission that was established on 9 January 1948, chaired by the Czech Karl Lisicky, with members from Bolivia, Denmark, Panama, and the Philippines, was informed by the British that they would not be allowed to enter the country. On 10 February, they requested armed assistance from the Security Council, but, with the Cold War well under way, the Americans would not concur in such a move against the British. With the British administration unwilling to see its troops and police killed in what had ceased to be a matter of national importance, Palestine was in a vacuum in which the complex work of constructing the Arab and Jewish states, the economic union, and the Jerusalem enclave could not even begin.

In these circumstances, it was hardly surprising that civil conflict broke out. Each side had been preparing. Haj Amin's cousin, Abd al-Qadir al-Husseini, led about 1,000 men in the Jerusalem area, as did Hassan Salameh, a supporter of Haj Amin, around Lydda. Neither man survived. Fawzi al-Qawuqji, leader of the 1925 rising against the French in Hama and a veteran of the 1936 Revolt in Palestine, commanded the 5,000-strong Arab Liberation Army.[25] But these formations lacked unity both strategically and politically, Haj Amin once again proving to be a divisive figure. By contrast, the Jewish Agency constituted the Palmach and the Haganah into a field army of six brigades, each covering a specific area. Their strategy was formed around Plan Dalet, which charged them with the defence of the areas allotted to the Jewish state and the protection of Jewish settlements in the proposed Arab state. It proved to be an unequal contest. As the mandate drew to its close, the Golani Brigade captured key positions in Galilee, and the Carmeli Brigade secured Haifa with its port facilities. Finally, three other brigades took Jaffa, a serious blow to the Arab cause.[26] These operations were accompanied by the flight, or removal, of thousands of Arabs. Atrocities were sadly to be expected. On 9 April, in a combined Irgun and Lehi operation, the inhabitants of the village of Deir Yassin just west of Jerusalem were massacred. Retaliation came with an attack on a Jewish medical convoy in Jerusalem in which seventy-seven doctors and nurses were killed.[27]

By the spring of 1948, it was clear that Jewish forces were gaining the upper hand in Palestine, but there was still a battle to come in Washington. Clearly resentful over the lobbying campaign, Truman attempted to disengage from the Palestine question, to the extent of making it clear that he would not meet any more extreme Zionist leaders. Other issues were weighing on him: principally the dangerously deteriorating situation in Europe as a result of the communist coup in Prague in February. The continuing turmoil in Palestine reaffirmed for Henderson and others in the Department of State their belief that Truman had been too easily persuaded by his political advisers that the Jewish state could be created without violence. They found an influential ally in the director of policy planning, George F. Kennan, author of the historic Long Telegram of 22 February 1946 that had predicted the onset of the Cold War. In an analysis submitted on 20 January, Kennan confirmed Henderson's view that the partition of Palestine could only be implemented through force, adding that this would have to involve the United States. Such a policy would alienate sections of the Muslim world, endangering western bases and oil concessions. He concluded that since the General Assembly partition plan had no reasonable hope of success, they should move to a federal state or trusteeship. From a different perspective, the director of United Nations Affairs, Dean Rusk, also concluded that they should look to trusteeship if a civil war were to develop. What Henderson, Kennan, and Rusk were advocating was, quite simply, a reversal of policy. If the Security Council could not implement the resolution, the matter would have to come back to the General Assembly. Truman's sibylline response approved this in principle but said that the imminent speech to the Security Council by the representative to the council, Ambassador Warren Austin, should not be seen as retreating from the stance taken in the General Assembly. With Truman's approval, on 24 February Austin told the Security Council that it was not permissible under the UN Charter to enforce a settlement.

The Department of State's campaign against partition seemed to have reached a successful climax on 19 March 1948 when Austin again addressed the Security Council in a speech, drafted by Henderson and Rusk's staff, which called for an end to attempts to implement partition and for the General Assembly to look instead for a policy of trusteeship. Truman's enraged reaction was that he had been undermined. The reason for his discomfort was that Truman had met Weizmann the previous day, assuring him he still stood by partition. On 16 April, the General Assembly convened to consider the idea of temporary trusteeship, but in the absence of any strong steer from Washington it never developed momentum. With the encouragement of his White House staff, Truman increasingly focused on the political dimension. A measure of the Jewish reaction to Austin's speech was a protest march in New York on 4 April of 40,000 war veterans, applauded by a crowd numbering some quarter of a million. Knowing that Marshall opposed Jewish statehood, Clifford and his colleagues prepared a contrary brief for Truman. Their document argued that the Jewish Agency had already succeeded in making partition an established fact. In recognising this, the United States would preempt a similar move by the Soviet Union. Much the same argument applied to the Republicans on the domestic front. At a meeting with Marshall and his under-secretary, Robert Lovett, convened by Truman on 12 May, Clifford developed his case, stressing that since the proclamation of the Jewish state was now inevitable, its recognition was in US interests. Marshall testily responded that Clifford's advice was based on domestic political considerations whereas the problems facing them were international. If Clifford's advice were taken, he said, then he would vote against Truman in the elections.[28]

With the British mandate due to end on 14 May 1948, clearly these views had to be reconciled somehow. Uneasy at the situation, Lovett kept in close contact with Clifford, and by the 14th Marshall had acquiesced in the need for recognition. The 14th was marked by the departure of General Cunningham from Haifa. Ben-Gurion and his colleagues met at Tel Aviv Museum where, standing beneath a portrait of

David Ben-Gurion proclaiming the State of Israel before the
Jewish People's Council in Tel Aviv, beneath a portrait of
Theodor Herzl, 14 May 1948. (World History Archive/Alamy Stock Photo)

Herzl, he proclaimed the state's independence and presided
over the signing of the Declaration of the Establishment of
the State of Israel. The ceremony concluded with the orchestra playing the Zionist anthem, 'Hatikvah' ('The Hope').[29]

Ben-Gurion was prime minister, and the provisional
Council of State elected Weizmann, who was still in the
United States, as president. Thirty-four signatures were on
the scroll, but, despite the fact that space had been left for
those of three who could not be present, to his great sadness
no provision was made for Weizmann's.[30] The declaration
came into effect at 6 o'clock Washington time. Truman's de
facto recognition of the new state came eleven minutes later,

followed the next day by that of Guatemala and on the 17th by the Soviet Union. Britain's de facto recognition waited until 13 May 1949. With the establishment of the new state, the political contours of the Middle East changed dramatically.

7

War and Revolution

On 15 May 1948, the secretary-general of the Arab League, Abdul Rahman Hassan Azzam, telegraphed his opposite number at the United Nations, Trygve Lie, announcing the league's intervention in Palestine. Noting the ending of the mandatory regime, the document argued that under the principles of self-determination recognised by the Covenant of the League of Nations and the United Nations Charter, a government of Palestine should be set up. The aim of the Arabs' intervention was held to be the creation of a United State of Palestine with guaranteed safeguards for its minorities.[1] But the political and military realities underpinning the league's action were far from secure. There was no unified Arab military command or general staff to coordinate the tactics – still less strategy – of forces that were widely dispersed across various theatres of operations. Two of the Arab armies, the Saudi Arabian and Lebanese, undertook little.

The Arab League offensive

The Syrian Army mounted offensives in conjunction with Fawzi al-Qawuqji's Arab Liberation Army north and south of the Sea of Galilee, but when these were repulsed in a series of hard-fought engagements, they settled for defensive operations.[2] The Iraqis succeeded in taking the strategic towns of Jenin and Tulkarm, potentially threatening the key port of Haifa just over ten miles away, but then they, too, went over to the defensive.[3] The Egyptians, free from 1945 of British military tutelage, committed a substantial force of five infantry battalions, a tank battalion, and accompanying artillery, deployed in two columns. Their air force could deploy British Spitfire and Hurricane fighters, which, if becoming obsolescent, had proved their worth in the war. But their field army was not well served by serious deficiencies in their headquarters in Cairo, and they had an extended line of communications across the Sinai.[4] Still, this was a challenge that Egypt could not ignore, if for no other reason than that Cairo was the headquarters of the Arab League. Strategically, and perhaps psychologically, Israel's possession of the Negev would drive a wedge between Egypt and the rest of the Arab world.

Closest to the fighting fronts was Jordan's Arab Legion, since 1939 under the command of the British Major-General John Bagot Glubb. Glubb had seen to it that the legion, which was from modest origins and recruited from Bedouin loyal to the Hashemites, was kept abreast of modern war. For active operations in 1948, the legion had four battalions of mechanised infantry, two artillery batteries with a total of eight guns, and fifty elderly British armoured cars, an operational strength in all of some 4,500 effectives. But its military problems were twofold: it had no system of reserves or replacements for men lost in action, nor did it have any air cover.[5]

There was also the political issue of the disconnect between the Arab League's stated objectives and the suspected ambitions of King Abdullah. For some time, the king had been of the view that the Jews had succeeded in establishing their state and that it was unrealistic to plan for its destruction. Equally unrealistic were the prospects for the Arab state envisioned in the UNSCOP proposals, its best hope lying in incorporation into his kingdom. He had to proceed warily. While some Palestinians were inclined to favour this latter outcome, it was anathema to Haj Amin and his supporters and, indeed, to the Arab League more widely. Abdullah had, for some time, had contact with the Zionists, and his ideas took shape at a secret meeting with the acting head of the Jewish Agency's Political Department, Golda Meyerson (later Meir), in November 1947. On the eve of war, disguised as an Arab woman, Meyerson undertook a highly dangerous secret mission to Amman in an unsuccessful attempt to dissuade Abdullah from joining the Arab League attack, but, as one of the league's leading figures, realistically he had no alternative.[6]

Formation of the Israel Defense Forces

Like their opposite numbers in the Arab League, the position of the Israelis had both advantages and disadvantages. The strangulated borders of the new state made any attempt at a defence in depth meaningless, but, unlike the Arab armies, scattered as they were around the periphery, the Israelis had the advantage of fighting on interior lines. The new country entered into independence with many of the attributes of an established state. For over twenty years, the Jewish Agency had been systematically working to create what was, in effect, a proto-state. Even more important was that the Haganah and the Palmach could instantly be converted into Tzahal, or the Israel Defense Forces (IDF), formally sanctioned on 28 May. The Irgun, now numbering in the thousands, and Lehi with several hundred, were not part of the IDF. Its main active units were the six brigades already set up, reinforced by a number of Palmach battalions. Behind their operations were numerous armed local defensive units. Many of these soldiers had recent military experience while serving with the Allied armies in the war. The Haganah had accumulated stocks of small arms and ammunition, and it had also manufactured large numbers of mortars, but the newly constituted IDF had no tanks, field artillery, or air support. Still, what was lacking in military hardware was more than compensated by the fighting spirit of the IDF, since for the Israelis the war was an existential one.[7]

United Nations mediation

Faced with the outbreak of open warfare, the United Nations General Assembly resolved on the appointment of a mediator. Charged with making an appointment, the American, British, French, and Soviet representatives turned to Sweden's Count Folke Bernadotte, a member of the royal family who was prominent in the International Red Cross. A descendant of Napoleon's Marshal Jean Baptiste Bernadotte, who had assumed the Swedish crown as Karl XIV Johan in 1818, Folke Bernadotte had undertaken hazardous journeys to Germany in the spring of 1945 where he had succeeded in negotiating with Himmler the release of some 30,000 concentration camp victims to Sweden.[8] As far as their backgrounds were concerned, the contrast with the man appointed by Lie as his principal aide, Dr Ralph Bunche, could not have been more pronounced. Bernadotte was descended from an imperial marshal, whereas Bunche's grandmother, who was a major influence in his upbringing, came from a family of enslaved people. Born into a poor African American family in 1904, Bunche had worked his way through university until a scholarship to Harvard enabled him to earn his doctorate, opening the way to an academic career at Howard University. Joining the United Nations in 1946, he had worked with UNSCOP and so was already familiar with the complexities of the issues when he was appointed principal secretary to the ill-fated Palestine Commission.[9] Joining Bernadotte and Bunche was a group of military advisers, mostly French, Belgian, and Swedish.

With their superior heavy weapons and air power, the Egyptian and Jordanian forces almost immediately threatened key Israeli positions. One Egyptian column advanced along the coast to within twenty miles of Tel Aviv, while the other captured Hebron and Bethlehem to approach the southern outskirts of Jerusalem. The Israelis and the Arab Legion fought bitter battles around the western approaches to Jerusalem, whose large Jewish population was in danger of being isolated from the coastal plain. While the Israelis succeeded in defending Jewish West Jerusalem, the legion secured the Old City within the walls. This was a particular blow to the Israelis, since the Old City included the long-established Jewish Quarter of some 1,700 inhabitants with their ancient synagogues clustered around the Western Wall, Judaism's most sacred site.[10]

A month-long truce was arranged by Bernadotte on 11 June 1948. Although the ceasefire was supposed to preclude bringing in men or supplies, Ben-Gurion's government eagerly seized the chance to remedy their deficiencies in heavy weapons and in the air. The key proved to be Czechoslovakia with its well-equipped armaments industry dating back to Habsburg days and large quantities of equipment left over from the war. An air lift was established from Czech bases that enabled material to be flown in. The cargo included crated former German Messerschmitt 109 fighter aircraft. Also smuggled in were some British Spitfire fighters and three American B-17 Flying Fortress heavy bombers. Once made operational, these assets gave the Israeli forces the weaponry needed for successful offensives.[11] The money for this armament came overwhelmingly from the American-Jewish community. Their generosity was galvanised by Golda Meyerson, who had left Israel on its first travel document for the United States to address meetings throughout the country.

The Irgun, too, had been active in weapons procurement. On 22 June, the *Altalena*, carrying almost 1,000 volunteers and loaded with rifles, machine guns, and ammunition that the Irgun had secured in Europe, ran aground off Tel Aviv. When negotiations for a distribution of its weapons between the Irgun and the IDF failed, the ship presented an open challenge to Ben-Gurion's authority. With the backing of his cabinet, he gave orders for the IDF to act. In the subsequent action, the ship was destroyed by artillery fire with concomitant loss of life. In the most public manner, Ben-Gurion had asserted the authority of the government, ensuring that there would be no state within a state. The Irgun was banned, but the rancorous aftermath of the *Altalena* affair was to be felt in Israeli politics in the years ahead.[12] Interestingly, at the same as taking on the Irgun, Ben-Gurion was preparing to curb the power of the Palmach, but such was its military reputation that any action against it had to wait.

The second campaign

With the end of the truce on 9 July, the IDF's new armaments enabled it to take the offensive. Its bombers took the war to the enemy, both Cairo and Damascus being bombed. But the key victories were on the ground: Galilee was secured, and many of its inhabitants were expelled. Christian and Druze villages and Nazareth, so important in the Christian tradition, were largely untouched, but altogether some 30,000 refugees left, mostly for Lebanon. Particularly bitter fighting took place close to Tel Aviv in and around the important Arab towns of Lydda, with its key international airport and railway junction, and Ramle. With his Arab Legion heavily engaged around Jerusalem, Glubb had little to spare for the towns' defence beyond a few hundred of his men and some irregular untrained and leaderless Jordanian tribesmen. When the towns fell on 12 July 1948, Ben-Gurion met his field commanders, seemingly indicating that the inhabitants, numbering some 50,000, be expelled.[13] The subsequent Lydda Death March in which hundreds died of exhaustion or dehydration in the summer heat as they made their way to the Arab lines some ten miles away at Ramallah, etched its way into the Palestinian memory. Visiting the refugees at Ramallah, Bernadotte recorded that he had never seen a ghastlier sight, with masses of people demanding food and a return to their homes.[14]

Glubb's decision that he had no alternative but to leave Lydda and Ramle to the Israelis, for which the legion was to be excoriated by the Palestinians and other Arabs, was the result of the pressure his forces were coming under on the Jerusalem front with a major battle taking place for the key position of Latrun, west of the city, a road junction that not only dominated communications linking Tel Aviv with Jewish West Jerusalem and Ramallah but also controlled the pumping station for Jerusalem's water supply. He believed that his force of 1,200 legionaries was defending the position against 6,500 Palmach troops.[15]

With the Israelis increasingly holding the strategic initiative, a second truce was arranged for 18 July 1948. During this period, the IDF was able to continue to receive its supply of munitions from Czechoslovakia and elsewhere. In the meantime, the political future of Arab Palestine was once again a source of division. On 20 September, the Arab Government of All Palestine was proclaimed under the presidency of Haj Amin with its base at Gaza. It was recognised by all the Arab states except Jordan, but nothing really came of it. The following day, an assembly of Palestinians and Jordanians denounced the Gaza government and appealed instead to King Abdullah.[16]

The Bernadotte Plan

Throughout this period, Bernadotte and his staff shuttled between the various parties exploring possibilities that might lead to a peaceful outcome. His own preference would have been for a unitary Palestinian state with rights for the Jews, but he recognised that Israel was functioning as a state and had been recognised by fourteen countries. As a result, he and his colleagues were agreed that the Jewish state should exist but ideally in some union with Arab Palestine and possibly Jordan. The Israeli conquest of western Galilee could be balanced by granting the Negev to the Arabs. These ideas formed the germ of the proposals that he submitted on 16 September 1948. By then, he had explored with the Israelis the question of the Palestinian refugees, whom he estimated at between 300,000 and 400,000, but since no concessions had been forthcoming, he recommended that they should be given the right to return or compensation should they not wish to do so. Lydda and Ramle should come within Arab territory and Haifa made a free port. The Jerusalem area, as defined in the 29 November resolution, should come under the United Nations. By this time, Bernadotte had expressed unease about the level of his personal security, but to no avail: based, it seems, on an earlier draft of his plan that was less favourable to Israel, Lehi members in Jerusalem ambushed and killed him on 17 September.[17]

Key elements of the Bernadotte Plan had already found

approval in the Department of State, officials seemingly believing that they had Truman's approval. On 21 September, Marshall, who was attending the United Nations in Paris, announced that the United States fully accepted Bernadotte's proposals. Truman, seeking the presidency against the popular Republican governor of New York Thomas Dewey, was undertaking his famous 'whistle-stop' tour when news reached him of Marshall's statement. At a critical meeting in Oklahoma City on 27 September, Clifford, Jacobson, and others persuaded him that he was losing millions of votes in New York and Pennsylvania. As a result, instructions were sent to Paris that no statement on Palestine be issued without his specific authority. On 3 November, Truman defied electoral arithmetic by winning the presidency against the votes of New York and Pennsylvania. Over in Britain, Bevin, too, accepted the Bernadotte Plan.[18]

The final phase

Bernadotte's assassination at the hands of Lehi members allowed Ben-Gurion to move forward with the process of national integration that he had begun with the *Altalena* affair. Lehi was outlawed, and Yellin-Mor and other leaders were arrested. Former members created a new political party, the Fighters Party, but Lehi had never been a mass movement, and its replacement collapsed after two years. One practical outcome of the *Altalena* fighting was the cessation of the Irgun's fighting role accompanied by Begin's formation of a new political party – Herut, or Freedom, heir in many respects to Jabotinsky's Revisionism – that over the next three decades was to challenge Mapai's political dominance. The Palmach, too, was fated to disappear, notwithstanding its excellent fighting record. Its command structure was wound up in September to October 1948, and its fighting units were disbanded the following summer. Much ill will had been generated, but with the demise of Lehi, the Irgun, and the Palmach, any potential threat to the integrity of the state from private armies had gone with them. The price was a bitter feud between Mapai and Herut.[19]

As the Bernadotte plan and Marshall's positive reaction to it had revealed, the major potential threat that the Israelis now faced was the loss of the Negev. On 15 October, they resumed fighting in the Negev at the strategic Fallujah crossroads. With fighting on the Jerusalem front effectively stalemated, five Egyptian brigades were matched by an equal number of Israeli brigades. Both sides fought fiercely, and each had its tactical successes, but Israeli air power and armoured strength proved their worth. On 7 January 1949, an international crisis threatened when five British Spitfires on reconnaissance flights from their bases in the Suez Canal Zone were brought down by the Israelis in controversial circumstances. The Israelis claimed that the aircraft were over Israeli air space in the Negev, while the British argued that their planes had been under orders not to cross the Egyptian border. Faced with the possibility of British intervention under the terms of Britain's treaty with Egypt, Ben-Gurion ordered his commanders, who were on the brink of cutting off the Egyptian forces around Rafah, to cease firing. The Israeli offensive had secured the Negev but not the coastal area that came to be known as the Gaza Strip.[20]

By the time of Israel's October 1948 offensive, it was apparent to almost everyone – with the possible exception of Egypt's King Farouk – that Israel was winning the war, but it was less clear how to end it. That task fell to Bunche, who had been appointed as the UN's acting mediator on 20 September. Bunche, who had been negotiating an armistice for months in 1948, was quick to take advantage of the ceasefire, convening a conference with Egyptian and Israeli delegations on the island of Rhodes on 12 January 1949. By 24 February, he had brokered an Egyptian–Israeli General Armistice Agreement intended to foster a permanent peace in Palestine. It was agreed that the non-military aspects relating to Palestine would not be part of the agreement but would be left for possible future negotiations. The critical part of the agreement was concerned with the Armistice Demarcation Line, which was not to be construed as a 'political or territorial boundary'. This agreement proved to be the template for others: with Lebanon on 23 March, Jordan on 3 April, and Syria on 20 July. Given what had preceded them, the armistice agreements were a testimony to Bunche's personal qualities and mediation skill. Fittingly, in 1950 he was awarded the Nobel Peace Prize, the first African American to receive this accolade.[21]

The Arab world after the war

Israel's success in the war permanently changed the dynamic of the Middle East. The Arabs, who had consistently opposed the creation of a Jewish state since Bloudan in 1937, now had to come to terms with its reality, especially after Israel's

admission to membership of the United Nations on 11 May
1949. Israel's membership was approved by thirty-seven
votes to twelve, with nine abstentions. In 1950, the Arab
League attempted to isolate Israel economically by reinforcing a boycott that had already existed since 1945. Israel was
widely viewed in the Arab world as a Western presence in the
Middle East, an impression that US support, and Soviet for
that matter, in the United Nations for its creation was hardly
likely to counter. Attitudes to Britain were more nuanced.
Although disliked for its authorship of the Balfour Declaration, Britain's policy under Bevin had become manifestly
pro-Arab; however, Arabs could not fail to compare Britain's
inability to counter the Jewish Revolt with its repression of
the pre-war Arab Revolt. Britain's abdication of authority in
the final months of the mandate led many Arabs to feel that
they had been let down. Resentment over Western actions
did not entirely cloud over a realisation that there had been
serious shortcomings in the Arab League's conduct of the
war.

At first sight it seemed that the main, indeed the only,
Arab beneficiary of the war was Abdullah, whose long-nur-
tured ambition for a kingdom on both banks of the Jordan
now lay within his grasp. On 11 April 1950, elections for a
new chamber of deputies were held across Jordan and the
remaining part of Palestine. Abdullah's action was opposed
by Egypt and Haj Amin, and there was rioting in Jerusalem
and elsewhere on what came to be called the West Bank.
However, on 24 April, Jordan's new prime minister, Said
al-Mufti, proclaimed the formal union of the West Bank
and the Hashemite kingdom. Abdullah had transformed

his country, now ruling East Jerusalem with its historic Old City, the strategic Latrun salient where his legionaries had held off Palmach attacks, and the important centres of Jenin, Nablus, Tulkarm, Qalqilya, Ramallah, Bethlehem, Jericho, and Hebron. Two major tasks confronted the ageing monarch. One was the extent to which he was able to reach an accommodation with Israel. More fundamental was how to forge a truly unified kingdom, two-thirds of its population now being Palestinians who felt no instinctive loyalty towards him, many of them unable to forgive what they saw as the betrayal of Lydda and Ramle by his legion.[22]

He never got the chance. On 20 July 1951, accompanied by his young grandson Hussein bin Talal, King Abdullah went for Friday prayers to the Al-Aqsa Mosque where he was assassinated. The inspiration for his fate seemingly came from Palestinians opposed to the policies he had pursued. While the assassin was immediately killed by his bodyguards, Hussein was also wounded in the attack. The reign of Abdullah's son, King Talal, was brief, since he had serious medical problems, and the succession passed to Hussein in August 1952, then a schoolboy at Harrow in Britain. After a brief spell at the Royal Military Academy at Sandhurst, the young king returned to face one of the most daunting challenges in the Middle East.[23]

The Palestinian al-Nakba

The sequence of events that had begun with UNSCOP and culminated in the 1949 armistice agreements had resulted in the devastation of Palestinian hopes and plans. There was no unitary Palestinian state in which they would have been a majority, as their representatives had claimed was their right under the UN Charter. Nor was there the partitioned Arab state that the 29 November 1947 UN Resolution had sanctioned. What remained to them was some 22 per cent of what had been Mandatory Palestine, and that was in two parts, the larger of which was incorporated into Jordan. The remaining part came to be called the Gaza Strip, basically that part of the coastal area held by the Egyptians at the time of the armistice agreements, with the ancient city of Gaza at its heart. This small area, some forty kilometres in length, much of its coast sand dunes, was retained by the Egyptians under the armistice agreement and administered, but not annexed, by them. Over 200,000 Palestinians remained inside Israel, with a major concentration in Galilee where towns like Nazareth and Umm al-Fahm retained a distinctively Arab character. With their rights guaranteed under Israel's Declaration of Independence, they initially had no alternative but to place their trust in the toleration of the new dispensation.

At the heart of what the Palestinians termed al-Nakba, or Catastrophe, was the fact that hundreds of thousands of them had fled or had been expelled from their homes to become destitute refugees during the 1948 war. Bernadotte's initial guess that they numbered between 300,000 and 400,000 proved to be far short of the mark; figures compiled by the UN numbered them at over 750,000. Some 350,000 were in the newly unified Jordan, 280,000 in the West Bank. Refugees from Haifa and Galilee were to be found in Lebanon and Syria, 97,000 and 75,000 respectively.[24] Some Palestinians still in their homes were classed as refugees since they had lost their land and were destitute. The Gaza Strip was completely transformed. Before the war, it had sustained a population of around 70,000, the principal cash crop being orange production. By the end of 1949, its population had risen to 270,000, in addition to which the Armistice Line had separated farmers from their lands, groves, and markets for their produce, which were now across the Israeli border.

Having left behind their homes and livelihoods, the immediate problem for the refugees was one of survival. While some found assistance from mosques, churches, and sympathetic fellow Arabs, most were in rudimentary camps. The Arab economies were not in a position to offer much help. The international community had other concerns. The refugees themselves rejected 'absorption' or 'resettlement' in their host countries, since this was seen as a way of preventing their return, although this aspiration increasingly seemed an unlikely prospect. On 11 December 1948, the UN General Assembly resolved that those refugees wishing to do so and who were prepared to live at peace should be allowed to return or offered compensation. Nothing was forthcoming from the Israeli government. The Economic Survey Mission was set up which proposed the establishment of an agency to assist the refugees. Their recommendation resulted in the creation of the United Nations Relief and Works Agency for Palestinian refugees (UNRWA) in December 1949. Seen as a temporary measure, the reality proved to be very different, with UNRWA providing essential support for generations in its refugee camps, providing food, shelter, education, and medical facilities.[25]

Israel after the armistice agreements

By any measure, Israel had emerged victorious, with borders considerably greater than those allotted under the 1947 partition resolution. But there were several caveats. The armistice agreements were not peace treaties, the borders created being only provisional. Israeli leaders had to reckon on possible future conflict with an Arab state or states. The borders made any in-depth defence impossible, since at one point the country was only nine miles in width, and the Jordanian-held Latrun salient was only a few yards from the Tel Aviv-to-Jerusalem road. Military preparedness, and the expense that this meant, was of the essence. The sense of isolation was reinforced by the Arab blockade, which prevented Israeli shipping and cargoes passing through the Suez Canal. Egyptian fortifications at Sharm el-Sheikh also effectively prevented Israeli traffic through the Straits of Tiran to their southern port of Eilat.

It was the position of Jerusalem that was most keenly felt. In December 1949, it was declared to be the Israeli capital, and the Knesset met there, although this decision was not recognised by the United States or Britain. The Jordanian-held Old City included Judaism's most sacred site, the Western Wall. Article 8 of the armistice agreement, which was to have confirmed the right of access to the Western Wall and other Jewish holy places, was never implemented by the Jordanians. Moreover, the armistice negotiations had left Mount Scopus to the east of the Old City, with its Hebrew University and Hadassah Hospital, as an Israeli enclave within Jordanian territory. Placed under UN protection, the enclave was allowed an Israeli police presence that was supplied by convoys under UN supervision. In short, there was ample potential for tensions in the city.[26]

There was an even greater financial problem that arose directly out of the very reason for the state's existence. In 1950, the Law of Return assured the right of every Jew to permanent settlement, followed in 1952 by the Citizenship Law, which conferred immediate citizenship on immigrants. The hope of Zionism had been that this would see a mass immigration from Europe, but, of course, the Holocaust had negated this, with only some 300,000 European Jews, many of them survivors of the camps, settling by 1951. Despite their support, few American Jews seemed to be attracted, little more than a trickle arriving. Mass immigration came only from the Jewish communities of the Middle East and North Africa, whose position had become increasingly precarious after 1945. Such was the surge that they came to form a slim majority of the Jewish population. With their very different cultural heritage, the costs of nation-building were inevitably high. These military and societal costs had to be met by an infant economy that enjoyed little in the way of natural resources. In particular, the country had problems with the most basic of all resources – water – with only one of the River Jordan's headwaters, the Dan, lying within its boundaries. As the population expanded in the 1950s, this issue became acute.[27]

Initial priming for the economy came from loans from the Export–Import Bank of the United States, but these were a palliative not a solution. In June 1952, Israel had to appeal to the Americans for a refunding of her debts. But financial relief was about to come from an unexpected – and, for many

Israelis, highly unwelcome – source. In September 1951, the newly established Federal Republic of Germany, led by the great European Dr Konrad Adenauer, had announced that it would make restitution to the Jews. For understandable reasons, many Israelis were outraged, but negotiations went ahead, culminating in the reparations Agreement signed in Luxembourg in September the following year. From 1952 to 1966, the Federal Republic transferred to Israel over three billion marks, mostly in goods and equipment, as well as payments to individuals.[28]

The Egyptian Revolution

The resentments that had long been present in sections of Egyptian society were to find their focus in the army, whose officers had experienced the government's shortcomings in the 1948–9 war. In the wake of the 1936 Anglo-Egyptian Treaty, the government opened up entry into the Military Academy to young men regardless of background. Many of those who joined came from the lower middle class, themselves sons of upwardly mobile peasant farmers. As army officers, they would have both status and the sense of serving their country. One of the first graduates, in 1938, Second Lieutenant Gamal Abdel Nasser, came from just such a background. The man who was to become the most celebrated Arab of his time was born in 1918 in Alexandria where his father worked in the post office. As his father's service was transferred to other branches, the young Nasser experienced much of the country at first hand. Later, Nasser spent much of the Second World War on garrison duty in the Sudan, but its remoteness from Cairo could not conceal the perception that the 1936 treaty had resulted in what was effectively a pseudo-independence. The sheer scale of the British military presence in the country would in itself have conveyed that, but what confirmed it was the direct intervention of February 1942, when the British had forced King Farouk to appoint a prime minister of their choice, which was bitterly resented.

By this time, Nasser had already formed friendships with two other young officers, Abdel Hakim Amer and Anwar al-Sadat, who were to become valued collaborators for much of his subsequent career. The latter had already moved in an overtly political direction, having made contact with the Axis.[29] The years 1948 and 1949 proved to be a watershed. Individual Egyptian units had fought well. The Fallujah garrison's dogged defence, in the course of which Nasser personally led a counter-attack, was recognised by allowing the garrison to leave with the traditional honours of war. The inadequacies of the supply and medical services told a different story, however, and their shortcomings were blamed on the incompetence of the government and the baleful legacy of imperialism.

In the aftermath of the war, Nasser was the driving force behind the formation of the secret Free Officers movement within the armed forces. In October 1949, together with Amer and others, a small committee was formed that in 1951 consisted of ten officers, including al-Sadat, representing different branches of the army and air force. These men were then able to organise within their own branch of the service. In preparing for a coup against the monarchy, they looked to

Brigadier-General Muhammad Naguib, a wounded veteran of the 1948–9 war.

The Free Officers made their move in a bloodless operation in Cairo and Alexandria on the evening of 22–23 July 1952. On 26 July, King Farouk was ordered to abdicate and leave the country, which he promptly did after naming his infant son, Prince Fuad, as his successor. There was no initial move to abolish the monarchy as such. Instead, a three-man regency council and a civilian prime minister, Ali Maher, were appointed. But real power rested elsewhere. The Free Officers committee was, in effect, a military junta with Nasser at its head as president of the Revolutionary Command Council and Naguib as its public face, the latter immediately being appointed army commander-in-chief. The monarchy and the vestiges of liberal parliamentary government were soon dispensed with. In January 1953, the Free Officers announced the dissolution of political parties and appointed Naguib as interim prime minister. There was only one logical outcome. On 18 June 1953, the Command Council declared Egypt to be a republic, with Naguib as president.[30]

Changing priorities in the Middle East

If the establishment of Israel changed the dynamic of the region, so, too, did the onset of the Cold War. In 1953, the Truman administration, which had done so much for Israel, was replaced by that of the Republican Dwight D. Eisenhower. It was a time of considerable uncertainty in international affairs, not least because of the death of Joseph Stalin in March 1953. For some time, the direction of Soviet foreign policy was, like that of Stalin's ultimate successor, uncertain. Nasser, King Hussein, and Eisenhower were as yet unknown quantities. Only Churchill, back in office since 1951, remained, but everyone knew that it was only a question of when he would be replaced by his foreign secretary, Anthony Eden. The new US secretary of state, John Foster Dulles, a veteran of the 1919 Paris Peace Conference, had no particular brief for Israel. This much became clear when he embarked on an early tour of the region, intending to engage Arab support in the Cold War. In both Egypt and Israel, Dulles signalled that his predecessor's policy had been overly influenced by Jewish groups. The reality of this new relationship came in September when Israel began work in the Syrian Demilitarised Zone established under the armistice agreement to divert water from the Jordan at Banat Yacoub: when Israel refused to comply with a United Nations demand to stop the project, Dulles suspended $26 million in aid.[31]

This dispute over the Jordan waters was compounded by a situation that had been maturing for some on the Israeli border where Arab farmers had been crossing the Jordanian Armistice Line to visit their old farms. Some were killed, and Arabs retaliated in kind. In response, the Israelis formed the small specialist commando unit, Unit 101, led by Ariel Sharon. Sharon, who over the following decades was to leave his mark on Israeli military and political life, was born in 1928 to well-educated parents in the cooperative settlement of Kfar Malal in central Mandatory Palestine where they worked the land. His military experience began in the 1948–9 war.[32] On 13 October 1953, an attack on the Israeli border village of Tirat Yehuda killed a young mother and her two children. Unit 101 was charged with retaliating against the Jordanian village of Qibya. In the course of destroying its buildings, sixty-nine people who were sheltering in them were killed, many of them women and children. The Americans denounced what had happened. The $26 million in aid was released when work was suspended at Banat Yacoub. The controversies over Banat Yacoub and Qibya were a sharp reminder of the instabilities that remained not far from the surface of the armistice lines.[33]

Nasser's rise to power

In 1954, an inevitable power struggle between the popular but politically rather artless Naguib and the ambitious but still relatively unknown Nasser was resolved in the latter's favour. Nasser's real power base was his presidency of the Free Officers and the Revolutionary Command Council that had emerged from it. Throughout much of 1954, the two men jockeyed for position, but with his grip on the army despite his comparatively junior rank, Nasser had a hunger for power and the stronger position. In April, in what was in effect a coup, Naguib remained as president but with Nasser as prime minister. With Naguib's removal in October, Nasser's triumph was complete.[34]

Although there were dissident voices, notably among the Muslim Brotherhood, the communists, and even some Free Officers, Nasser never hesitated to strike against them whenever he felt his position threatened. Having escaped an attempted assassination by a member of the Muslim Brotherhood in October, he acted ruthlessly against the group, hanging six of them and imprisoning many others, including its leader, Sayyid Qutb. Relations between the Free Officers and the Brotherhood were never entirely straightforward, but, after disturbances at Cairo University in January 1954, it was decided to ban the latter. Even so, its influence in the countryside and among elements of the army meant that it could not discounted, and, as result, it maintained an envi-able ability to survive.[35] On the other hand, since there was little by way of an industrial proletariat, the communists were a negligible factor.

Nasser's initial priority was to free Egypt from the last ves-tiges of imperialism, which meant ending the British mili-tary presence along the Suez Canal Zone. The Canal Zone was a network of strategically placed military bases and air-fields, housing some 80,000 soldiers and airmen. Its status was increasingly questionable. The 1936 treaty had specified that British troops could remain for twenty years, at which point the question would arise as to whether the Egyptian Army had the resources to ensure the security of naviga-tion through the canal. In any event, in October 1951 King Farouk's government unilaterally abrogated the treaty. This was followed by a succession of Egyptian attacks on the zone with considerable British and Egyptian casualties. Like the three Irish treaty ports that were ceded to Éire in 1938, the positions along the canal were only viable in the context of a friendly hinterland, and this was palpably lacking. Moreo-ver, with Indian independence in 1947, part of the reason for a continued British military presence had gone. In October 1954, British foreign secretary Eden concluded a new agree-ment whereby the British military presence would be ended within twenty months, much to the fury of a section of his own party.[36] The last British troops departed from Port Said on 13 June 1956.

At first, relations between the Americans and the new regime in Cairo were not clouded by a legacy of imperial interference in Egyptian affairs. Fearful of what they perceived to be improving Egyptian–American relations, the Israelis undertook a covert mission to discredit Nasser, bombing the United States Information service offices in Cairo and Alexandria. But the scheme unravelled: the agents were arrested and put on trial, two being sentenced to death and others to long prison sentences. Approaches to the Americans for intervention to have the sentences reduced were unheeded. By the end of 1954, Nasser had secured his secured his position internally, with a major foreign policy success to his credit.

The Gaza Raid and the arms race

Seeing the young Egyptian leader as having the credibility to stand over a Palestinian settlement, British and US officials worked in secret on Project Alpha in the hope that a positive channel could be opened up between Egypt and Israel. For his part, Nasser signalled that he was not averse to a settlement that might involve Egypt acquiring the Negev, thus removing the land barrier from the Arab world, in return for Israel gaining the Gaza Strip. But the Gaza Strip was presenting other problems, since it had become the base for the armed Palestinian Fedayeen guerrillas, who were crossing the Armistice Line to attack Israeli settlements. Ben-Gurion had attempted retirement, but, in the light of these disturbing events, in February 1955 he returned to the cabinet as defence minister. Following a series of Palestinian guerrilla raids that had penetrated close to Tel Aviv, on 28 February the Israelis attacked Gaza. Although described as the Gaza Raid, Operation Black Arrow was, in fact, a major military operation led by Sharon, whose Unit 101 had merged with the paratroopers to form an elite counter-terrorism force. The paratroopers' target was the Egyptian Army's headquarters in Gaza. In the ensuing fighting, eight Israeli and thirty-eight Egyptian soldiers were killed.[37]

If the Israelis had hoped that Operation Black Arrow would convince the Egyptians to cease their support for the Palestinian raids, they were to be confounded: instead, Nasser concluded that he needed to build up his armed forces. The following months were to see a growing tension between the Egyptian leader and the West, not that it had ever been part of his purpose to be in thrall to the latter. His growing estrangement from the Americans really began when, contrary to their advice, he attended the Bandung Conference of non-aligned states in Indonesia in April, a major priority of which was anti-colonialism. Here, Nasser encountered the prime minister of the People's Republic of China, Zhou Enlai – a particular American *bête noire* – with whom he raised the possibility of acquiring arms from the Soviet Union. The Soviet leadership was quick to see their chance of gaining a bridgehead in the Middle East. Contrary to US advice, on 30 September 1955 Nasser announced an arms agreement apparently with Czechoslovakia but actually with Moscow. True to their word, in addition to automatic light weapons, the Soviets also supplied tanks, armoured personnel carriers, and self-propelled artillery. What really worried the Israelis, however, was the arrival of MiG-15 jet fighters and Ilyushin Il-28 jet bombers. Once operational with trained pilots, the latter placed Tel Aviv and the other Israeli towns within minutes of attack from air bases in the Sinai. These shipments thus marked the start of an arms race. The Israelis and the French found a common interest, since in 1954 the latter were faced with a widespread rebellion in Algeria which they believed was partly inspired by Nasser. In April 1956, the French supplied Israel with 12 Mystère Iv jet fighters, followed by contracts for a further 72 Mystères, 120 AMX light tanks, and 40 Super Sherman tanks. A future conflict between Egypt and Israel would no longer be fought with Second World War cast-offs.[38]

This escalation in the military equation was not the only danger sign in the region. Britain's old ally in the Middle East, Iraq's Nuri al-Said, was pursuing his own agenda at the heart of which was a security pact. In February 1955, he concluded a defence agreement with Turkey, known as the Baghdad Pact, which was then joined by Britain. Iran and Pakistan subsequently also became members. While on the surface this appeared to be a formidable combination, its inherent weakness was that Iraq was the only Arab member. The fellow Hashemite monarch of Jordan, King Hussein, seemed an obvious candidate, but a visit by Britain's General Sir Gerald Templer to pursue this merely exposed the degree of opposition that Hussein faced from both Cairo and the Palestinians. On 1 March 1956, Hussein abruptly dismissed the veteran Glubb from his command.[39] The removal of

British officers from an Arab army need not in itself have seemed a matter of great moment, but, in the febrile state of the Middle East, it was seen as a victory for Nasser, not least by Anthony Eden, who had at last replaced Churchill as prime minister in April 1955. Although recently in poor health brought on by gallstones, Eden had a military cross from the First World War, held a first-class degree in oriental languages, and had a long and honourable record as foreign secretary. He appeared ideally placed to help settle the Middle East, but the Fates were to decide otherwise.

8

From War to War

By 1956, Nasser had done enough to arouse the fears of the Israelis and, albeit for different reasons, the suspicions of the Americans, British, and French. That he was seeking to chart a genuinely neutral course for a country that had only just emerged from decades of imperial domination was neither understood nor appreciated; instead, his initiatives tended to be seen through the prism of the 1930s, despite the fact that Nasser's Egypt was not Mussolini's Italy, still less Hitler's Germany. Egypt had long-standing domestic problems that needed to be addressed. The country's population had multiplied fivefold over the previous century, but the stock of fertile land watered by the Nile remained relatively finite. There was, in short, an urgent need to expand the stock of available farmland if the country's population were to be sustained. Harnessing the Nile waters held the answer. In addition to this, Egypt was woefully deficient in its electricity infrastructure, a problem that hydroelectric power generated by a dam could redress. The height of the barrage built by the British at Aswan in 1902 had twice been increased, but this had proved to be a palliative rather than a cure. In November

1954, Nasser announced that his government was going to build a high dam at Aswan. The barrage across the Nile was to be almost two-and-a-half miles in length, resulting in the creation of one of the world's largest manmade lakes at the cost of resettling tens of thousands of peasant families. Some of the country's finest monuments, notably the temples at Abu Simbel, would be submerged unless money could be found to rescue them.

The technology needed for this massive civil engineering project was provided by the Germans, but this was only one part of the equation – the other was the necessary finance. Since Egypt's fiscal state meant that it could not cover the project's full cost, a complex financial aid package was put together by the World Bank and the US and British governments, which were initially concerned that Nasser would turn to Moscow for aid. Grants from the two governments were to be made towards the first stage. The second phase was to be the provision of a loan from the World Bank, with Anglo-American support.[1] The package was put to Nasser in December 1955, but over the following months substantial opposition grew in Washington to money being given to a regime that seemed increasingly anti-Western. The latter sentiment was powerfully reinforced when on 16 May 1956 Nasser announced Egypt's recognition of the People's Republic of China. On 19 July 1956, Dulles met the Egyptian ambassador to Washington, informing the astonished diplomat that the US offer of financial aid for the dam project had been withdrawn. Dulles concluded this bleak encounter with the patronising advice that the Egyptians ought to concentrate on less monumental projects. Apparently not consulted in advance by Washington, the British announced that they, too, were withdrawing their offer of a grant. At this point the final domino, the projected World Bank loan, toppled, too.

The Suez Crisis[2]

Having so far enjoyed something of a Midas touch in international affairs, Nasser was soon confronted with the sometimes brutal realities of great-power politics. The news of the collapse of the financial package for the dam was made all the more humiliating for him since it reached him just as he was returning from a conference in Yugoslavia with its leader Marshal Tito and India's premier Jawaharlal Nehru that had burnished his image as a leader in the non-aligned world. His riposte came in a major speech at Alexandria on the fourth anniversary of King Farouk's abdication on 26 July 1956. On a prearranged code word in the speech – 'Ferdinand de Lesseps' – soldiers took over the key installations of the Suez Canal Company at Port Said, Ismailia, and Suez. As they did so, Nasser announced the company's nationalisation.

The company, which was responsible for the canal's operation and had its headquarters in Paris, operated under a lease that was due to expire in 1968. Its shareholders were to receive compensation, and Nasser emphasised that the canal would continue to work normally under its existing staff who were forbidden to resign.

Both Eden and his French counterpart, the socialist Guy Mollet, favoured the preparation of a military expedition, although this was tempered by the fact that, while both the

President Nasser addressing crowds after his return from
Alexandria where he proclaimed the nationalisation of the
Suez Canal, July 1956. (RBM Vintage Images/Alamy Stock Photo)

Royal Navy and Royal Air Force were in a position to move quickly, it would take almost two months for the British Army to organise the force needed to seize the entire length of the canal. The British paratroopers, in particular, required retraining. The British land force, painstakingly assembled, was to comprise an infantry division, a parachute brigade, and a Royal Marine Commando brigade. France was immediately able to offer the tough paratroopers of the 10th Airborne Division, with four regiments, including the French Foreign Legion, which had seen action in Indo-China, and the 7th Fast Mechanised Division. There was no quick answer to collecting the number of ships, especially landing craft, that would be needed for a seaborne landing. In political terms, it was unclear whether the purpose of such a military intervention was to return the canal to international control or to overthrow Nasser. If the latter, who or what was to replace him was opaque. From the start, the US response was more cautious. While castigating Nasser's action at a meeting in London on 1 August, Dulles emphasised the need for a negotiated settlement. He had brought with him a letter from Eisenhower counselling against the use of force at that time. Failure to read US intentions correctly would cost the emergent Israeli-French-British enterprise dearly. In the meantime, the task of assembling a viable Anglo-French force at bases in Malta and Cyprus was taking time, and Nasser was ensuring that the canal was working normally, thus obviating the need for any military action.

The Protocol of Sèvres

Faced with this situation, in September 1956 the French explored possible options with the Israelis. Ben-Gurion, once again prime minister, and Shimon Peres, the young director-general of the Ministry of Defence, were keen to respond. A meeting in Paris on 30 September–1 October prepared the way for cooperation. But the French had already agreed that their forces would come under British command, and they would certainly need the British air and naval bases in Cyprus and Malta. At a meeting on 14 October, General Maurice Challe, French deputy chief of staff of the air force, offered what seemed to be the winning formula: the Israelis would mount an offensive in the Sinai Peninsula, giving the British and French a reason to land at the canal to preserve it and separate the two combatants. On 22–24 October, Ben-Gurion, accompanied by Peres and chief of staff Moshe Dayan, met representatives of the British and French governments at a highly secret meeting at Sèvres outside Paris and reached an agreement for such an operation. The Sèvres Protocol sanctioned an Israeli offensive in the Sinai Desert on 29 October. Britain and France would then call for a ceasefire and for the Israelis and Egyptians to withdraw their troops ten miles from either bank of the canal. If this did not happen, the two countries would begin their operation against Egypt on the 31st. The plan, not wholly welcomed by the entire British Cabinet, was flawed in conception and, as it turned out, in execution. The country to be attacked by the Anglo-French forces, Egypt, was actually the victim of an offensive. But what proved to be the fatal misreading that undermined the whole enterprise was a fundamental failure to anticipate the likely US response.

Operation Kadesh

There were, in effect, two military campaigns against Egypt in 1956: that of the Israelis, which was a conspicuous success, and that of the British and French, which ended in humiliation. The military driving force behind the Israeli offensive was Lieutenant-General Moshe Dayan, chief of staff since December 1953. Born to immigrant parents from Ukraine in Degania in 1915, Dayan had taken part in the bitter fighting against Vichyite troops in Syria in 1941. Badly wounded, he lost the sight of his left eye, the resulting black eye patch marking him out as a distinctive figure, although he would gladly have dispensed with it. In the 1948–9 war, his command had been active in both the Lydda–Ramle and Jerusalem fronts.[3]

The canal had not been at the forefront of the Israelis' military thinking; what really rankled with them was the blockade of the Straits of Tiran from Sharm el-Sheikh. Operation Kadesh, the Israeli offensive into Sinai launched in accordance with the Sèvres Protocol on the morning of 29 October, was relatively modest in scale. The spearhead was an airborne drop east of the strategic Mitla Pass 150 miles inside Egyptian lines, close enough to the canal to justify the Anglo-French cover story of issuing an ultimatum. It was a dangerously exposed position, relief coming across the desert from the rest of Sharon's elite 202nd Parachute Brigade which arrived on the 31st. In heavy fighting inside the pass, both sides took substantial losses: some 260 Egyptians and 38 of Sharon's paratroopers were killed. The scale of the Israeli losses engendered controversy between Dayan and Sharon, but the Israelis held the initiative in the Sinai. The other principal Israeli action was to send the 9th Brigade overland to capture the coveted prize of Sharm el-Sheikh, potentially opening the blockade of the straits, which they reached on 5 November. Egyptian resistance in the Gaza Strip ended on 3 November. The Israeli part of the tripartite plan had ended.[4]

Operation Musketeer

The Anglo-French ultimatums had been delivered to the Egyptians and Israelis on 30 October. While in some respects identical, the message issued to Egypt requested that British and French troops temporarily occupy Port Said, Ismailia, and Suez in order to ensure safe shipping through the canal and separate the two armies. The two sides were to withdraw their troops ten miles from the canal, which would have ensured Israeli control over virtually all of the Sinai. If there was no acceptance of these terms within twelve hours, then Anglo-French forces would intervene. The Egyptians ignored the ultimatum, triggering the start of air operations against them.

These events were unfolding as a major tragedy was developing elsewhere. On 23 October 1956, as the Israelis, French, and British were conferring at Sèvres, large-scale rioting broke out in Budapest, which led to the reformist Imre Nagy becoming prime minister. On 1 November, he proclaimed Hungary's neutrality in the Cold War, a course that the Kremlin could not tolerate. On 4 November, the Red Army attacked Budapest, brutally suppressing the Hungarian freedom fighters. Nagy and his colleagues were later executed. There was nothing that the West could do to assist the Hungarians, and the two crises could not have come at a worse time for President Eisenhower, who was facing re-election on 6 November. In his 1952 election campaign, Eisenhower had pledged to 'roll back' communism, which was clearly not happening in Hungary, while he had not been consulted by his closest allies in London and Paris over the Anglo-French-Israeli operation.

The Anglo-French air operation, which began on 31 October, was tightly focused on the Egyptian air bases and destroyed most of Egypt's aircraft except for some that had been hidden, a precondition for the landing at the canal. This part of the operation began in the early morning of 5 November when over 1,000 men of the 3rd Battalion, Parachute Regiment and the 2nd Marine Parachute Regiment were dropped at Port Said. Time was of the essence, since domestic opinion in Britain and, more significantly, international pressures had been mounting against the Anglo-French action. As more airborne troops arrived, the local Egyptian commander at Port Said negotiated a temporary ceasefire, opening the way it seemed for an Anglo-French advance along the canal to Ismailia and Suez. The seaborne assault, painstakingly assembled, began on the morning of 6 November when men of Britain's 40 and 42 Commando, supported by the 6th Royal Tank Regiment, landed at Port Said in what proved to be one of the briefest operations in British military history.

As the fighting continued during 6 November, Eden's government was facing a crisis of a different kind, one that was to determine the fate of the expedition. Britain's chancellor of the exchequer, Harold Macmillan, saw that his currency reserves were fast draining away and that the country faced financial ruin, and he was also aware of the lack of US financial support, which soon took tangible form. Confirmation came that the United States Treasury was opposing Britain's attempts to protect sterling by drawing money from the International Monetary Fund. Other factors were at play. The Soviet leadership had issued threats, hinting at possible intervention in the Middle East. More importantly, United Nations Secretary-General Dag Hammarskjöld was raising an International Peacekeeping Force, initially proposed by Canada, thus invalidating the reason given for the intervention. With Macmillan and senior colleagues arguing against continuing the operation, Eden saw no alternative but to concur. A bitterly divided French cabinet also agreed. Both the British and French military commanders had been preparing for a military operation on the 7th to try to reach Ismailia, but with the ceasefire coming into effect at 2 a.m. local time, these were stillborn.

The aftermath

The advance detachments of Hammarskjöld's hastily assembled United Nations Emergency Force (UNEF) of Danes and Norwegians arrived on 21 November. They were followed by Indians and Yugoslavs under the overall command of Canadian Lieutenant-General E. L. M. Burns. Their presence enabled the British and French troops at Port Said to be evacuated with a measure of dignity on 23 December. The following day de Lesseps's statue was blown up before a large crowd. Eden went to Jamaica in an attempt to restore his health, returning to London in mid-December, but he did not feel able to carry on and resigned the premiership on 9 January 1957. Honoured as the Earl of Avon, he was respected as a faithful servant of the state, although the Suez affair was to affect his legacy. His successor, Harold Macmillan, saw the restoration of good relations with the Americans as a clear priority. The re-elected Eisenhower administration had already rewarded Britain for the ceasefire by supporting financial aid through the International Monetary Fund. The Suez affair was an embarrassing end both to Britain's lingering aspiration to be a great power and to its longstanding role in the Middle East, although its presence in Aden and the Gulf continued for another decade. For the French, Suez contributed to the sequence of events that saw the army revolt in Algeria in May 1958, which brought General de Gaulle back to power in the hope of preserving French Algeria. Four years later, he was to give Algeria its independence.

Eisenhower moved quickly to confirm America's leading role in the region, announcing on 5 January 1957 the Eisenhower Doctrine by which armed force was promised to any Middle Eastern country that requested help against communism. At the same time, he and Dulles were adamant that Israel could not retain her military conquests. With his troops controlling much of the Sinai Peninsula, Ben-Gurion hoped to be able to bargain for retention of the Gaza Strip and Sharm el-Sheikh, which had, after all, been the Israelis' main objective all along. When the Israelis rejected the offer of UNEF in return for a full withdrawal, Eisenhower went on television to assert that the Israelis could not exact conditions for a withdrawal from positions that they had invaded. In private, he threatened Israel with sanctions that would have affected both foreign aid and pro-Israeli fundraising in the United States. Faced with this pressure, Golda Meir, now foreign minister, announced in the United Nations General Assembly on 1 March 1957 that Israel would withdraw from the Gaza Strip and Sharm el-Sheikh. Asserting that the Gulf of Aqaba was an international waterway, Meir said that any interference with Israeli shipping there or through the Straits of Tiran would be met with all necessary measures. Israel was offered reassurance in the form of UNEF stationing in the Gaza Strip and the Sinai, including Sharm el-Sheikh. More pertinently, Nasser gave a secret assurance that the Straits of Tiran would be regarded as an international waterway.[5]

In the aftermath of the crisis, it seemed that Nasser could do little wrong. No Arab, before or since, has enjoyed such acclaim, both among his own people and in the wider Arab world. His portrait could still be seen in Arab homes decades after his death. In 1958, the Soviet Union announced that it would provide the necessary finance to proceed with the Aswan High Dam project, which formally opened in 1971. The resulting Lake Nasser provided many of the anticipated benefits to the economy, although there have been questions about its environmental impact. The Great Temple of Ramses II at Abu Simbel was preserved through financial assistance from UNESCO. But some of the sureness of touch that had marked Nasser's earlier career seemed to desert him. In the early 1960s, he increasingly resorted to hyperbole in his public speeches.[6] Nasser's role in the wider Arab world continued. In September 1962, for instance, Imam Muhammad al-Badr, the ruler of Yemen, was overthrown in a military coup led by Brigadier Abdullah al-Sallal who proclaimed a republic. But Badr, who had escaped, raised tribal forces loyal to him. Faced with civil war, Sallal asked Nasser for military help. Egyptian military involvement, which lasted until December 1967, drew in a third of the army, putting the economy under further strain. Nasser's rule became increasingly autocratic. His only real friend was his trusted colleague from his early military days, Amer, who became a field marshal and commander-in-chief. The relationship was to end in tragedy.

1958: The Middle East in revolution

The year 1958 saw Nasserism at its peak across several parts of the Middle East, particularly at the popular level. The first manifestation of this phenomenon came in Syria, which had struggled to find political stability since independence. The country was initially led by Shukri al-Quwatli who had been instrumental in leading it to independence, but his credibility was undermined by the army's lacklustre performance in the 1948–9 war. In March 1949, he was overthrown in a bloodless military coup. Two further coups followed that year, which resulted in the coming to power of Colonel Adib al-Shishakli. Another military revolt in February 1954 saw Shishakli removed, and he eventually fled to Brazil where he was later assassinated. In 1955, Quwatli returned to power, mirroring Nasser in fostering links with the Communist Bloc. Nasser, too, was increasingly seen as an effective ruler, especially after 1956.

On 18 November 1957, a group of Syrian and Egyptian parliamentarians unanimously resolved to work towards a federal union. There was genuine support for this in Syria, especially in the army and the Ba'ath Party, which supported the idea of Arab unity. Such was the enthusiasm for the project that on 1 February 1958 Nasser and Quwatli met in Cairo, announcing that their two countries would be united as the United Arab Republic (UAR) with its capital at Cairo. The new country would have a common army and a single parliament and foreign service, but otherwise devolved administrations. The name was designed to induce other Arab countries to join, but many Egyptians, proud of their heritage, were dismayed that Egypt did not feature in the title. Neither, for that matter, did Syria, which became the Northern Region of the UAR. When emotion subsided, it was clear that it was an unequal union, most obviously because the population of Egypt was much higher than that of Syria. Quwatli was dignified as the First Arab Citizen, but the real power in Syria rested with Amer who was dispatched to Damascus. The key decisions were Nasser's.[7]

Despite its complex multi-confessional composition, the Lebanese state seemed to find stability for a time based upon the 1943 National Pact, which shared the major offices of state between the various groups. But what was in any case a somewhat uneasy coalition came to be challenged in two ways. In the course of 1948–9, Lebanon became the refuge for some 97,000 Palestinian refugees, mostly from Galilee, with UNWRA providing camps such as Tel al-Zaatar, Sabra, and Shatila. Although they were not Lebanese citizens, the refugees' presence impinged on the country's delicate demographic balance. The Maronite Christian Camille Chamoun, who became president of Lebanon in 1952, did not take kindly to the way in which the country's large Sunni community responded to the message of pan-Arabism coming from Cairo. Instinctively pro-Western, Chamoun remained neutral during the Suez Crisis and then accepted the Eisenhower Doctrine. Rumours circulated that he was going to seek a constitutional amendment to enable him to have a further term as president. With tensions rising, on 8 May 1958 the murder of an opposition journalist triggered civil war, with Chamoun's supporters pitted against those led by the Druze leader Kamal Junblatt. The Maronite army commander, Fuad Shihab, prudently remained neutral. The conflict was only resolved in the backwash of the dramatic events in Baghdad on 14 July.[8]

As in Egypt and Syria, the army in Iraq was the source of covert opposition to the regime, the monarchy of King Feisal II. His principal advisers were his uncle, Crown Prince Abd al-Ilah, and the veteran Nuri al-Said, a long-standing prop of the Hashemites who had returned to the premiership in 1954. Essentially pro-Western, Nuri held no brief for the wave of pan-Arabism surging through the region, forging links instead with Turkey, Iran, and Pakistan. As he did so, the idea of a coup was maturing in the officer corps where the Supreme Committee was formed. Its chair was Brigadier Abd al-Karim Qasim together with Colonel Abd al-Salam Arif, who actually mounted the coup in Baghdad on 14 July

1958 where the king, the crown prince, and other members of the Hashemite family were murdered, as was Nuri.[9]

The Iraqi Revolution threatened the Western position in the region and those who supported it. Faced with this crisis, both Chamoun and Jordan's King Hussein appealed for Anglo-American military assistance. The powerful United States Sixth Fleet was in a position to respond immediately, and its marines came ashore at Beirut on 15 July. They were followed two days later with the landing of British paratroopers at Amman, deploying at the airport to avoid provocation. The Anglo-American interventions were bitterly denounced at the United Nations, but they did help to cauterise what was in danger of escalating into a regional crisis. On 31 July, the Lebanese conflict was ended when the warring parties agreed that General Shihab would assume the presidency when Chamoun's term ended, with the Sunni Rashid Karami as prime minister. With the crisis over, the marines were evacuated by 25 October. British troops left Jordan by 2 November.[10]

The Palestinian revival

As these events in Damascus, Beirut, Baghdad, and Amman were attracting the world's headlines, far-reaching changes were quietly maturing among the Palestinians. That they had barely featured in the great Middle Eastern crisis of 1956 seemed confirmation that they were becoming the forgotten people of the region, at best characterised as refugees, at worst as a propaganda tool. From that basis, young Palestinians began to look for ways in which their cause could be revived and sustained. The man to drive this movement was Mohamed Abdel-Raouf Arafat al-Qudwa al-Husseini, commonly known by his youthful nickname Yasser Arafat. Born in Cairo in 1929 to parents of Jerusalem and Gaza origins, Arafat moved to Jerusalem as a child. Following service in the 1948–9 war, he studied engineering at university in Cairo. In 1958–9, together with his friend Khalil al-Wazir, a native of Ramle, he was the driving force behind two initiatives. The first was the journal *Filastinuna*, 'Our Palestine', which preached the Palestinian cause. The other was the formation of Fatah, the Palestine National Liberation Movement, a reverse acronym of Harakat Tahrir Filastin. Ten years later, Arafat was to become the unchallenged leader of the Palestinians with Fatah their principal instrument.[11]

The uneasy peace

For much of the 1960s a calm seemed to have settled on the Middle East, but this proved to be illusory. The tide of Nasserism appeared to be receding, and Syrians increasingly saw themselves as an Egyptian colony. This was understandable. Amer, in effect Nasser's viceroy, enjoyed full powers. Reform measures went in tandem with restrictions on civil liberties, enforced by a secret-police network. The interunion customs system discriminated in favour of Egyptian goods. Perhaps the final blow came in August 1961 when Nasser revoked the devolved administrations to create a single UAR government. On 28 September 1961, Syrian army officers mounted a coup in Damascus. Their initial demand for autonomy within the union met with a stony response. Believing that the revolt was confined to Damascus, Nasser ordered the men of the Third Army to march on the city, but they refused. A force of Egyptian paratroopers dispatched to Syria surrendered. Nasser had no alternative but to bow to the inevitable. The end of the union was proclaimed, with the country established as the Syrian Arab Republic.[12]

Domestically, Nasser faced a potential challenge from Qutb who, like others before and since, had put his time in prison to good use, refining his message that society had to be recast on an Islamic basis and condemning the secular nature of Nasser's regime. Prison proved to be an excellent source of recruits to his cause. While in jail, he was contacted by members of the secret revolutionary Islamic group al-Tanzim with a view to his assuming leadership. His writings inspired many, and on his early release from prison in 1964 he was closely involved with the group. But this was a highly dangerous course of action which was abruptly brought to an end when the security forces stumbled on the organisation in 1965 and rounded up its members. Qutb was hanged on 29 August 1966, but his teachings continued to inspire many Muslims, not just in Egypt but across the Middle East.[13]

Post-revolutionary Iraq proved to be no more politically stable than the UAR, if for different reasons. From the start, it was evident that there were clear differences between Qasim, who assumed the presidency, and the younger Arif, who believed that he had spearheaded the opposition to the monarchy. Arif openly admired Nasser and his pan-Arabism, while Qasim, of mixed Sunni–Shi'a origin, was clearly focused on Iraq. An early conspiracy against Qasim associated with the veteran Rashid Ali, who had returned after the revolution, was uncovered. Both Rashid Ali and Arif were condemned to death but reprieved. Qasim withdrew from the Baghdad Pact, cultivated ties with the Soviet Union, and encouraged the Iraqi communists, none of which made him any friends in the West. His international isolation was demonstrated further in 1961 when he seemed to threaten Kuwait. Britain, which had not abrogated its commitments in the Gulf, responded militarily when the Kuwaiti ruler appealed for support. This use of British forces found support in the Arab League, which sent troops to replace them. Arif had his allies in the army and among the Ba'athists, who mounted a successful coup on 9 February 1963. Qasim was executed. After a brief Ba'athist interlude, another coup brought Arif to power in November. His leadership saw a rapprochement with Egypt, but Nasser, having just experienced one failed attempt at union, was not inclined to rush into another. The question did not arise in any case, since in April 1966 Arif perished in an air crash.[14]

Despite these events in Lebanon, Syria, and Iraq, or perhaps because of them, Israel enjoyed a period of relative tranquillity in the years immediately after the Suez Crisis. The presence of UNEF seemed a guarantee of stability on its borders with the Gaza Strip and Egypt and of navigation through the Straits of Tiran. The country's economy moved forward after it had surmounted the economic crises of the early years. The ageing Ben-Gurion resigned the premiership in June 1963, being succeeded by the veteran Zionist Levi Eshkol. Eshkol's foreign minister was the highly experienced diplomat Abba Eban who brought with him wide experience in Washington and at the United Nations. The policies these two men pursued did not sit well with Ben-Gurion, who formed a new political party, Rafi (Israel Workers List), on 16 June 1965 which attracted two influential supporters in Dayan and Peres.[15] They were perfectly positioned to act as informed critics of Eshkol and Eban as the country experienced a new wave of Palestinian attacks.

By 1963, the construction of Israel's National Water Carrier had progressed to the stage where it could begin to connect the waters of the Jordan with the arid Negev. With the principal headwaters of the Jordan flowing from Lebanon and Syria, there was a strong Arab reaction to what they saw as the theft of water that rightly belonged to them. As the political temperature rose, Nasser, who knew the Arabs were unprepared for war, held a conference in Cairo in January 1964. The main outcome was agreement for a political organisation to represent the Palestinians, the Palestine Liberation Organisation (PLO), which was formed in May 1964. Its chair, Ahmad Shukairy, was a protégé of Nasser, who essentially controlled the organisation. Judged harshly by the Palestinians, including Arafat for his lack of leadership, Shukairy's main political vehicle was propaganda.[16] The PLO's one asset was the creation of the Palestine Liberation Army under Egyptian command recruited from refugees in Syria and Gaza.

Fatah's armed campaign, carried out under the cover name of Asifa (the Storm), began on 1 January 1965 with an attack on Israeli water installations and then continued throughout the year. Never in themselves a realistic threat to Israel, the raids were a reminder that the state had to be constantly on its guard, and Fatah's actions were certainly stoking tensions in the Middle East. From February 1966, its operations assumed a new potential when the Syrian government decided to increase support for Fatah, enabling it to be more ambitious. Israel inevitably retaliated, not always with much impact, since it did so against targets in Lebanon and Jordan. In November 1966, a major Israeli operation against the village of Samu in the West Bank inside Jordanian territory, believed to be harbouring guerrillas, resulted in a battle with the Arab Legion, fuelling the belief that Israel was avoiding a confrontation with the Syrians and increasing domestic pressure on the Eshkol government. The same month, at the urging of the Soviet Union, Damascus and Cairo composed their differences to the extent of concluding a mutual defence pact. There were also the ongoing tensions between Israel and Syria over water and the demilitarised zone, with Israeli communities in the north-east vulnerable to Syrian artillery on the Golan Heights. Even so, it was not at all obvious that 1967 would see another major war in the Middle East, especially as Nasser was signalling to the Americans that the pact with Syria would not lead him into war.

The Six-Day War[17]

As Nasser had it, the crisis was triggered on 13 May 1967 when a message was conveyed to the Egyptians from the Syrians and the Soviet Union that between eleven and thirteen Israeli brigades were massed on the Syrian border with a view to invading. This warning was untrue. For the Israelis to have deployed a force of this scale would have required their previous mobilisation, and this had not happened. Nasser's initial response to this apparent threat to his ally was to send two armoured divisions into the Sinai on 14 May. The Israelis responded with an armoured brigade and then, on 16 May, by mobilising reserves. These moves called into question the role of UNEF, the force that Hammarskjöld had conjured up in the aftermath of the Suez Crisis. On 16 May, Nasser ordered UNEF to concentrate in the Gaza Strip, but this did not include its withdrawal from the two key areas of Gaza and Sharm el-Sheikh. Israel had made it clear that any blockade of the Straits of Tiran at Sharm el-Sheikh would be treated as an act of war. UNEF, only some 1,400 strong, was never anything other than a diplomatic trip wire, with any questioning of its position being referred to the UN General Assembly in the expectation that negotiations would run their course. The burden now fell on UN Secretary-General U Thant, who had succeeded on Hammarskjöld's tragic death in 1961. Without reference to the General Assembly, he decided that the UN could not have troops on Egyptian territory without its consent and that the entire force would have to leave.

The decision to withdraw UNEF, Nasser was to claim, left him with no alternative but to activate the blockade at Sharm el-Sheikh. Realising this, Israel ordered full mobilisation on 20 May, followed the next day by the Egyptian blockade of the straits. By then the situation had moved beyond that of taking pressure off Syria. Nasser was in a dilemma. While his speeches threatened Israel, he sent backchannel messages through the Soviets to Washington that he would not attack. Both Moscow and Washington had concluded that, if war came, Israel would win swiftly. Nasser, it seems, was being counselled by his trusted lieutenant, Field Marshal Amer, that his forces were ready for war. Although Amer's confidence was soon to be confounded, there was some basis for it. The Egyptians had invested heavily in the military infrastructure of the Sinai, constructing strongpoints, bases, and roads to the extent of creating a new strategic pass, the Gidi, to supplement the Mitla. Under the command of General Abdel Mohsin Murtagi were 100,000 men, consisting of four infantry, two armoured, and one mechanised division, with almost 1,000 tanks. In addition, the air force had been equipped with 200 of the latest Soviet fighters, the MiG-21, and 30 Tu-28 heavy bombers.

A diplomatic mission by Eban yielded nothing. The British and French would not move without the Americans, who had too many problems of their own in Vietnam. President Lyndon Johnson advised Eban that Israel would not be alone unless it went alone, and the Americans subsequently arranged for Egypt's vice-president to come to Washington on 7 June. But time was not on the side of diplomacy as regional tensions rose. On 29 May, Nasser spoke to the People's Assembly announcing that the issue was no longer the straits but the rights of the Palestinians. A military pact with Jordan was concluded the following day, a decision that constrained King Hussein's freedom of action. General Abdel Munim Riad arrived in Amman to take command of the Jordanian forces. A poorly delivered speech by Eshkol did nothing to reassure an increasingly fearful Israeli public, and a role was demanded for Dayan, who had retained the aura of the 1956 Sinai campaign. On 1 June, a government of national unity was formed, with Dayan as defence minister and including Begin as minister without portfolio. Without consulting the Americans, and by a divided vote, on 4 June the new government decided on war.

The plans that were set into operation in the early hours of 5 June had been prepared in meticulous detail under the direction of two Palmach veterans: Rabin, who was appointed chief of staff in 1964, and Brigadier-General Mordechai Hod, the air force commander since 1966. Their weapons were devastating pre-emptive air strikes against the Arab air forces, the Egyptians especially. The latter had the potential to overwhelm Israel's towns and cities. Observing radio silence, virtually all of Hod's air fleet of French-built Mirages, Mystères, and Ouragans flew out over the Mediterranean at low level before turning towards Egyptian air space. Their attacks on the airfields were timed for 7.45 a.m. as the Egyptian fighters had landed after their dawn patrols. On returning to base, Israeli ground crews had the planes refuelled and rearmed in eight minutes ready for further strikes. Within three hours, Egyptian air power – all of its bombers and 135 fighters – were wiped out. This operation was quickly followed by others, which destroyed twenty-two Jordanian and fifty-five Syrian aircraft. Hod's crews had opened the way for the army. The Egyptians did their Jordanian and Syrian allies no favours by sending misleading messages that they had mastered the Israeli Air Force.

The military campaign against Murtagi's army in the Sinai was conducted by Southern Command under General Yeshayahu Gavish who deployed three divisions under Major-Generals Sharon, Israel Tal, and Avraham Joffe. With a mixed force of armour and paratroopers, Tal isolated the Gaza Strip

and advanced to El Arish. Sharon was charged with taking
the supply routes across the central Sinai, enabling Joffe's
division to advance between himself and Tal. Lacking air
support, the Egyptian Army stood no chance against this
coordinated offensive. By 8 June, Gavish's command had
taken the entire Sinai, reaching the Suez Canal and inflicting over 10,000 casualties. The Israelis sent messages to King
Hussein to keep out of the conflict. His air and ground forces
no match for the Israelis, Hussein had everything to lose by
taking part – but with his forces under Egyptian command,
the king's room for manoeuvre was limited. Had he stood
aside, his large Palestinian population would have erupted.
Hostilities were triggered when Jordanian artillery began to
bombard the isolated Israeli position on Jerusalem's Mount
Scopus. Hussein could field eight infantry brigades, seven of
them in the West Bank, and two armoured brigades. With
the IDF engaged against the Egyptians in the Sinai, Israel's
Central Command under General Uzi Narkiss had a mechanised brigade and the 16th Jerusalem Brigade, composed of
reservists. But the pace of advance enabled Gavish to release
the 55th Parachute Brigade, which on 7 June captured Jerusalem's largely undefended Old City. The rest of the West
Bank quickly followed, a ceasefire with Jordan coming into
effect later that day. For Israelis, the emotional climax of the
war came when Dayan, Rabin, and Narkiss entered the Old
City through the Lions' Gate, which their paratroopers had
earlier breached.

Apart from some air action, the Syrian front had so far
been largely inactive. But once the fighting against Egypt
and Jordan had ended, the Israelis were able to reinforce

Major-General David Elazar's Northern Command. On paper, the Golan Heights presented a formidable challenge, dominating as they had done much of northeastern Israel. With Soviet help, the Syrians had constructed a series of defensive strongpoints. Manning them were nine infantry, one mechanised, and two armoured brigades. The Israeli assault on the Golan Heights began on 9 June, and, by the time a ceasefire came into play the following evening, they controlled the area, including the provincial capital of Quneitra and one of the summits of Mount Hermon, the key to observing any military activity in the region. But the war ended on a controversial note for Israel. On 8 June, a sustained naval and air attack was mounted on the US electronic surveillance vessel the USS *Liberty* cruising off the Sinai coast in which thirty-four seamen were killed.[18] The Americans were sceptical of the Israeli claim that she had been wrongly identified as an Egyptian warship, although it was the probable explanation.

The implications of defeat and victory

On 9 June 1967, Nasser announced his resignation, but massive demonstrations caused him to withdraw it the following day. An immediate consequence of the defeat was his breach with Amer, the two men seemingly blaming each other for the disaster. Resigning his position, Amer retained some support in the army. Suspicions about his intentions and a campaign against him resulted in his death, tragically by suicide, on 14 September. Other army and air force officers were cashiered or tried by military courts. Nasser retained power but as a reduced figure, humiliated by the turn of events. Egypt was forced to turn to the Arab monarchies for assistance and to the Soviet Union to rebuild the military. If the war was a humiliation for Egypt, it was a disaster for Jordan, which had lost much of its territory, including the vital arable land and water resources of the West Bank – and, perhaps above all, East Jerusalem, a magnet for pilgrims and tourists with all the revenue they generated.

Israel's victory left it in control of the entire Sinai, with a border at the Suez Canal and including the prize of Sharm el-Sheikh, the Gaza Strip, the Golan Heights, East Jerusalem, and the whole of the West Bank. The view of the Eshkol government was that most of these territories could be exchanged for peace agreements. There were two exceptions. Some 5,000 Arabs were expelled from the strategic Latrun salient. But the real prize for Israel was East Jerusalem. On 27 June, the Knesset passed legislation extending Israeli jurisdiction and administration and thereby uniting the two parts of the city. The city's mayor, Teddy Kollek, demolished the ancient Mughrabi, or Moroccan, quarter in the Old City to create an open plaza in front of the Western Wall. The possible threat to the Haram al-Sharif alarmed the Islamic world. The Israelis established a position, allowing Muslims to enter and worship at the Haram al-Sharif/Temple Mount, while members of other religions could enter it but not worship there, except for Jewish worship at the Western Wall. Israel's unilateral annexation of East Jerusalem went unrecognised, the UN General Assembly on 4 July declaring it to be invalid by ninety-nine votes to nil with twenty abstentions.

9

The Middle East Transformed

In the immediate aftermath of the Six-Day War, it became clear that the United States was going to break out of the straitjacket of Vietnam to engage more directly with the Middle East than had been the case for some time. On 19 June 1967, Johnson broadcast what he termed 'Principles for Peace in the Middle East'. There had to be, he announced, an end to threats against the existence of any nation, justice for the refugees, no interference with maritime rights, restrictions on the arms race, peace based on recognised boundaries, and recognition of the special interests of the three Abrahamic religions in the holy places of Jerusalem.[1]

United Nations Security Council Resolution 242

Johnson's 'principles' were reflected in the British-sponsored Security Council Resolution 242 passed with the support of the five permanent members on 22 November 1967. The text had to be carefully calibrated to ensure the support both of the United States and the Soviet Union. It emphasised 'the inadmissibility of the acquisition of territory by war', acknowledged 'the sovereignty, territorial integrity and political independence of every state in the area', recognised the need to guarantee freedom of navigation, called for 'a just settlement of the refugee problem', and 'withdrawal of Israel armed forces from territories occupied in the recent conflict'. The last of these proved to be problematic: the Arabs claimed this wording meant 'all' the territories, while the Israelis replied that it did not. The British sponsor, Lord Caradon, contended that 'the inadmissibility of the acquisition of territory by war' meant that beyond minor rectifications such as the Latrun salient and the Mount Scopus enclave, Israel could not retain the territories it had conquered. Eban, by contrast, argued that Israel had only accepted the resolution on assurances by the United States and Britain that the words 'all the' had been excluded from before 'territories'.

The resolution was to be the basis for all subsequent negotiations, and by accepting it both Egypt and Jordan had acknowledged Israel's right to exist. The Palestinians, however, were not prepared to be categorised as a 'refugee problem' and were soon to pursue their own agenda. Resolution 242 was intended to be the basis of peace negotiations under the aegis of the United Nations, which appointed the Swedish diplomat Gunnar Jarring as its special representative.[2] Jarring worked conscientiously, eventually submitting a plan to the Egyptians and Israelis in 1971 which was rejected, although some of its elements were to surface in later negotiations. The problem was that, in the immediate aftermath of the war, the positions of the two parties were too asymmetrical. Israel was too powerful militarily to see the need for hasty concessions. Meanwhile, the Arabs' defeat had been so comprehensive that they had virtually nothing to concede except direct negotiations and recognition of Israel – both of which they had explicitly rejected at a summit held in the Sudanese capital of Khartoum in September 1967.

Arafat and the PLO

No one felt the defeat of 1967 more keenly than the Palestinians, not least since the remaining 22 per cent of pre-1948 Palestine was now in Israeli hands. Three Arab armies had been defeated with seemingly little prospect of their imminent recovery, while the PLO had proved to be a feeble vehicle for their hopes. From this dismal base, Arafat and Fatah began to chart a way forward. Basing himself initially in Nablus on the West Bank, Arafat began organising Fatah networks both there and inside Jordan, but their guerrilla actions were quickly countered by the Israeli forces. On 21 March 1968, Israel mounted a major operation involving 15,000 troops against the Jordanian village of Karameh where 300 guerrillas put up strong resistance, doing much to restore Arab morale. With this credibility behind him, Arafat restructured the PLO in July 1968 at a meeting of the Palestine National Council. Fatah became its leading element, but the PLO also came to include a number of smaller groups, the most powerful of these being Dr George Habash's Popular Front for the Liberation of Palestine (PFLP) and Saeqa, which had Syrian links. The meeting rewrote the original Palestinian National Charter of 1964 and sanctioned armed action as the way forward. Denying the legitimacy of the Balfour Declaration, the 1947 partition, and the establishment of Israel, the new charter affirmed that within its mandatory boundaries Palestine was indivisible. At a subsequent meeting of the Palestine National Council on 3 February 1969 in Cairo with Nasser present, Arafat became chair of its executive committee. As chair, Arafat was to dominate Palestinian affairs until his death in 2004. His revolutionary credentials and his skill in raising finance from among Palestinians in the wider world copper-fastened his position, but his wider political abilities remained to be tested.[3]

In reality, Israel's control was such that little by way of armed struggle could be managed in the West Bank, although Fatah was able to operate in Gaza until 1971. What really captured the world's headlines was the PFLP's tactic of attacks on civilian aircraft. Israel's national carrier, El Al, was an obvious target, but so were other airlines flying to the country, one of these attacks destroying a Swissair flight to Tel Aviv in February 1970. Guerrilla activity also threatened the position of King Hussein, whose authority seemed to be slipping, while Israeli retaliatory raids on the Palestinians were causing casualties. While the guerrilla groups were by no means united, under the broad umbrella of the PLO a state within a state was fast emerging. On 1 September 1970 came the second of two Palestinian attempts on King Hussein's life. Days later the PFLP hijacked airliners belonging to Swissair, the US Trans World Airlines, and Britain's BOAC, diverting them to Dawson's Field in Jordan and holding 300 passengers and crew hostage. Most were released, but over fifty were removed to hiding places and the three planes were blown up. The action presented King Hussein with a challenge that he could not ignore. On 17 September, his troops attacked the main guerrilla centres in Amman and elsewhere. Palestinian casualties were heavy as the Syrian Army, but not Hafez al-Assad's air force, intervened in the north of the country. As the situation appeared to escalate, King Hussein responded to an appeal from Nasser to a peace conference in Cairo on 27 September, which resulted in a ceasefire.[4] The following day, Nasser collapsed with a fatal heart attack. He was mourned by millions of his fellow Egyptians. The civil war in Jordan came to be called Black September.[5]

OPEC and the oil revolution

While these dramatic events were taking place, a revolution of a different sort was maturing in various parts of the Arab world. Petroleum was the one commodity that marked out the Middle East's place in the world economy. In September 1960, at a meeting in Baghdad, five countries – Iran, Iraq, Kuwait, Saudi Arabia, and Venezuela – formed the Organization of the Petroleum Exporting Countries (OPEC), its purpose being to coordinate petroleum policies and safeguard the interests of its members. Abu Dhabi (later the United Arab Emirates), Qatar, Algeria, Indonesia, Libya, and Nigeria joined, with a succession of others following. A further refinement followed in 1968 when Saudi Arabia came together with other Arab producers to form the Organization of Arab Petroleum Exporting Countries (OAPEC). These two bodies gave their members greater negotiating positions with the oil companies. In meetings in the summer of 1973, OPEC decided to implement a new pricing policy. This was confirmed at meetings in November and December 1973 when the price of Saudi Arabian light crude oil, the 'marker crude' that set international oil prices, which had stood at $3.011 a barrel in early October, was more than trebled to $11.651. This change of pricing policy was to transform the economic fortunes of the Middle Eastern oil-exporting countries. What had been fishing villages along the Gulf morphed into major players in the world economic system, triggering spectacular economic growth. With some 20 per cent of the world's proven oil reserves, Saudi Arabia was the region's economic powerhouse. With oil production the underpinning of the monarchy's economy, it was understandable that the Saudis would wish to control it, which they did by carefully measured stages, acquiring a 25 per cent share in Aramco in January 1973. In June 1974, this was increased to 60 per cent, and by the end of the decade the oil industry was fully in Saudi hands. Other Arab countries were doing the same. In short, the economic balance of much of the Middle East had tilted dramatically in favour of the producers.[6]

Britain's withdrawal from the Middle East

The Suez Crisis did not quite mark the end of Britain's presence in the Middle East. Aware of Aden's strategic position near the narrow Bab al-Mandeb Strait, through which commercial and naval traffic entering or leaving the Red Sea had to navigate, Britain hoped to make it their military base, which would have become a southern counterpart to the Sovereign Base Areas that they had retained after Cyprus gained independence in 1960. The British also still had treaty arrangements with the Sultanate of Muscat and Oman and the Trucial States in the Gulf, which had traded for decades under British protection. Aden proved to be no more immune to the call of Nasserism than other parts of the Arab world. The British sought to counter the challenge of the National Liberation Front (NLF) with the formation of a South Arabian Federation of Aden and a group of emirates, which was, like most of the federations they created, a failure. In 1963, an insurgency broke out that soon had the British government accepting the inevitable. As attacks on British troops in Aden gained momentum, on 29 November 1967 the rearguard departed by helicopter. The NLF immediately established the People's Republic of Southern Yemen, soon to be renamed the People's Democratic Republic of Yemen.

The final blow to the British position was inflicted by its economic weakness. Faced with the need for devaluation and the erosion of its financial reserves, the British government announced that it would withdraw from east of Suez by 1971. An attempt to create a federation of the Trucial States foundered on the opposition of Bahrain and Qatar, which became independent. The remaining small emirates of Abu Dhabi, Dubai, Sharjah, Umm al Quwain, Ajman, and Fujairah came together in 1971 as the United Arab Emirates (UAE), with its capital at Abu Dhabi, Ras al Khaimah joining them the following year. The basis for its future transformation came in 1958 with the discovery of oil resources in Abu Dhabi, which allowed the new state to participate in the activities of OPEC and OAPEC. Abu Dhabi was to become a major exporter in the international energy market, with its oil resources the engine of future prosperity. In fact, the UAE and Qatar were to become key actors in the region's diplomacy.

Oman, which had long enjoyed a distinctive status, presented two problems. First, there was the nature of its regime under Sultan Said. On 23 July 1970, his son, the Sandhurst-educated Saiyyid Qaboos, seized power in a bloodless coup. Since 1964, there had been a stubborn rebellion in the less economically favoured Dhofar region in the south of the country. With seconded British military help, Qaboos brought the rebellion to an end in March 1976. Assisted by his country's key strategic position on the Indian Ocean shipping lanes and fuelled by the discovery of oil and gas, he presided over his country's steady economic development until his death from cancer on 10 January 2020.

Neighbouring Yemen followed a markedly different path. In May 1990, the People's Democratic Republic of Yemen that had replaced the British merged with the Yemen Arab Republic to the north to form the Republic of Yemen, but the new polity failed to find political stability. The key development was the rise of the Shi'a Ansar Allah movement. Commonly known as the Houthis, from the prominent Houthi family, in 2004 they began a rebellion against the country's internationally recognised government. That conflict continued intermittently over the next two decades, with the Houthis gaining control of the capital, Sana'a, and the bulk of the population. In 2015 the government made Aden its temporary capital. In the bitter civil war, the government was backed by Saudi Arabia, while the Americans believed that Iran was supporting the Houthis. The conflict was to beggar much of the country that was already one of the poorest in the region.[7]

US initiatives and new leaders

As Britain's position in the Middle East was fast fading, the United States was becoming more deeply involved, seeing Iran and Saudi Arabia as possible strategic substitutes for a British military presence. Israel was also looking to Washington for military supplies. This was partly the result of French President de Gaulle's spurning of Israel for ignoring his advice not to go to war in 1967, but it was also partly a result of the fact that the Soviet Union was putting substantial resources into rebuilding the Egyptian and Syrian armed forces. By 1969, some 400 aircraft had been provided to Egypt, and thousands of Soviet advisers and technicians were at work there. The Israelis, meanwhile, wanted to replace their ageing French air fleet with the US supersonic McDonnell Douglas F-4 Phantom fighter. The backbone of air operations over Vietnam, the Phantom was a sophisticated aircraft. After lobbying in Congress, Johnson authorised the sale of fifty Phantoms to Israel. Support for the measure in Congress was mustered in part by the American Israel Public Affairs Committee (AIPAC), an influential lobbying organisation that had been formally established in 1959 by the journalist I. L. Kenen who had been at the forefront of pro-Israeli activities for some years.[8]

In 1969, the widely travelled Republican Richard Nixon succeeded Johnson. Keen to make his mark in foreign policy, Nixon appointed to the position of national security adviser the distinguished Harvard academic Dr Henry Kissinger, who had come to the United States as a Jewish refugee from Hitler's Germany. In the Middle East, new leadership was also emerging. Eshkol's sudden death in March 1969 saw the veteran Golda Meir become prime minister. She did so at a difficult time in Israeli politics: in January 1968, Mapai, the left-wing party that had long dominated politics, joined with Rafi and the small Ahdut HaAvoda party to form the Israeli Labour-Party, a move that brought her into coalition with the high-profile figures of Dayan and Peres, the former retaining his key portfolio of minister of defence. Initially, too, Meir inherited an uneasy coalition government that included Begin's right-wing Herut party. On the wider front, Israel was engaged with Egypt in the War of Attrition, launched by Nasser along the Suez Canal in September 1967. In the course of the fighting, the veteran Israeli warship *Eilat* was sunk by an Egyptian missile with heavy loss of life. The conflict was only brought to an end by the Americans in August 1970, an event that saw the right-wing members resign from its government. Long excluded from power, the right then made moves to mount a credible challenge to Labour. These climaxed in 1973 when, on his retirement from the army where he had latterly held the key Southern Command, Sharon called for a right-wing coalition. On 14 September 1973 the Likud (Unity) Party was formed under Begin's leadership with Sharon as his election manager.[9] In Egypt, Nasser's successor was his vice-president and former army colleague Anwar al-Sadat, while in November 1970 air force general Hafez al-Assad mounted a coup in Syria. A Ba'ath supporter and a member of the minority Alawite community, Assad's political abilities enabled him to stay in power until his death in 2000.

On 9 December 1969, Nixon's secretary of state, William Rogers, unveiled his thoughts on what might create a lasting peace. Based on Resolution 242, Rogers affirmed the right of navigation in the Straits of Tiran and the Suez Canal. On borders, he confirmed that any change should not reflect the weight of conquest, which was really code for the Latrun salient. He could not support Israel's action in unilaterally annexing East Jerusalem, but he argued that it should be a unified city in which both Israel and Jordan would play a role. Rogers departed from Resolution 242 in one key area: he referred not to refugees but, in a politically charged change of gear, to 'the Palestinians'. The Egyptian response was one of wait and see, but in Israel and among its US supporters there was an enraged reaction. On the ground, measures were set in hand to ensure Israeli control of East Jerusalem, including sanctioning the construction of apartments for 25,000 Israelis. Privately, Nixon had already reassured the Israelis that the plan would not be followed up, but it was not repudiated by the Americans.[10]

Preparations for war

Syria's Assad and Egypt's Sadat had a clear priority: the return of their national territories, respectively the Golan and the Sinai. Although the vital task of rebuilding his military potential was being undertaken by the Soviet Union, Sadat saw the United States as crucial to progress. In July 1972, he ordered the removal of all Soviet personnel from Egypt, but, although this dramatic move opened up channels between Cairo and Washington, no US intervention was forthcoming. The alternative was to prepare for war. The Egyptian armed forces were being transformed by a group of highly able officers under the overall leadership of the commander-in-chief, General Ahmed Ismail Ali. The air force was entrusted to Air Chief Marshal Hosni Mubarak. Together with their Syrian colleagues, the Egyptians devised a strategy whereby the Egyptians would surprise the Israelis by crossing the Suez Canal in massive numbers, and the Syrians would seize Israeli positions on Mount Hermon. Both would then engage in a war of attrition, preventing the Israelis from pursuing the kind of mobile warfare that had been so successful in 1967. Well aware that the key to Israel's victory in the Six-Day War had been its air strikes, the Egyptians with their Soviet advisers had devised a system of air defence that would enable their ground forces to operate unhindered. The secret here was the supply of large numbers of Soviet surface-to-air missiles. Soviet batteries were also delivered to the Syrians. Another area of Israeli military expertise had been armoured warfare, and this was to be countered by handheld rocket-propelled grenades and anti-tank missiles. Sadat's commanders went to great lengths in training so that formations became familiar with their designated tasks, to the extent of using replicas of the Suez Canal and Israeli defences. Finally, previous educational deficiencies were addressed by extensive recruitment of university graduates, with officers learning Hebrew. In short, by 1973 the Egyptian Army bore no resemblance to its 1967 incarnation. The Syrians, too, had reorganised their forces and rehearsed repeatedly. The hope was that the war of attrition would lead the Israelis to make political concessions. The final date for their joint operation was set for 6 October when the waters in the canal were at their most suitable. It was also Yom Kippur, the most sacred day in the Jewish year, when Israelis would be celebrating the holiday.[11]

From the start, possession of the east bank of the Suez Canal presented the Israelis with a strategic dilemma. On one level, the Israelis had the luxury of a 150-mile barrier between the canal and their frontier. The canal itself presented the Egyptians with a formidable water obstacle – for, although their commandos had penetrated it on a number of occasions, crossing it with armoured formations was a very different matter. But an adequate defence of a waterway that stretched for some 120 miles was virtually impossible for Israel's standing army. Israel had two possible options, each with influential advocates. Sharon and his colleague from the 1967 Sinai offensive, Israel Tal, wanted to keep the armour at a distance from the canal as the basis for a mobile defence. In contrast, the chief of staff, Lieutenant-General Chaim Bar-Lev, and Major-General Gavish, responsible for Southern Command, favoured holding the water line, especially in areas where the Egyptians might cross. The resulting Bar-Lev Line, completed in 1969, was based on a series of fortified positions along the line of the Canal, each garrisoned by 100 men. But the Israeli command was never quite of a mind as to whether the line was intended to offer defence or to serve as a trip wire to allow counter-attacks to be mounted. When hostilities began on 6 October, the men of its regular garrison were on home leave celebrating Yom Kippur, and the line was held by reservists of the 16th Jerusalem Brigade.[12]

On the Syrian front, there was no defensive equivalent of the Bar-Lev Line; the Israelis instead relied on their strategic positions on Mount Hermon to alert them to any possible attack. The underlying Israeli assumption was a failure to realise just how deeply the Egyptians and Syrians felt about their 1967 defeat and the seriousness with which they were working to remedy this. A major preoccupation for the Egyptians was how to deploy two armies totalling some 100,000 for the offensive without alerting Israeli intelligence, which had installations both in the Golan and on Mount Hermon. Elaborate deception plans were made by both countries. On 5 October 1973, the Israelis learned of the evacuation of Soviet families from Syria. Meir later felt that she should have ordered mobilisation, but on advice that the two Arab armies were in defensive positions this was not done. It was only on the morning of the 6th that the cabinet learned of an imminent Egyptian and Syrian attack. The government decided not to send a pre-emptive air strike since it was felt that, as the country would look to the international community for help, it should not attack first.[13]

The Syrian and Egyptian offensives[14]

What the Arabs came to call the October War and the Israelis the Yom Kippur War began at 2 p.m. on 6 October with an artillery barrage on the Bar-Lev Line and a helicopter-borne assault by Syrian commandos on the Israeli installations on Mount Hermon. The small Israeli force, most of them intelligence experts, was overwhelmed. Invaluable intelligence-gathering equipment was captured, which was eagerly snapped up by Soviet advisers. This operation was the prelude to a major offensive on the Golan positions by three infantry divisions with 540 tanks. Behind them were two armoured divisions with a further 460 tanks. The Israeli brigades facing them were hopelessly outnumbered. In the first two days of fighting, the two brigades stemmed the offensive in an epic of defensive fighting, but at enormous cost in men and tanks. With northern Israel facing invasion, fresh troops were rushed to the Golan, aided by the Syrians' failure to capture the bridges over the River Jordan. The Israeli Air Force was also heavily engaged in holding the front, but at the cost of some forty aircraft. By 9 October, the Syrian offensive had been held, but hard fighting continued.

Because of its lack of strategic depth compared with the Sinai front, the northern front was the more urgent danger for Israel. Responsibility rested with Northern Command under Major General Yitzhak Hofi, whose force built up to three divisions. On 11 October, Hofi's divisions began the Israeli counter-offensive. As the Syrians were steadily pushed back, they were joined by units from Iraq and Jordan, but effective coordination across this hastily assembled force proved to be difficult and their losses were considerable. On 21 October, a combined force of paratroopers and infantry was sent against the Syrian position on Mount Hermon, which was taken by the Israelis the following morning.

For the assault on the Bar-Lev Line, the Egyptians had formed two armies. The Second Army, three divisions strong, commanded by Lieutenant-General Saad Mamoun was to attack north of the Bitter Lakes, while Lieutenant-General Abdel Munim Wassel's Third Army, with two divisions, was responsible for operations south of the Bitter Lakes. Each division was reinforced by an armoured brigade as well as commando units and engineers. A marine brigade was assigned to cross the Bitter Lakes, the junction between the two armies. The leading elements of the two armies crossed the canal by boat, overwhelming Israel's thinly held Bar-Lev Line. By the following day, engineers had erected five bridges, enabling the Egyptians to deploy tanks in support of their infantry. Although the bridges were damaged by the Israeli Air Force, Egyptian engineers were able to repair them. On 8 October, the full invading force was across the canal, consolidating behind bridgeheads. Israel's Southern Command was the responsibility of the recently appointed Major-General Shmuel Gonen. As mobilised reserves reinforced his command, Gonen divided it into three divisions. On 8 October, the chief of staff, David Elazar, planned a counter-attack against the Second Army, but his brigades were confronted with the new reality of the Egyptian bridgehead's defensive shield, and after a series of engagements they were forced to withdraw having lost some fifty tanks. Thus far, the Egyptian plan was working well.

With no sign of the fighting dying down, on 9 October the Israeli ambassador to Washington, Simcha Dinitz, confided in Kissinger, the recently appointed secretary of state, that the IDF had so far lost forty-nine aircraft and 500 tanks. Such an attrition rate was not sustainable without US supplies. Failure to provide supplies could inhibit US efforts to influence the course of events, but Nixon and Kissinger were anxious to avert any Arab oil boycott. They decided to resupply the Israelis, with an assurance that tank losses would be made good after the war, enabling the IDF to release its reserves. Even so, the initial scale and pace of the resulting operation frustrated the Israeli government. The airlift was at first confined to El Al's seven jets, with urgent supplies sent by the Americans as far as the Azores. Phantom jets were a problem but fourteen were allocated. It was not until the 14th that American C-5A Galaxy transports started to land at Lod (formerly Lydda) Airport. Once the commitment to send supplies had been made, the Americans saw no merit in holding back sending twenty transports a day.[15]

As serious fighting continued in the Sinai, the IDF commanders worked on a plan they thought would enable them to tear a hole in the Egyptian front. The concept was to break free from the battles of attrition by sending a major force across the canal to the west bank where they would be able to fight a mobile campaign. The recently retired Sharon had returned to service. A reconnaissance force from his division discovered that the boundary between the Second and Third Armies at Deversoir just north of the Great Bitter Lake was only weakly held. On 14 October, Egyptian forces moved out of their positions along the canal in a major offensive into the Sinai, but, as they lacked the missile protection in the bridgehead, they were defeated in a massive tank battle. The battle opened the way for the planned canal crossing, which was entrusted to Sharon's division. On 15 October, Sharon's leading elements were ferried across the canal, establishing a fragile bridgehead. Although the Egyptians tried hard to contain or cut off the bridgehead, once the Israelis succeeded on the evening of the 18th in manoeuvring a bridge into position, at the cost of heavy casualties, the way was open for a major advance. While Sharon probed north to Ismailia, two brigades advanced south along the Bitter Lakes towards Suez, imperiling the entire position of the Third Army on the east bank.[16]

The diplomatic front[17]

Although there were no formal channels of communication between Cairo and Washington, from the start of hostilities Sadat had been sending assurances that the war was being fought for limited aims. On 16 October, Sadat confirmed as much in a speech to the People's Assembly when he announced that, in return for Israel reverting to the 1967 borders, he would attend an international peace conference and try to persuade the Palestinians of the need for peace based on the rights of all the peoples of the area. While this was valuable information for Nixon and Kissinger, it was only the start: the diplomatic context was far from straightforward, quite apart from the truism that it is easier to start wars than to end them, especially since Sharon's canal crossing was giving Meir's government the prospect of avenging their earlier defeats. The Nixon administration was committed to a policy of détente with the Soviet Union. It was not in the interests of either party to see any of the protagonists that they were supporting militarily humiliated. Equally worrying from a Western perspective was that the Arab world was mobilising its economic resources in support of the Egyptians and Syrians. At a meeting in Kuwait on 17 October, Arab petroleum ministers condemned the United States for its support for Israel, deciding to reduce oil production by 5 per cent of the September total and then by a further 5 per cent each month until Israel withdrew from its 1967 conquests and the rights of the Palestinians were restored. When, on the 19th, Nixon requested a supplementary $2.2 billion from Congress to pay for the airlift, a total oil embargo was placed on the United States and the

Netherlands. Because of the critical role of the oil facilities of the port of Rotterdam, this threatened to undermine the economy of Western Europe.

The outbreak of the war had coincided with a period of acute political crisis in Washington, partly generated by the fallout from the 1972 Watergate affair. Although Nixon was not completely detached from the crisis in the Middle East, Kissinger was able to act from a position of strength, buttressed by the extent of US aid to Israel. Sadat could plausibly argue that he could fight Israel but not the United States as well. It was, however, the Soviets who were able to convince Sadat, with information gleaned from their satellite intelligence, that Sharon's canal bridgehead threatened military disaster. On 20 October, at the Soviet request, Kissinger flew to Moscow with plenipotentiary powers. He presented a draft document, which had been agreed to by the Soviet leadership and endorsed on the 22nd as UN Security Council Resolution 338. The resolution called for the two sides to observe a ceasefire in twelve hours in the positions they then occupied, for the subsequent implementation of Resolution 242, followed by negotiations for a just and durable peace. Perceiving this as the two superpowers combining to thwart Israel from exploiting its successes, Meir's government insisted that Kissinger come to brief it. While he was able to reassure the Israelis that there was no superpower pact to force them to return to their 1967 borders, Kissinger made a concession that came close to undoing the package. There had been a communications failure in conveying the document to the Israelis, and, in compensation, Kissinger hinted that they might overrun the time of the ceasefire by a few hours. The Israeli commanders, however, interpreted it more broadly. When Egyptian artillery opened up, the Israeli forces raced south from the Bitter Lakes to the Gulf of Suez, effectively trapping the city of Suez and the Third Army.

This action imperilled the entire package that Kissinger had negotiated in Moscow, since neither Sadat nor the Soviets could contemplate the surrender or starvation of the encircled Third Army. The Soviets made threatening moves, deploying warships in the eastern Mediterranean and putting seven airborne divisions on alert. The US response was to increase the state of alert of their armed forces from DEFCON 4 and DEFCON 5 to DEFCON 3, that is maximum readiness without war being imminent. They then offered the Soviet leadership the face-saving formula that they could could join the Americans in truce supervision. It proved to be enough to defuse what had threatened to become one of the most dangerous encounters of the Cold War, and, in the event, it was not needed. On 24 October, after a second Security Council Resolution, the ceasefire came into effect, although violations continued for some days. The fate of the Third Army remained unclear, with Kissinger determined to prevent its destruction because of the ceasefire violations. The Egyptians conceded that in return for a supply convoy under UN and Red Cross auspices and an end to violations, they would agree to direct talks between representatives of the two military at Kilometre 101 on the Cairo–Suez Road. On 28 October, Lieutenant-General Abdel Ghani al-Gamasy, the operations officer of the Egyptian Army, and Major-General Aharon Yariv, who had acted as a spokesman for the IDF, met at Kilometre 101 in an unprecedented encounter and began setting out how the ceasefire would work.

Kissinger's step-by-step diplomacy[18]

This was a war that neither side had really won, although all three protagonists had fought with skill and bravery. Still, the Egyptian and Syrian armies had restored their military pride, and the wider Arab world had shown that it could wield the oil weapon. Meanwhile, the early setbacks had shaken the confidence of the Israeli public. Meir's Labour Alignment held on in the Knesset elections of 31 December, but then support steadily ebbed away. By coincidence, the man who had long personified a sense of national confidence, David Ben-Gurion, died on 1 December 1973 at the age of eighty-seven. On 1 April 1974, the official inquiry into the war was published, its initial findings pointing to military and intelligence failings. Although Meir's actions were not criticised in the report, she felt that she had to resign, which she did on 11 April, to be replaced by Yitzhak Rabin. Although the Soviet leadership had in the main acted prudently, it was clear that the way forward was in the hands of the Americans and that Kissinger had proved that he was uniquely placed to act. Appreciating the gulf of mistrust between Israel and the Arabs, his approach was to move forward by a series of carefully calibrated steps that would build confidence leading to further steps.

The most pressing problem for Egypt was the position of the Third Army, while the Israelis were anxious for the return of prisoners. Kissinger's first success was to broker an agreement with Meir and Sadat signed by Gamasy and Yariv at Kilometre 101 on 11 November that allowed for the movement of supplies to Suez and the Third Army, replacement of Israeli checkpoints by the UN, the exchange of prisoners, and discussions on the separation of forces. Given what had just been happening, it was a significant act of faith on the part of everyone involved. Kissinger then embarked on a rapid tour of Middle East capitals to test the ground for the conference that Resolution 338 had sanctioned. Sadat was keen, but the Israelis were wary, knowing that they would be under pressure to make withdrawals. Assad could not be won round but indicated that he would not stand in the way. Their meeting opened up the path for a possible future relationship. The conference, which met for a day, convened at Geneva on 21 December. Its significance lay in the fact that for the first time Egypt and Jordan were in the same room as the Israelis, and it cleared the way for Kissinger's next moves.

Kissinger returned to the Middle East on 11 January 1974, armed with imaginative proposals that Dayan had brought to Washington. The latter suggested that Israel would withdraw its forces from the western bank of the canal, allowing Egypt to occupy the east bank up to a depth of four to six miles. In turn, Israel would occupy a line to the west of the strategic Mitla and Gidi passes with a UN buffer zone between the two. Egyptian forces east of the canal would be restricted to two or three battalions with no tanks. Dayan expected Sadat to reciprocate by ending the state of war and allowing Israeli ships and cargoes through the canal. Israeli security would be underpinned with continuing US arms supplies. Although reluctant at first, Sadat conceded that the Israeli line should be west of the passes, not east as he had wanted. Agreement turned on the nature of Egyptian forces east of the canal, Sadat insisting on divisions, the Israelis on battalions. The eventual compromise was that Egypt could deploy eight battalions and thirty tanks with an assurance from Sadat that the latter would not be implemented. He also gave a secret assurance that he would allow Israeli cargoes through the canal once it was cleared. An agreement to that effect was signed by the two chiefs of staff at Kilometre 101 on 18 January 1974, opening the way for a disengagement of forces that was completed by 5 March. Israel had withdrawn not just from its west-bank bridgehead but from the first tranche, however small, of its 1967 conquests, its security now firmly linked to the Americans. For Sadat, Egypt now garrisoned both banks of the canal.

With the situation along the canal stabilised, Kissinger could turn his attention to the Golan where the Israelis were positioned to threaten Damascus, a mere twenty miles distant. While the negotiations over the canal had been held in the context of positive messages coming from Sadat, there had been no echo of this from Assad. Assad's position appeared simple: he demanded the evacuation of the Israeli salient and the return of the Golan Heights. He was, however, a pragmatic leader who was prepared to settle for less, as long as it involved the return of the provincial capital of Quneitra. No Israelis lived there, but they had built settlements only two-and a-half miles away. Both sides were aware of the strategic importance of Mount Hermon. Kissinger began his mission on 28 April 1974, and it was to last thirty-two days. The context could hardly have been worse, since radical Palestinians were poised to undermine any settlement. They attacked the northern border town of Kiryat Shmona on 11 April killing eighteen civilians, followed on 15 May by the massacre of school children at Ma'alot. More promising was the ending of the oil embargo on 18 March. Quneitra proved to be the key. Kissinger was told that what mattered to the Israelis was not the city but the strategic hills around it. With that knowledge, he proposed a line to the west of Quneitra, a UN demilitarised zone, and a limit on Israeli troops on the hills. On 31 May 1974, Assad agreed to this and signed an agreement at Geneva. He further conceded a limitation on his forces in front of Damascus to nine brigades and that surface-to-air missiles would not come closer than fifteen or so miles from the front. On the Palestinian issue, Assad would make no public statement that could be seen as abandoning them, but he gave an assurance on violations of the border. The shattered city of Quneitra was returned, satisfying Syria's honour. Although no further progress was made with Syria, Assad was to respect the obligations he had made under the agreement.

When Kissinger returned to the Middle East in March 1975, his personal stock stood high, but his position was not quite what it had been. The previous August, Nixon had felt compelled to resign over the Watergate affair. His successor, Gerald Ford, was well respected but inevitably lacked the authority of an elected president. Moreover, the United States' standing in the world had been undermined by the evident failure to sustain South Vietnam despite enormous sacrifice. The Mitla and Gidi passes were at the heart of the renewed negotiations, with Egypt demanding a line to the east, while Israel insisted that it remain to the west. For his part, Sadat insisted that he would not issue a declaration of non-belligerency while Israel was on Egyptian territory, but he was again ready to offer assurances. Rabin's government was not convinced by this, and their position stiffened when on 5 March 1975 eight Fatah guerrillas landed on the Tel Aviv waterfront, killing eighteen people at the Savoy Hotel.

With negotiations stalled, on 22 March Kissinger announced that he was returning to Washington to begin a 'reassessment' of Middle East policy. Rightly concluding that this process could only work to Israel's disadvantage, Rabin's government decided to mobilise its diplomatic muscle. Senior figures including Abba Eban, General Yariv, and Dayan came to the United States. Dayan alone spoke at twenty-one colleges, putting forward his country's case. The Israelis rallied support in Congress. On 21 May, a letter, signed by fifty-one Democrat and twenty-five republican senators, was sent to Ford, pointing out that Israel was a reliable ally, supporting its need for defensible borders and the necessity for a peace treaty. The politicians further affirmed that the reassessment should rest on the premise that the two countries stood together and that the United States should be responsive to Israel's military and economic needs. The 'reassessment' had seemingly been checkmated, but the letter made no real difference, since Kissinger continued with his pressure on Rabin's government.

But the diplomatic mission effectively failed. On 4 September 1975, Egypt and Israel signed the second Sinai disengagement agreement at Geneva by which Israel withdrew from east of the passes and also restored to Egypt the small Abu Rudeis oilfield in Sinai. In return, Egypt conceded that non-military cargoes to and from Israel would be permitted through the Suez Canal, while overall the two parties pledged that the conflict between them would be resolved by peaceful means and not by military force. Israel secured from the United States assurances that it would guarantee its energy needs and be fully responsive to its military needs. Moreover, the Israelis were guaranteed that the United States would not recognise the PLO as long as it refused to acknowledge Israel's right to exist and did not accept Security Council Resolutions 242 and 338.

The PLO after the war

Despite the renewed Arab pride after the 1973 war, the PLO faced the prospect of being marginalised. Its leaders knew that Sadat was waging war and negotiating in a strategy that would likely end in a settlement with Israel that would render it safe from further attack. Kissinger was looking to King Hussein for the next move forward. There was also a gnawing feeling that Egypt and Jordan had come to acknowledge, if only by their acceptance of Resolution 242, the reality of Israel's presence in the Middle East. That being so, the end result for the Palestinians would be the establishment of a state in the West Bank and Gaza in contravention of the National Charter. This would do little, if anything, for those Palestinians in the refugee camps in Jordan and Lebanon. After much debate, the Twelfth Palestine National Council in July 1974 sanctioned the establishment of sovereignty on every part of Palestine that was liberated, an inevitably elliptical definition of policy but one that pointed in a certain direction. A Jordanian option was headed off at an Arab summit in Rabat on 28 October, which affirmed that the PLO was the sole legitimate representative of the Palestinian people. On 13 November, Arafat addressed the UN General Assembly, choosing to explain to delegates the Palestinian case rather than announce any new policies. The PLO was granted observer status at the UN, enhancing its international position, but its progress was on the point of being eroded by events in Lebanon.[19]

The Lebanese Civil War

Lebanon appeared to flourish under President Shihab after the 1958 upheaval, becoming a commercial and recreational hub for much of the region, but this was deceptive. Its Shi'a population felt at arm's length from the dominant Maronite–Sunni governing elite, finding their voice in the Movement of the Disinherited founded by Musa al-Sadr. Stability was also threatened by the position of the Palestinians, who were never really integrated into the state. As earlier in Jordan, the PLO in Lebanon was becoming a state within a state.

After King Hussein's attack on the PLO in September 1970, Lebanon became the organisation's main base, the refugee camps providing a ready source of recruits. The PLO's activities were opposed by two right-wing Christian parties: former President Camille Chamoun's National Liberal Party and the long-established Kataeb, or Phalange Party, of Pierre Gemayel. Kamal Junblatt's National Movement did not share their opposition to the PLO. Civil war was triggered on 13 April 1975 when gunmen killed four people as Gemayel attended the consecration of a church in Beirut. In response, rival militiamen attacked a bus, killing twenty-seven Palestinians and Lebanese Muslims. As the situation deteriorated, rival groups formed their militias. Musa al-Sadr created a Shi'a militia, Amal, in 1975. The two main Christian groups, the National Liberals and the Phalange, combined in the Lebanese Front, with Chamoun as leader and Gemayel's son Bashir leading its military wing, the United Military Command, later renamed the Lebanese Forces. The group was subsequently taken over by the Phalange. The Maronite Marada Brigade was formed by Tony Frangieh.

These Maronite groups appeared to be under severe pressure from Junblatt's National Movement and the PLO. The Israelis and the Syrians were anxiously watching the situation, with Assad apparently fearing that the confessional tensions exposed in Lebanon might be repeated at home. The Americans were able to broker an arrangement whereby the Israelis acquiesced in a Syrian military intervention in Lebanon so long as this did not cross a 'red line' six miles south of the Beirut–Damascus axis. The Syrian deployment began on 1 June 1976, but it did not end the fighting, which reached a climax on 12 August when Christian militiamen captured the Tel al-Zaatar Palestinian refugee camp after a bitter siege. By the end of 1978, Kamal Junblatt had been assassinated, as had Tony Frangieh together with his wife and young daughter, while Musa al-Sadr had disappeared. But, as no obvious end to the conflict seemed in sight, world attention turned to dramatic developments elsewhere in the Middle East.[20]

10

The Search for Stability

As a result of Kissinger's efforts, much of the Middle East enjoyed a measure of stability after the major wars of 1967 and 1973, but this was yet to be translated into peace agreements. The opportunity to pursue this goal, however, was denied to him by the victory in the 1976 presidential election of the Democrat Jimmy Carter, who was determined to move the United States away from the traumatic legacies of Watergate and Vietnam. A devout Christian who had visited Israel in 1973, Carter believed that the United States should uphold human rights and that this had to include the issue of the West Bank.[1] He assembled a strong foreign-policy team under the secretary of state, Cyrus Vance – several of whom, notably the national security adviser, Zbigniew Brzezinski – were familiar with Middle Eastern issues. In particular, the latter had been associated with a report issued by the prestigious Brookings Institution, which had posited Israel's reversion to the 1967 border but had also brought into the public domain the need for a Palestinian state, either as an independent entity or federated with Jordan, provided that the Palestinians accepted Israel.[2] Carter had discussed these findings with Brzezinski. In these circumstances, the first contacts between the administration and the local leaders took a predictable course. In a visit to the region, Vance found Sadat to be responsive to the idea of linking the West Bank and Gaza with Jordan but Rabin hostile to the idea of a Palestinian state, however configured. When Carter met Rabin on 7–8 March 1977, the Israeli premier received unwelcome news when Carter floated the idea that the PLO might be involved in negotiations. On 16 March, Carter told a meeting at Clinton in Pennsylvania that the Palestinians would have to have a homeland.[3]

Begin's electoral victory

Although Carter was setting a fast pace, nothing could be done before an Israeli general election in May. By then, Rabin was no longer prime minister. He had decided to step down over a personal matter and was replaced by his party rival Peres.[4] Labour had never really escaped blame over the 1973 war, and after three decades in power was no longer fresh. Despite a temporary breach with Sharon, Begin and his Likud party mounted a vigorous campaign successfully targeted at Labour's perceived failings.[5] Revisionist Zionism, so long confined to the political margins, had come into its inheritance, with Begin in his first television address as prime minister honouring Jabotinsky's memory and message. With the right-wing electoral victory in the May election, the tectonic plates of Israeli politics appeared to have shifted.

Begin made two key appointments. Once the two men were reconciled, Sharon was appointed minister of agriculture, a portfolio that enabled him to carry forward Likud plans for settlements on the West Bank, or Judea and Samaria as they defined it. There were already settlements in the Jordan valley, built under Labour for strategic reasons. Defensive considerations had also led to the construction of a belt of settlements in Sinai, including the towns of Ofira near Sharm el-Sheikh and Yamit near the Israeli border. Likud's approach was driven by ideology and was much more ambitious, although the legalistic Begin insisted that only state land be used. In October 1977, the cabinet sanctioned Sharon's plans for a network of settlements, as a result of which sixty-four were set in hand during his tenure as minister.[6] More surprising was the appointment of Dayan to the Foreign Ministry, given his prominent position in Labour and the fact that he was opposed to extending Israeli sovereignty over the Occupied Territories. But Dayan had already demonstrated that he had flexibility of mind when it came to foreign policy and was to do so again.[7] The main point at issue was the mismatch between Carter's expression of hopes for the Palestinians and Begin's passionate commitment to the West Bank, although not to Gaza. This became clear at the first meeting between the two men in Washington in July when Begin confirmed his opposition to a Palestinian homeland and asked Carter to stop using the term.

Sadat's initiative

On 4 September 1977, Dayan made the first of a series of highly secret visits to Morocco at the invitation of King Hassan II where he held discussions with Egypt's deputy prime minister, Dr Hassan Tuhami. A close confidant of Sadat, Tuhami was at pains to emphasise that the Egyptian leader was fully committed to reaching a peace settlement and believed that Begin and Dayan were the strong leaders who could deliver it.[8] These contacts prepared the way for the announcement that astonished the world, including the US administration and some of Sadat's own advisers, made by Sadat to the People's Assembly on 9 November 1977 that he was prepared to go to the Knesset to talk to the Israelis. Sadat was embarking on a bold course of action that involved him going to Jerusalem for face-to-face negotiations, something the Israelis had been demanding for years, thus hopefully setting the conditions for peace. His unilateral initiative meant that the Americans were, for a time, sidelined. In a historic occasion, watched by television audiences across the world, on 20 November Sadat and Begin addressed the Knesset. Sadat spoke at length of the barriers that existed between them, but he assured the Israelis that their country had the right to live in the region in security and safety. He appealed for a peace settlement that would see Israel withdraw from all the Arab territories including East Jerusalem, stressing that there had to be a recognition of the Palestinians' right to a state. Begin followed in a polite but cautious tone that indicated that he was not going to allow the emotion of the moment to override what he regarded as Israel's vital interests.[9]

If Sadat believed that his dramatic initiative would lead to rapid progress, he was soon brought up against Begin's tough negotiating skills. A summit meeting at Ismailia on 25 December merely confirmed the gulf between them. An

early irritant was the Israeli construction of a group of settlements in Sinai. In discussions with the Americans, Begin
claimed that he had proposals for a withdrawal from Sinai,
and he had introduced the concept of autonomy for the
West Bank and Gaza. Exactly what autonomy meant in the
context remained to be teased out. It became clear to Carter
and Sadat that progress would require America's involvement. A more substantive impediment to progress was a Palestinian raid on the coast between Tel Aviv and Haifa on 11
March 1978, inflicting many fatalities including an American
woman. In response, Israel sent a force estimated at 20,000
into Lebanon, which advanced to the Litani River. Appalled
as he was by the Palestinian action, Carter nevertheless put
pressure on Israel to withdraw. This took place under the
auspices of the United Nations Interim Force in Lebanon.
These events formed the backdrop to a visit by Begin to
Washington from 21–23 March, when Carter charged him
with being committed to six 'no's: that he would not withdraw from the West Bank, that he would not halt settlement
construction, that he would not withdraw settlements from
the Sinai, that he would not put these settlements under
the United Nations, that he would not concede that resolution 242 applied to the West Bank and Gaza, and that he
would not allow the Palestinians to determine their future.[10]
With the negotiations at an impasse, and no positive chemistry between Begin and Sadat having developed, on 31 July
1978 Carter decided that they would be invited to a summit
meeting at the president's country retreat, Camp David, in
Maryland.

The Camp David Summit

Accompanied by their key advisers, the three leaders met at Camp David on 5 September. Success was not preordained, and the intensity of the negotiations was confirmed by the fact that agreement was only reached on the 17th. The strength of the Israeli position was that they had little to lose should the conference fail. Their primary aim was a bilateral agreement with Egypt that would secure their southern flank, if possible, by retaining their Sinai settlements and their air bases of Etzion and Etam. Begin did not want to make concessions in the West Bank and Gaza beyond his autonomy formula. By contrast, knowing that he had isolated Egypt from much of the Arab world, Sadat needed a positive outcome. Total Israeli withdrawal from Sinai was naturally his top priority, but he also had to achieve something for the Palestinians. Carter, too, had placed much of his credibility on the conference's success. At a ceremony in the White House on 17 September, the three leaders signed two frameworks, subsequently known as the Camp David Accords.

'A Framework for the Conclusion of a Peace Between Egypt and Israel' met Sadat's key demands in important aspects. Egyptian sovereignty was to be restored over the entire Sinai, with the withdrawal of Israeli armed forces and the air bases confined to commercial use. Israeli shipping was to be given free passage through the Suez Canal, and the Gulf of Aqaba was confirmed as an international waterway. The goal of the framework was agreed to be the conclusion of a peace treaty within three months. Many Israelis felt that they had given up tangible positions in return for a peace treaty that might prove transient, but for Sadat it was simply the

Sadat, Carter, and Begin signing the Camp David Accords
at a ceremony in the East Room of the White House,
17 September 1978. (Newscom/Alamy Stock Photo)

return of Egyptian national territory. The other document,
'A Framework for Peace in the Middle East agreed at Camp
David', was more far-reaching and ultimately more problematic. Its avowed aim was the achievement of peace treaties
based on Security Council Resolutions 242 and 338 and, as
such, it addressed the future of the West Bank and Gaza.
There were to be transitional arrangements for a period not
exceeding five years during which Egypt, Israel, and Jordan
would negotiate a self-governing authority for the West
Bank and Gaza. When the self-governing authority had been
established, the three countries and elected representatives
from the West Bank and Gaza would negotiate their final

status. At the heart of the framework, however, was that the transitional arrangement was 'to provide full autonomy to the inhabitants'. This phrase was to undermine the framework from the start. On his return home, Begin insisted that what he had conceded was the personal autonomy of the inhabitants.[11] As the result of Sadat's initiative, Egypt, on the other hand, was now isolated in the Middle East, with the PLO, Syria, Jordan, Saudi Arabia, Libya, Algeria, and Yemen severing diplomatic and economic relations.

In the months that followed, the Carter administration had to confront the developing crisis in Iran, but at the same time it could not ignore the necessity to put flesh on what had been agreed at Camp David. It took a visit by Carter to Egypt and Israel to secure real progress, but once again Carter's relations with Begin were sulphurous. A joint address to the Knesset went badly, prompting Dayan to negotiate a final text with Vance. On 26 March 1979, the 'Peace Treaty Between the State of Israel and the Arab Republic of Egypt' was signed in Washington, formally terminating the state of war between the two countries. Israel agreed to withdraw all its armed forces from Sinai over which Egypt would have full sovereignty. The treaty confirmed that Israeli ships and cargoes and cargoes coming from or going to Israel would have free passage through the Suez Canal and that the Straits of Tiran and the Gulf of Aqaba were international waterways. In a letter to Carter, the two leaders pledged to conduct negotiations for the self-governing authority for the West Bank and Gaza as set out in the other Camp David framework.[12] Negotiations did begin, but, as the Carter administration was increasingly consumed by the problem of Iran, these never developed the necessary momentum.

New leaders

Just as Carter and his officials were negotiating to turn the aspirations in the Camp David Accords into political realities, events in Iran were developing at bewildering speed. By November 1978, widespread discontent with the rule of the Shah was being expressed, and his authority quickly eroded. On 16 January 1979, together with his family, the Shah flew into exile, never to return. On 1 February, Ayatollah Ruhollah Khomeini returned from exile in France to assume unquestioned power as the religious and political leader of what would soon become the Islamic Republic of Iran. The events in Tehran turned out to be far more profound than mere regime change. The Islamic nature of the revolution inspired others in the Middle East, including Hezbollah, the 'Party of God', based in the Shi'a areas of southern Lebanon. But the Shi'a character of the revolutionary regime set Iran on a different trajectory to the predominantly Sunni Arab Middle East, especially its neighbour across the Gulf, Saudi Arabia.[13] The immediate manifestation of this was to be war with Sunni-led Iraq. When the exiled Shah came to the United States for a cancer operation, on 4 November a crowd of revolutionary Iranians seized the US embassy in Tehran, taking sixty-six hostages. Attempts to resolve the hostage crisis, including a failed rescue mission, were to dominate what turned out to be the final months of the Carter administration.[14]

While these events were unfolding, a revolution of a very different kind happened in Iraq. The country had long been prone to political uncertainty, but in July 1968 the Ba'ath Party seized power under Ahmed Hassan al-Bakr, with the youthful Saddam Hussein holding the powerful position of responsibility for internal security. Born in the Sunni heartland near Tikrit in 1937, Saddam Hussein had long worked for the Ba'athists, steadily reinforcing his claim to be the natural successor to al-Bakr. When the latter resigned in July 1979, Saddam Hussein was appointed president of the revolutionary Command Council and of the republic. Skilled in the ways of Iraqi politics, he was to wield unquestioned power for almost quarter of a century, never brooking opposition, often ruthlessly so. Like previous regimes in Iraq, his core power base lay with his fellow Sunni Arabs, especially in the military and Republican Guard, but he was well aware of the need to be more inclusive.[15]

Leadership in the United States and Egypt also changed, the former democratically, the latter not. In the 1980 presidential election, the Republican Ronald Reagan defeated Carter, altering the direction and tone of US policy. Whereas Carter had focused on the Israeli–Palestinian question and the achievement of an Egyptian–Israeli peace agreement, Reagan's prime concern was how the Middle East fitted into the Cold War, especially since the Soviet Union's invasion of Afghanistan in December 1979 and the overthrow of the United States' main regional ally in Tehran. His initial instinct was to attempt the creation of a new 'regional consensus' embracing Israel, Egypt, Saudi Arabia, Oman, Somalia, and Kenya, but this failed to materialise. An agreement was signed between the United States and Israel, but was almost immediately suspended when in December 1981 the Knesset sanctioned the de facto annexation of the Golan Heights, contrary to US policy.[16]

Sadat's great moment had been on 6 October 1973 when his soldiers had successfully stormed across the Suez Canal. On the anniversary in 1981, while observing a great military display in Cairo, he was assassinated by a group of soldiers. He was immediately replaced by his vice-president, the air force general Hosni Mubarak. Mubarak punctiliously observed the peace treaty, reassuring those Israelis who had feared that it might not outlast its author. Israel's Knesset elections in June 1981 saw Begin and Likud returned, but, in one significant move, Sharon changed his agriculture portfolio for that of minister of defence. In that capacity he had to oversee the task of removing the settlers from Sinai under the terms of the peace treaty. Ofira and the smaller settlements were handed over intact to Egypt in stages, but since Yamit lay close to the Israeli border Sharon saw no alternative to its destruction. This was accomplished in April 1982 in an operation bitterly opposed by extreme-right-wing protestors.[17]

With so many changes in leadership, the political dynamic in much of the Middle East had altered significantly.

The Iran–Iraq War

Saddam Hussein was not long in power before his attentions focused on Iran. The most obvious issue between the two countries had been the Shatt al-Arab waterway, where the border with Iran ran along the middle of the navigable channel but which Iraqis believed rightfully belonged to them. Beyond the Shatt al-Arab was the south-western Iranian province of Khuzestan with its rich oil resources and a population that was largely ethnically Arab, even if they were long reconciled to being Iranian. A further consideration was the attraction of Ayatollah Khomeini's regime to Iraqi Shi'as. The upheaval caused by the Iranian Revolution seemed to provide the ideal conditions for a successful campaign that would burnish Saddam Hussein's ambitions to be a leader of the Arab world. Hundreds of officers of the Shah's army had been dismissed or executed or had deserted. On 17 September 1980, Saddam Hussein publicly asserted Iraqi sovereignty over the Shatt al-Arab, leading to air strikes and a ground offensive against Iran. Not for the last time, he made serious misjudgements, not the least of which was the commitment that Iranians brought to the defence of their revolution. The Arabs of Khuzestan did not rally to the Iraqi invaders. The Iraqi armed forces were organisationally weak, even to the extent of failing to make proper reconnaissance of the enemy dispositions, with too many commanders chosen for their loyalty to the Ba'ath regime.

Vastly superior to the Iranians in tanks and artillery, the nine Iraqi invading divisions should have overwhelmed their ill-prepared opponents, but tactical opportunities were missed. The only early success was their capture of Khorramshahr, although they suffered heavy casualties in the process. Iraq's lacklustre performance in the early phases of the invasion gave the Iranians time to plan their counter-offensives. These began in January 1981, with heavy fighting continuing throughout much of the year. Particularly noteworthy was the role of the Islamic Revolutionary Guard Corps, which was initially poorly trained but which more than compensated for this by its determination to uphold the Islamic Revolution. Having retaken Khorramshahr, by May 1982 the Iranians had reoccupied all of Khuzestan. This success persuaded the Iranians to move over to an offensive into the Shi'a areas of southern Iraq. In a series of offensives that continued through until 1986, the Iranians were confronted by an Iraqi army that proved to be more adept at defence than it had been at invasion. It was becoming clear that the military stalemate had to be broken or that the war be brought to an end. Saddam Hussein was also faced with an insurgency in the Kurdish areas in the north.

Heavy casualties at the hands of the Iranians in 1986 prompted a reconstruction of the Iraqi Army. The largely Shi'a infantry divisions had been fighting tenaciously in defence, but something more was needed to galvanise the war effort. Part of the solution was the expansion and equipping of the Republican Guard, a mainly Sunni formation originally created to defend the regime. But the transformation of the armed forces came at a heavy price, with loans from Saudi Arabia, Kuwait, and the Gulf states leading to a substantial burden of debt. The decisive Iraqi moves came in 1988, this time with a series of well-planned and well-executed offensives that culminated in a ceasefire in July. The ceasefire allowed Saddam Hussein to turn the weight of his armed forces against the Kurdish insurgents in a ruthless campaign that lasted until September. None of his strategic objectives in invading Iran had been achieved, and his country was now a debtor state.[18]

Operation Peace for Galilee[19]

Meanwhile, in the late spring of 1981, tensions mounted appreciably along Israel's border with Lebanon. The Palestinians had acquired Katyusha rocket launchers and other artillery capable of reaching targets inside Israel, and, with the civil war still raging, the Lebanese authorities were powerless to control them. Faced with a deteriorating situation, which inevitably involved Israeli counter-strikes, in July the Americans were able to broker a ceasefire. The Israelis and the Phalange both had reasons for wishing to develop some form of cooperation between them. Bashir Gemayel had emerged as the key figure on the Maronite side. In January 1982, Sharaon, accompanied by two key aides, made a secret helicopter mission to the Christian-controlled part of Lebanon to meet him, together with other leading Maronites. The Maronite leaders saw an Israeli intervention as a means of countering the Syrian presence of some 60,000 troops, which their militias lacked the strength to do. Sharon discussed the problems that Israel was facing along its Lebanese border and probed the possibility of an Israeli–Lebanese peace treaty, without much of a response.[20] The following month, Bashir Gemayel came to Jerusalem to meet Begin. While a possible Israeli–Maronite alliance was maturing, it is possible that the former was reading too much into it: Gemayel was a Lebanese patriot who would not welcome being seen as Israel's proxy. It was to prove something of an arm's-length relationship for the short period of its duration.

With the evacuation from Sinai completed, it seemed likely that the Israelis would look to the security of their northern border. In fact, their operation in southern Lebanon was triggered by an unforeseeable event: an attempt on the life of their ambassador to London, Shlomo Argov, on 3 June 1982. Badly wounded, Argov died in 2003, having spent the intervening years in permanent hospital care. Intelligence from London was that the attackers had belonged to a dissident group hostile to Arafat and the PLO, but this did not affect the course of events. On 6 June, the IDF began a major operation in southern Lebanon called Operation Peace for Galilee. The stated aim of the offensive was to create a twenty-five-mile *cordon sanitaire* in southern Lebanon that would put the northern Israeli communities out of rocket and artillery range. As the offensive pressed ahead, outnumbered PLO fighters fought hard, with heavy casualties incurred on both sides. Israel faced the obvious danger of provoking a conflict with Syria, which had a substantial military presence in Lebanon. And, indeed, air and ground fighting with Syria began on 9 June. As fighting continued, the IDF moved incrementally towards Beirut, reaching its western and southern suburbs by 13 June and making contact with Bashir Gemayel's Phalangists. Israel's policy had been not to enter an Arab capital militarily, but there was a fine line between the city and its extensive Muslim suburbs in which some 6,000 Palestinian guerrillas were embedded.

In early July 1982, Israeli artillery began bombarding predominantly Muslim west Beirut. As US officials worked to defuse the situation, it became more acute with repeated Israeli air strikes that began on 1 August. These provoked a personal intervention by President Reagan who contacted Begin on 12 August, castigating him for what was happening and appealing for an end to the attacks. A ceasefire followed that day. The situation on the ground seemed to be grid-locked. The PLO fighters were no match for the IDF either in numbers or equipment, while unease over the nature of the war was steadily growing in Israel. Painstaking negotiations had resulted in a plan that would see an evacuation of the PLO fighters from Lebanon overseen by a multinational force (MNF) drawn from the United States, France, and Italy. Arafat's main fear was that this would leave the refugee camps vulnerable to the Christian militias, but he seemed reassured by the presence of US military. The Israeli and Syrian governments also acquiesced to the plan. On 21 August, the first contingent of French Foreign Legion paratroopers landed at Beirut port to supervise the evacuation of PLO men to Tunisia and Yemen, soon followed by their Italian and US colleagues. The MNF's mission was defined as guaranteeing the safety of the departing PLO and of others in Beirut and restoring Lebanese government control over the Beirut area. The first part of the plan worked to perfection, with 8,144 PLO men evacuated by sea, most of them to Tunisia, and 6,254 – many of them Palestine Liberation Army personnel – escorted overland to Syria. But the operation was timed to last thirty days, and how the position of the remaining Palestinian civilians in west Beirut was to be ensured once the MNF had gone was unclear.

Sabra and Shatila

The Americans intended the operation to be the prelude for a peace plan that Reagan unveiled on 1 September. Stressing his personal commitment to Israel, he cautioned against further settlements in the West Bank. The essence of the plan was self-government for the Palestinians of the West Bank and Gaza in association with Jordan. Begin instantly spurned the proposals, stressing that for him the West Bank was Judea and Samaria. The Americans knew that the plan would take time to negotiate, but no one could have foreseen the sequence of events that robbed it of any chance of success.

On 23 August 1982, Bashir Gemayel was elected president of Lebanon, but at a meeting with Begin he made it clear, to the latter's consternation, that he could not move to an early peace treaty.

Whatever future directions he was contemplating must be conjectural, since on 14 September he was killed in a massive bomb explosion at his party headquarters. He was almost immediately succeeded by his brother Amin Gemayel, who held the presidency until 1988. The Israelis' response to the loss of their ally was to send troops back into west Beirut. They were accompanied by Christian militiamen who were permitted to enter the Sabra and Shatila refugee camps in pursuit of 'terrorists'. On 16 September, the militia entered the camps killing many hundreds of defenceless inhabitants.[21] As the enormity of the event started to emerge, the world was shocked, and a mass protest rally was held in Tel Aviv, forcing the government to concede an independent inquiry. When it reported in February 1983, Begin was criticised for his detachment and a number of officers were censured, but the main conclusion was that Sharon bore a responsibility for allowing the militia into the camps and recommended that he should not continue as defence minister. The findings prompted his resignation, although he continued in the government as a minister without portfolio.[22] These events coincided with the death of Begin's wife, Aliza. In September 1983, he resigned the premiership, dying on 9 March 1992. The new Prime Minister was Yitzhak Shamir, a Lehi veteran. After the following Knesset election, he entered into a rotation agreement with Labour, which saw Shimon Peres as prime minister and himself as deputy, but the two men were too far apart ideologically for it to be an easy partnership.

Multinational Force II and the Lebanese conflict

In view of these events, the MNF was reconstituted, Reagan announcing his agreement to this on 20 September 1982. Two days later, the IDF began to withdraw from west Beirut. When constituted, the troops of MNF II were deployed across the city, with 1,500 French in the port area close to Christian east Beirut and 1,400 Italians in the central sector covering the refugee camps. The US marines, some 1,400 strong, later joined by a small British contingent, were stationed in the south adjacent to Beirut International Airport and the Israeli positions. Their area was potentially vulnerable to bombardment from the nearby Chouf Mountains, a stronghold of the Druze militias, and attack from the Shi'a suburbs of south Beirut. It was perhaps inevitable that the men of MNF II would be perceived by the Shi'as and the Druze as a prop of Amin Gemayel's government, drawing them into the still festering situation in the country. Then, on 15 March 1983, an Italian soldier was killed. This proved to be the prelude to a massive car-bomb explosion at the US

Embassy in Beirut on 18 April, in which some sixty people died. Among the seventeen American dead were the CIA's station chief and seven of his operatives, who were meeting the agency's Middle East analyst, who was also among the victims. By then it was clear that the Reagan Plan had no prospect of success.

The IDF began to pull back away from the city on 2 September 1983, leaving the Americans exposed to firing from the Chouf Mountains, which they countered with the heavy guns of the Sixth Fleet, but the decisive blow came on 23 October, when suicide car bombers from south Beirut drove into the marines' compound and the French headquarters, killing fifty-eight French soldiers and 241 marines. American public support for what seemed a pointless mission plummeted. On 7 February 1984, Reagan announced that the marines would be 'redeployed' to ships offshore, and the French, Italians, and British also left.[23] Israeli public opinion, too, saw little point in carrying on. The IDF in southern Lebanon was increasingly harried by Hezbollah. In 1985, the Israelis withdrew from the country, retaining only a small 'security zone' along the southern border until that, too, was evacuated in 2000.

The withdrawal of foreign troops, with the exception of the Syrians, did not mean that Lebanon's travails were at an end. The civil war had a dynamic of its own, with much of the country effectively controlled by the rival militias. The war had taken its toll of political leaders. Two of the elder statesmen on the Maronite side, Pierre Gemayel and Camille Chamoun, died in 1984 and 1987 respectively, while the Sunni Prime Minister, Rashid Karami, was assassinated in June 1987. As he was about to leave the presidency in September 1988, Amin Gemayel appealed to the army commander, General Michel Aoun, to form a temporary government. The Saudis and Americans worked to broker a settlement, convening a meeting of Christian and Muslim deputies at Taif in Saudi Arabia. The Taif Accord, signed on 22 October 1989, proposed a revised parliament composed equally of Christians and Muslims, but since the latter were divided between Sunnis and Shi'as, the Christians retained some advantage. The Syrians were also accorded a supporting role. Even so, the civil war still had some way to run. On 5 November 1989, René Moawad became president, but he was assassinated within the month. His successor was Elias Hrawi, but his appointment triggered a conflict with Aoun's supporters that was only ended by the intervention of the Syrian Army in October 1990, forcing Aoun into exile. Effective power passed into the hands of the Sunni prime minister, Rafiq Hariri. This final crisis brought the long-running civil war to an end, leaving the task of how to restore a shattered economy and political consensus.[24]

Given the legacies of what had happened, neither task proved to be straightforward. An experienced businessman, Hariri worked to galvanise the economy, but in February 2005, like so many before him, he was assassinated in Beirut. His death did nothing to ease the country's divisions. Although Syrian troops left, Hezbollah remained a powerful force. Then, in May 2005, to the delight of his supporters, General Aoun returned to Beirut from exile. In October 2016, he was elected president, with Hariri's son, Saad, Prime Minister.[25]

The Intifada and the rise of Hamas

By 1987, it seemed that the Palestinians of the West Bank and Gaza could expect little progress on either the Camp David framework or the Reagan Plan, especially since US eyes were understandably focused on fast-changing events in the Soviet Union and Eastern Europe. That year marked two decades of occupation in the course of which Israel had acquired a more pervasive presence as its number of settlements increased. When Shamir returned to the premiership in 1986, a further forty-eight settlements were authorised for the West Bank and Gaza. Israeli acquisition of land amounted to some 50 per cent of the West Bank and 30 per cent of the Gaza Strip. Although not all of this area was settled, Palestinians saw this as a portent for the future.

There was apparently no organised plan for the uprising that was triggered on 8 December 1987 when an Israeli military vehicle accidentally crashed in the Gaza Strip, killing four people. But rumour had it that this was a retaliation for the killing of an Israeli in the city two days earlier. Strikes, rioting, and demonstrations quickly followed across Gaza, the West Bank, and Arab East Jerusalem, and the Israeli security forces were increasingly hard pressed to contain the situation, which became known as the Intifada, or Uprising. The leadership of the Intifada lay with a shadowy Unified National Command (UNC), which had little trouble finding replacements once members were arrested. With a solid base of support in the West Bank and Gaza, the UNC had stolen the initiative from the PLO in Tunisia. Even so, in April 1988 the Israelis mounted an operation in Tunis in which Khalil al-Wazir, the leading PLO figure who had been Arafat's right hand in the foundation of Fatah, was killed.[26]

In fact, the PLO and Fatah, both secular organisations, were about to face a very different challenge, one that was to alter the face of Palestinian politics in the decades ahead. The Intifada was still in its early stages when the quadriplegic charismatic religious teacher Sheikh Ahmed Yassin launched Harakat al-Muqawama al-Islamia (the Islamic Resistance Movement), or Hamas. Inspired by the teachings of the Muslim Brotherhood, the movement's covenant pledged the creation of an Islamic state in the whole of pre-1948 Palestine. Hamas members worked hard at social and religious issues, steadily attracting grassroots support, notably in the Gaza Strip. Yassin's imprisonment by the Israelis from 1989 to 1997 did not impede its steady growth. In 1991 its military wing, the Izz ad-Din al-Qassam Brigades, named in honour of the revolutionary leader killed in 1935, was formed.[27]

Despite the unpromising political situation, diplomatic attempts were being pursued, not least by the Americans. An initial portent of change came at the PLO National Council in Algiers on 15 November 1988, which declared an independent Palestine, a formula that could imply recognition of Israel, although Arafat would not move too far or fast. A speech to the United Nations in Geneva on 15 December that failed either to renounce terrorism or recognise Israel fell flat. It was only at a press conference the following day that Arafat was able to announce what the Americans had been pressing for all along: a rejection of terrorism and an acceptance of the right of all nations in the area to live in peace and security. Not all Palestinians agreed with Arafat's move, and, although his declaration had opened up a dialogue with the US, an abortive attack on Tel Aviv by a dissident faction in June 1990 closed it again.[28]

Saddam Hussein and the Gulf War

Iraq's principal legacy from Saddam Hussein's fruitless war with Iraq was massive indebtedness to other Arab countries, neighbouring Kuwait alone being owed $30 billion. He also accused the country of a pricing policy that depressed oil prices. Kuwait was especially vulnerable both in terms of its militarily porous border and because Iraq had nurtured ambitions towards it, as it had shown in 1961. As threatening noises started emanating from Baghdad in 1990, OPEC adopted a new pricing structure, agreed with Kuwait, that promised to help Iraq. Nevertheless, on 2 August 1990 the Iraqi Army invaded, and Kuwait was annexed as a province of Iraq. The Iraqi invasion was a clear violation of Article 51 of the United Nations Charter, and the Security Council condemned it, demanding a withdrawal. Equally significant was the decision of the Council of the Arab League, including Egypt and Syria but not Jordan or the PLO, to condemn the invasion. Saddam Hussein's ultimate aims were unclear, but with Kuwait's oil production added to that of Iraq, Saddam became a major regional leader. Equally alarming to the Arab states was his movement of substantial armed forces to the border with Saudi Arabia, potentially threatening its vital oil producing region. Saudi Arabia could not match Iraq's military potential should it be threatened or invaded.

The US administration of President George H. W. Bush

was quick to rally international support in opposition to the Iraqi action. Britain's cooperation was readily assured, as was the acquiescence of the Soviet Union. On 5 August, Bush announced that the Iraqi aggression would not stand, but an immediate military option was not available. Air power and lightly armed paratroopers could be quickly deployed, but US Central Command's General Norman Schwarzkopf reported that it would take eight to ten months to assemble the six divisions with the necessary logistic support that he believed he would need to liberate Kuwait. Before any such deployment could be contemplated, Saudi Arabia's consent was essential. Operation Desert Shield was quickly joined by Britain, France, and others, and steps were taken to ensure Arab military participation. Egypt and Syria each contributed two divisions, and the Saudi military was, of course, also involved. Not all Americans were convinced about military action to free Kuwait, but on 19 November 1990 UN Security Council 678 stated that unless Iraq withdrew by 15 January 1991 all necessary means could be used.

With no sign of Iraqi compliance, a sustained air assault of what was now called Operation Desert Storm was launched by the US, British, French, Italian, and Saudi air forces. Within days, Iraqi air defences had been overwhelmed, while much of its air force had flown to Iran, leaving the ground forces exposed. On 24 January 1991, Schwarzkopf began his ground offensive. His western flank was secured by the French division and three US divisions of the XVIII Airborne Corps. The central assault fell to the four armoured divisions, including one British, of VII Corps. A marine expeditionary force, together with a corps of Saudi and

Egyptian troops, was the other main prong, but military contingents from Syria, Canada, Italy, and other Arab countries took part, too. There was also a major naval presence in the Gulf, prominent among which were the two Second World War vintage battleships, USS *Missouri* and USS *Wisconsin*, whose Tomahawk missiles could strike far inland and whose sixteen-inch gun batteries offered invaluable fire support to the land campaign. The Iraqi forces could not compete with this overwhelming deployment. On 26 February, Iraq announced that it would evacuate Kuwait, and a ceasefire was agreed on 3 March. The reality was that the coalition had triumphantly fulfilled the Security Council Resolution and that any further operation into Iraq would not have been supported internationally. Some had expected that this overwhelming defeat would lead to the overthrow of Saddam Hussein and the Ba'ath Party, but this did not happen. Risings in the Kurdish north and the Shi'a south were suppressed. Saddam Hussein's Republican Guard still stood by him. Two other consequences of the war should be noted. Saddam Hussein had hoped to disrupt the Arab coalition against him by firing Scud missiles into Israel, provoking its retaliation. While the Israeli public was understandably nervous about being under bombardment, the government understood what Saddam Hussein was out to achieve by the missile attacks and stayed their hand as far as retaliation was concerned. In contrast, the PLO's support for Iraq left it isolated in the Middle East, especially from its sources of finance.[29]

In the immediate aftermath of the war, Bush and his secretary of state, James Baker, succeeded in organising a peace conference at Madrid in October 1991 jointly with the Soviet leader Mikhail Gorbachev. Although nothing actually came of it, the fact that Israel was in face-to-face negotiations with three Arab countries – Egypt, Syria, and Lebanon – signalled a leap forward. Just as significant was the presence of a Palestinian delegation drawn from representatives who had no links with the PLO but were residents of the West Bank and Gaza. Relations between the Bush administration and Shamir's Israeli government were poor, since the latter proved reluctant to make concessions, but the prospects for progress seemed to change on 23 June 1992 when Knesset elections returned Labour to power with Yitzhak Rabin head of a coalition and Shimon Peres as his foreign minister. Labour's coalition enjoyed a bare sixty-one to fifty-nine majority in the Knesset, however. Rabin had over time come to view the West Bank and Gaza very differently to his Likud predecessors, while Peres was open to working towards negotiations with the PLO. Any relationship that the new Israeli government could develop with Bush and Baker proved to be ephemeral, however, since the Democrat William J. Clinton won the 1992 presidential election.

The Oslo process

On 13 September 1993, millions of people throughout the Middle East – and indeed beyond – watched as Yasser Arafat and Yitzhak Rabin shook hands in a ceremony presided over by President Clinton on the South Lawn of the White House. The two leaders had come to Washington to sign an agreement between the state of Israel and the

In the presence of President Bill Clinton, PLO chairman
Yasser Arafat shakes the hand of Israeli prime minister
Yitzhak Rabin after the signing of the Israeli–PLO
peace accord. (REUTERS/Alamy Stock Photo)

Palestine Liberation Organisation that had been gestating
for months in a secret location in Norway, hosted by Norwe-
gian intermediaries, and that they had confirmed in separate
letters four days earlier. Arafat's letter conceded what Israel
had long wanted: the PLO's recognition of its right to exist
in peace and security, the removal of part of the Palestine
National Charter that had denied that right, and a renun-
ciation of terrorism. Rabin's letter accepted that the PLO
was the representative of the Palestinian people. Under the
agreement, Israel was to withdraw its troops and administration from the Gaza Strip and the city of Jericho on the West

Bank, and this would be followed by elections for a Palestinian Council for the West Bank and Gaza for a five-year period during which time a final settlement would be negotiated. Jericho was symbolic for a later extension in the West Bank. Since Arafat would never have accepted a Gaza-only option, Jericho was to be the standard bearer for the rest of the West Bank. The agreement reflected a pragmatic acknowledgement on part of both parties that, as a result of the Gulf War and the ending of the Cold War, the international order had changed significantly. Neither leader held any illusions about the pitfalls that would inevitably lie ahead, nor, it seems, did Rabin ever really develop any warmth towards Arafat. Given their respective paths, perhaps that was unsurprising. The critical element between them would be trust, not personal rapport.[30]

11

The Middle East in Turmoil

While the handshake in the White House garden was historic, potentially far-reaching, and possibly painful, measures would have to be undertaken by both sides if it were to be translated into reality on the ground.

Creating the Palestinian Authority

Both leaders faced serious obstacles to progress. Rabin and Peres viewed the West Bank in a fundamentally different way to their Likud opponents. For Rabin, the West Bank was both a strategic liability and a demographic threat to Israel's Jewish identity, while for Likud it was an essential part of the Jewish inheritance. Many of the settlers in the West Bank also held tenaciously to the latter view; now numbering some 120,000, they could not be ignored, not least because of the hinterland of support that they enjoyed in sections of the general Israeli population. The Israeli public was now also being asked to place its trust in what for years had been castigated as a terrorist organisation. When the Knesset voted on the agreement, it was approved by sixty-one to fifty votes – but with eight abstentions. Rabin's tenuous hold on the Knesset rested on the votes of Arab and communist members. A reminder of the intensity of feeling came on 25 February 1994 when a Jewish doctor massacred twenty-nine worshippers at the Hebron mosque before being killed himself. Retaliation came on 6 April when a suicide bomber attacked a bus queue in Afula, killing eight people and injuring over thirty.[1]

Palestinian support ultimately hinged on Arafat's control of Fatah, not all of whose members were sympathetic. Overt opposition came from Hamas and Islamic Jihad. Attacks on Israelis were intended to undermine support for Rabin and Peres and, by extension, Arafat. Arafat's own political skills, which had been those of a revolutionary leader, would inevitably be tested in the new dispensation that was being opened up. In fact, the year 1994 seemed to confirm the possibilities that were arising as a result of what was being called the Oslo peace process. At a meeting in Cairo in May, Rabin, Peres, and Arafat were able to fine-tune some of the key elements in their agreement. In Gaza, the Israelis agreed to redeploy their troops to guard the settlements there. The Palestinian Authority (PA) was to be set up, enjoying many of the symbols of sovereignty. Elections to the Palestinian National Council were clearly won by Fatah, with Arafat becoming president. In May, he returned to Gaza, and in June came to Jericho.

The Washington Declaration and the Israeli–Jordanian peace treaty

With the PLO's recognition of Israel, there was no obvious reason why Jordan should not move to a peace treaty. Moreover, in the aftermath of the Gulf War, Jordan was left somewhat adrift diplomatically and in terms of US goodwill. For years, there had been channels of communication between King Hussein and the Labour leaders, whose views on a final settlement were not far apart. On 25 July 1994, the White House lawn was once again the setting for reconciliation, this time of the Washington Declaration by King Hussein and Rabin, which opened the way for a peace agreement. Important details were yet to be agreed – not least on the vexed question of water rights – but once these were resolved, the peace treaty between the two countries was signed on 26 October in Clinton's presence by Rabin and the Jordanian premier, Abdul Salam al-Majali, on the border at Wadi Araba. It was a wide-ranging treaty that proposed cooperation between the two countries in such areas as agricultural development, postal and telephone links, tourism, and the joint development of the twin cities of Aqaba and Eilat at the head of the Gulf of Aqaba, but, above all, it ended the state of war that had existed since 1948.[2] Having succeeded to the throne as an untried schoolboy in the most unpromising of circumstances, King Hussein had surmounted many challenges, the most obvious of which was the loss of much of his kingdom in 1967, to become one of the Middle East's most enduring and respected rulers. Having undergone treatment for cancer, he died on 7 February 1999, his eldest son succeeding him as King Abdullah II.

The assassination of Rabin

Progress over the West Bank proved to be slow. It was not until 28 September 1995 that the two sides signed a new agreement in Cairo, encouraged by the presence of Clinton, Mubarak, and King Hussein. Its purpose was to carry forward in a tangible manner the principles embodied in the earlier Oslo Accords. For its part, Israel agreed to withdraw its forces from most of the West Bank towns and villages by 30 March 1996. The Palestinians agreed to make the necessary amendments to the National Charter that threatened Israel's existence. Sensing the need to reinforce their domestic position in the face of criticism, Rabin and Peres decided to call a peace rally in Tel Aviv's Malchei Yisrael Square for 4 November 1995. The event was a great success, attended by an estimated 100,000 people. The two Israeli leaders, rarely the most comfortable of colleagues, embraced. They then accompanied the crowd singing 'Shir Lashalom', 'A Song for Peace'. As he left the rally, Rabin was shot and mortally wounded by a young Israeli opposed to his policies.[3]

In some respects, the assassination had no immediate implications for the peace process, or so it seemed. Peres, who had succeeded his colleague, did not seek an early electoral mandate but pressed ahead with implementing what had been agreed at Cairo: evacuating the main cities of the West Bank. Elections for the Palestinian Council on 20 January 1996 confirmed Arafat's position as Palestinian leader, and the PLO, as it had promised, removed the sections of its National Charter that called for Israel's destruction. But as far as the Israeli public was concerned, the Oslo process had rested on a knife edge from the start. Attacks by

Palestinians opposed to the agreements were able to undermine Israeli public confidence. In early 1996, bombs in Jerusalem, Ashkelon, and Tel Aviv resulted in multiple fatalities. For many Israelis, Peres did not seem to have much to show for his peace agenda.[4]

The Oslo process under Likud

Peres's successful rival for power was Benjamin Netanyahu. Born in 1949 when the state was barely in its infancy, Netanyahu represented the coming of age of a new generation of politicians. When his historian father, Benzion Netanyahu, took up an academic appointment in the United States, he came to know the country at first hand, graduating from the prestigious Massachusetts Institute of Technology. His early career was as a combat soldier in the IDF's elite special forces unit. His elder brother, Yonatan, became a national hero when he was killed leading a commando operation to rescue hostages from a hijacked airliner at Entebbe airport in Uganda in July 1976. A subsequent diplomatic career saw him represent Israel at the United Nations. Netanyahu's specialism was in security and counter-terrorism, on which, in 1995, he published *Fighting Terrorism*. Two years previously, he had explained his views in *A Place Among the Nations: Israel and the World*.[5] His was thus a profile that resonated with large sections of the population, faced as they were with the seemingly unstoppable wave of bomb attacks. Although the election result was tantalisingly close for both major parties, Netanyahu was able to assemble the necessary coalition for him to form a government.

Although his party had been opposed to the agreements Rabin and Peres had concluded, Netanyahu's new Likud government was bound by them. When Netanyahu and Arafat met in August 1996, they pledged to pursue the peace process, but yet again it ran into serious difficulties over the holiest sites for Jews and Muslims in Jerusalem. Any proposed building or archaeological activity in the vicinity of the Haram al-Sharif/Temple Mount was regarded with great suspicion, so when the Israelis opened an entrance to the ancient Hasmonean Channel near the site in September 1996, there were widespread protests across the West Bank and Gaza. In the course of the demonstrations, the Israeli security forces and the Palestinian police exchanged fire, with widespread fatalities. The last major city to be evacuated by the Israelis under the Cairo Agreement was Hebron, always a particular focus of tension and all the more so in the light of the 1994 massacre there. With Labour support, Netanyahu secured Knesset agreement to withdraw from 80 per cent of the city.

On the broader agenda that had featured in the Oslo process, however, there was little sign of progress. It took the personal involvement of President Clinton and a desperately ill King Hussein to move things forward, bringing Arafat and Netanyahu in October to the Wye River Conference Center in Maryland in October 1998. After nine days of negotiations, Arafat agreed to a raft of measures designed to prevent attacks on Israel, including the involvement of the US Central Intelligence Agency. Israel was to set in hand further evacuations from the West Bank, putting 40 per cent under Palestinian control. The Wye River Memorandum did not significantly add to the previous agreements, the only critical difference being that it was being made by Likud.[6] Clinton put his full weight behind it in a historic visit to Israel and Gaza in mid-December when he delivered a powerful speech to the Palestine National Council in Gaza, watching while the council eliminated from the National Charter those sections calling for Israel's destruction. Accompanied by Arafat, Clinton opened a new terminal at Gaza Airport, which would open up communications for the Gazans.[7] For his part, Netanyahu faced serious dissent from within his government. With the prospect looming of losing a vote of confidence in the Knesset, he called an election for 17 May 1999.

Netanyahu's challenger in the May election was a retired general, Ehud Barak, who had replaced Peres as Labour leader in June 1997. A much-decorated veteran, Barak had the necessary credentials with the electorate to lead Labour back to power: after a distinguished combat record leading special forces in hazardous missions and experience in command of armoured troops, Barak had been made head of the Military Intelligence Department, then given Central Command, responsible for the West Bank, before becoming chief of staff in 1991. On leaving the IDF, in 1995 he had entered political life in the Labour interest, becoming a member of Rabin's cabinet. Running for election in 1999, Barak was committed to the country's security, pledging to continue with the Oslo Agreement, negotiate with Syria, and to evacuate the remaining Israeli troops from southern Lebanon. Barak won a substantial victory over Likud and was able to put together the necessary coalition.[8] Netanyahu, meanwhile, resigned the Likud leadership, to be replaced by Sharon.

Barak moved quickly to establish contact with Arafat,

meeting him in Gaza in July 1999 when the two men promised to work together on the peace process. In September,
they agreed to settle the questions of borders and Jerusalem
within a year. This was followed by the opening of a land
corridor between the West Bank and Gaza, thus enhancing
the identity of the Palestinian Authority. Hezbollah's access
to rockets meant that the 'security zone' no longer offered
protection to northern Israel. The final legacy of Operation Peace for Galilee was completed by the following May
with Israel's withdrawal from Lebanon. Barak's bid for a settlement with Syria was less productive. Negotiations went
ahead, but Assad, holding to the view that the entire Golan
was Syrian national territory, was in failing health. He died
in June 2000, not long after an unsuccessful summit with
Clinton in Geneva in the spring.[9]

The Camp David Summit[10]

With differences starting to surface among his coalition
partners and his Knesset majority eroding, Barak persuaded
Clinton to bring the Israeli and Palestinian leaders together
for a summit at Camp David that ran from 11–25 July 2000.
Clinton and his negotiating team saw the shape of an agreement that would give the Palestinians most of the pre-1967
West Bank border but with modifications that would transfer the bulk of the settlements to Israel with the possibility of
land compensation in return. The Jordanian border would
try to reconcile Palestinian sovereignty with Israel's security
concerns. An international fund would be set up for the refugees. The unique position of Jerusalem would be approached

from the standpoint that it had administrative needs, that it was sacred to Jews, Christians, and Muslims, and that there were political considerations.

Barak's imaginative response went beyond anything that an Israeli leader had so far contemplated. Crucially, he was prepared to consider Palestinian rule in 91 per cent of the West Bank, with Palestinian sovereignty in seven outer Arab neighbourhoods in Jerusalem and over the Muslim and Christian quarters of the Old City, with Muslim custodianship of the mosques on what for the Israelis was the Temple Mount. Arafat's reply to Clinton essentially rested on the argument that, since he had accepted Security Council Resolution 242, the borders had to be those of 4 June 1967. He proposed an international commission on the refugees and that Jerusalem be either an international city as set out in the 1947 General Assembly Resolution or that East and West Jerusalem would be the capitals respectively of Palestine and Israel, the 4 June 1967 again being the dividing line between them. Clinton and his negotiators put forward a compromise that would give the Palestinians full sovereignty over the outer areas of East Jerusalem, with a link to the Haram al-Sharif and a special regime for the Old City. Arafat was not convinced by the argument that the offer was the best that he could expect, at which point Clinton ended the summit.

The al-Aqsa Intifada

The Haram al-Sharif/Temple Mount lay at the heart of the Israeli–Palestinian dispute, as the Camp David negotiations had shown. Sharon proposed visiting the complex. It was not his first visit, but it seems to have been prompted by his belief that Barak had conceded too much at Camp David. Sharon's move posed Barak with a dilemma. While the proposed visit was evidently a political statement aimed at his government and at the Israeli public, Barak could only prevent it on security advice that it would be a threat to public order or security. But the advice did not reflect such a threat, and on 28 September 2000 Sharon made a brief visit accompanied by 1,000 police officers. The visit was not in itself the cause of what subsequently happened, but it helped to bring into focus the discontentment simmering among the Palestinians.[11] The following day, after Friday prayers, large-scale demonstrations against the visit were held in the course of which five Palestinians were killed. This proved to be the start of what Palestinians called the al-Aqsa Intifada. This Intifada differed from its predecessor in key respects, not least because the Palestinian security forces were armed. Palestinian attacks came to be characterised by the use of suicide bombers, against whom there was practically no defence beyond pre-emptive strikes against potential bombers. The Israeli security forces had recourse to heavy weaponry.[12]

In this unpromising situation, Clinton, who was in the final weeks of his presidency before power passed to the Republican George W. Bush, attempted a breakthrough with the so-called Clinton Parameters. At their heart was a sovereign Palestinian state in Gaza and 94–6 per cent of the West Bank, with a land swap of 1–3 per cent, which would transfer most of the settlers to Israel. Once again, the key issues were the refugees and Jerusalem. The refugees were to have the right of return to the State of Palestine, while Israel could indicate that it might take some. On Jerusalem, there would be de facto Palestinian sovereignty on the Haram al-Sharif/Temple Mount, together with Israeli sovereignty over the Western Wall. The Parameters were accepted by the Israeli cabinet, contingent on Palestinian agreement. But a meeting between Clinton and Arafat in Washington on 2 January 2001 failed to reach that agreement, despite a warning from Clinton that the Parameters would lapse with the end of his presidency. A subsequent meeting of Israeli and Palestinian representatives at Taba in Egypt on 27 January also failed. Days later, Barak lost to Sharon in the Knesset elections. By then, the prospects for Israeli–Palestinian relations seemed far removed from the hopes that had been generated by the scene at the White House on 13 September 1993 that had riveted audiences across the world.[13]

Any optimism that the Oslo process had encouraged was dispelled as the cycle of violence seemed to acquire a dynamic all its own. The year 2002 began with the interception by the Israelis of the ship *Karine A*, which they claimed was carrying an arms consignment to Gaza. Although Arafat denied involvement, Bush broke off relations with him.[14] As suicide attacks and retaliatory strikes escalated, in March a suicide bomber struck a Passover gathering in Netanya, killing twenty-nine people. In response, Sharon launched Operation Defensive Shield in the West Bank, striking initially at Ramallah and effectively confining Arafat to his headquarters, the Muqata, in the city. In a major incident at the Jenin refugee camp, the IDF lost twenty-three men, and at least fifty Palestinians were killed. In the course of the operation, much of the economic infrastructure of the nascent PA was undermined.

Israel's ultimate defence against the suicide bombers was the construction of a formidable security fence. Started in 2002, it was steadily extended to include East Jerusalem, separating historic neighbourhoods like Ar Ram in the north of the city and cutting off Bethlehem with its reliance on the pilgrim trade. If its construction served to reassure an Israeli public, it could offer no defence against rocket attacks.[15]

9/11 and the Iraq War

George W. Bush was only months in office when, on 11 September 2001, the United States suffered a trauma on a scale that few could have imagined. On the morning of 9/11, as the tragedy came to be known, two aircraft that had taken off from Boston were hijacked and crashed into the twin towers of New York's World Trade Center demolishing them; a third aircraft that had just left Washington was targeted on the Pentagon, while a fourth hijacked flight that had left Newark was brought down by its passengers before it could reach its target. According to the official estimate, this action claimed the lives of over 2,600 people at the World Trade Center, 125 at the Pentagon, and 256 on the four aircraft. The perpetrators of the attack were young men of Middle Eastern origin, the coordinator being an Egyptian. It was soon clear that the attack was the work of a fundamentalist Islamist group called al-Qaeda (the Foundation), then based in Taliban-controlled areas of Afghanistan. It was led by a Saudi expatriate, Osama bin Laden, whose inspiration had been the work of Qutb, the Egyptian Islamist leader executed under Nasser in 1966. Al-Qaeda's origins lay in part in the long campaign to drive the Soviet Union out of Afghanistan, which had attracted many young Muslims. With their success, many of its members focused on what they saw as the Western dominance of the Middle East. By 1988, bin Laden had assumed the leadership of al-Qaeda, steadily building up the organisation until in February 1998 he issued a fatwa, or declaration, against the United States.[16]

No president could ignore the 9/11 attacks. Although al-Qaeda was operating from Afghanistan, its leader and the 9/11 hijackers were Middle Eastern. The international 'war on terror', a military campaign declared by the US in the wake of 9/11 but waged under the auspices of the NATO alliance, was directed against al-Qaeda and the Taliban and conducted in Afghanistan. Even so, bin Laden was able to survive in hiding until an American operation killed him at his headquarters in Pakistan in 2011.

The Americans' attention soon turned to Iraq, based on the belief that Saddam Hussein had secretly maintained stocks of chemical and biological weapons such as those that had been used against the Kurds in 1988, and which might become available to terrorists. The debate over weapons of mass destruction (WMDs) dominated the discourse over Iraq for the next twelve months. In the event, no WMDs were ever found, but throughout that period Saddam obfuscated and repeatedly defied attempts to establish the true position.[17] It may well have been, as he later told US interrogators, that he did not want to appear weak to the Iranians. But in January 2002, Bush made a speech in which he castigated an 'axis of evil' comprising North Korea, Iran, and Iraq, which, he claimed, had something to hide. It was only after the adoption of UN Security Council Resolution 1441 in November 2002 that UN arms inspectors were allowed into the country, by which time the United States was already contemplating a multinational military force with a view to intervention. On 19 March 2003, the aerial phase of Operation Iraqi Freedom began, followed by a land invasion from Kuwait. A British force occupied Basra and the south of the country, while the Americans advanced on Baghdad, capturing it on 9 April. With Saddam in hiding, the military phase of the operation was over, but the task of rebuilding the country lay ahead.[18]

Post-war Iraq: The search for stability

From its creation by the British out of the three former Ottoman vilayets of Baghdad, Basra, and Mosul, Iraq had been an uneasy amalgam of Sunni and Shi'a, Arab and Kurd. But power resided in the hands of the Sunni Arab minority, latterly through the Ba'ath Party under Saddam Hussein and their dominant position in the officer corps of the armed forces. In the aftermath of the 2003 war, that polity shattered, and Saddam Hussein was captured in December. Together with some associates, he was tried for crimes against humanity in 1982 at the town of Dujail, found guilty, and subsequently executed in 2006.[19]

The military victory had been only the first phase; Iraq's reconstruction would present problems of a different order. The immediate governance of the country fell to the victorious coalition, with the British responsible for the southern area based on Basra, but the directions of policy rested with the Americans in Baghdad. The latter initially governed through the Office of Reconstruction and Humanitarian Assistance. In May 2003, the experienced US Ambassador L. Paul Bremer III became administrator of the Coalition Provisional Authority (CPA).

Key decisions were taken by the Authority in two areas. Its first was to pursue a policy of what was termed the country's de-Baathification, in which an attempt was made to identify those who had been the senior party loyalists under Saddam Hussein; these were to be excluded from the administration. On the defeat of Saddam Hussein's regime, the army had disintegrated, with desertions among the Shi'a rank and file. Once confirmation had come from Washington, the Authority's second order was signed on 23 May 2003 abolishing all the existing military and security formations, including the Defence Ministry. Effectively, a new Iraqi army, which was to reflect all sections of Iraqi society, was to be created *de novo*, while payments were to be made to soldiers of the former army.[20] In June 2004, power was assumed by an Iraqi interim government, but, as its title indicates, it was merely holding the ground until a viable new structure could be found. Elections in December 2005 saw the coming to power of the Shi'a-dominated Dawa (Call) Party, led by Nouri al-Maliki.

As the country struggled to adjust to these new realities, radical new groupings emerged, not least among the Sunni community which felt disempowered for the first time in the country's history. Although the British also came under serious challenge in the Shi'a south, an insurgency in the Sunni heartland in Anbar Province around the cities of Tikrit and Fallujah was by 2006 threatening the very fabric of the state. In August 2003, a car bomb killed the United Nations Special Representative Sérgio Vieira de Mellow. The insurgency was also taking a mounting toll of US and allied forces. Days later, a bomb at the Imam Ali Mosque at the Shi'a holy city of Najaf killed Ayatollah Muhammad Baqir al-Hakim with many of his followers. In November 2004 alone, 137 Americans were killed when marines attacked Fallujah. As the security situation showed no sign of improvement, it was inevitable that calls would come for an end to the operation, but Bush and his military advisers concluded that the only viable option was the deployment of more troops. On 10 January 2007, Bush broadcast his change of strategy with the commitment of more than 20,000 additional soldiers. The surge, as it was termed, committed an extra five brigades to Baghdad and two to Anbar Province, as well as additional Iraqi troops promised by al-Maliki.[21]

The road map for peace

The cycle of violence had led Bush to conclude that the only way forward in the Middle East was the creation of a Palestinian state that would reject terror and work for peace with Israel. He had articulated this position in a statement at the White House on 24 June 2002, calling upon Israel to support a 'credible Palestinian state'. Castigating the Palestinian leadership for supporting terrorism, he appealed for the election of new leaders 'not compromised by terror'. The situation with the regard to Iraq was, of course, the main US preoccupation, but in a speech in February 2003, Bush argued that the removal of Saddam Hussein would encourage the Palestinians to choose new leaders who would work for peace, in return for which Israel would be expected to support a Palestinian state. The new start in the Palestinian leadership that he was looking for seemed to be signalled in March 2003 when the Central Council of the PLO appointed a veteran of the Oslo negotiations, Mahmoud Abbas, as prime minister of the PA.

With the fall of Baghdad and Abbas's confirmation as Prime Minister, Bush unveiled the 'Performance-Based Road Map to a Permanent Two-State Solution to the Israeli–Palestinian Conflict' on 30 April 2003. The road map was to follow three stages to be completed by 2005. In Phase I, the Palestinians were to confirm Israel's right to exist and bring an end to violence. Their security forces were to operate against those engaging in terror. The Israelis, too, were to end violence against Palestinians and affirm their commitment to a sovereign Palestinian state. What's more, Israel was to end settlement activity and dismantle settlement outposts created since March 2001. Phase II, which would follow Palestinian elections, would see an international conference establish the provisional borders of a Palestinian state. In 2004, Phase III would see another international conference intended to reach a final-status resolution dealing with borders, Jerusalem, refugees, and settlements. A lack of detail in Phase III would mean hard negotiations ahead, but once again voices expressed immediate opposition. Hamas and Islamic Jihad rejected the road map. Sharon, meanwhile, convinced his cabinet colleagues, by a divided vote, to endorse it. On 4 June 2003, Bush, Sharon, and Abbas met at Aqaba. Abbas confirmed that he would end the Intifada, while Sharon acknowledged the need for the Palestinian state to be contiguous. But the summit was soon followed by a massive suicide bombing in central Jerusalem, with the Israelis killing a Hamas leader in Gaza in a rocket attack.[22] Once again, the auguries for the peace process seemed bleak.

Changes in leadership

Gaza had long presented problems all of its own, with its rapidly increasing population lacking viable economic outlets and prospects, while Israelis disliked service there. Its problems were compounded by the presence of some twenty-one Israeli settlements. Sharon enraged many of his supporters by announcing a disengagement plan that would involve a unilateral withdrawal from Gaza, including the settlements. When Palestinian suicide bombers targeted Ashdod, the Israelis killed the Hamas leader Sheikh Yassin in a missile attack in March 2004. His successor, Dr Abd al-Aziz al-Rantissi, was killed in a similar attack the following month. These strikes seem to have increased support for the movement, however. Nevertheless, Sharon confirmed that he had decided on a total evacuation of Gaza, ending any Israeli responsibility for its inhabitants. In addition, four settlements in the north of the West Bank were to be evacuated.[23]

In the autumn of 2004, Arafat's health deteriorated. He was worried that if he left for more advanced medical treatment abroad he would not be allowed to return to Ramallah. When he had assurances that this would not be the case, he was flown to a military hospital in France via Amman on 29 October, but he died on 11 November. After a funeral in

Cairo, he was buried in the grounds of the Muqata. Thousands of Palestinians gathered in Ramallah to mourn the leader who had for so long personified their cause. His successor as PLO chair was Mahmoud Abbas. With the strong support of Fatah members, he was also elected president of the PA. Abbas wasted no time in meeting Sharon together with Mubarak and King Abdullah II at Sharm el-Sheikh in February 2005 to proclaim an end to the Intifada and military operations. Hamas was, however, not a party to this.[24]

Notwithstanding popular protests and dissent in his party, Sharon honoured his pledge to withdraw from Gaza. Settlers were given forty-eight hours to leave, and on 12 September 2005 the military presence was ended. On 21 November, he treated the Israeli body politic to an earthquake by resigning the Likud leadership to form a new secular political party, Kadima ('Forward'), committed to a peace policy. He was immediately joined by the Labour veteran Peres and by Ehud Olmert who had been the Likud mayor of Jerusalem. Sharon's move heralded a new alignment in Israel politics, but on 18 December he had a mild stroke, followed on 4 January 2006 by a cerebral attack which rendered him unconscious until his death on 11 January 2014.[25]

Renewed violence: Lebanon and Gaza

Under Olmert's leadership, Kadima did well in the March 2006 Knesset elections, forming a coalition with Labour. March elections in the PA resulted in a profound change in Palestinian politics when Hamas, which had built up its credibility by its involvement in social work, decisively defeated Fatah. Ismail Haniyeh of Hamas became the PA prime minister, subsequently leaving Gaza to become head of Hamas's political bureau. Relations between the two Palestinian organisations quickly fractured. In June 2007, open fighting between them resulted in Hamas controlling Gaza and Fatah holding on to the West Bank. Now in control of the Gaza Strip, Hamas could strengthen its position by the construction of an intricate network of tunnels that allowed it to conceal its activities and intentions. These events coincided with a serious clash with Hezbollah, which killed eight Israelis in a raid. In subsequent fighting, it is believed that 144 Israelis and over 1,000 Lebanese were killed, with 4,000 rockets launched into Israel.

In November 2007, Bush attempted to regain the initiative with a major conference at Annapolis where the two sides pledged to work for a two-state solution by the end of 2008. But, once again, realities on the ground proved to be more powerful than diplomacy.[26] In the course of 2008, Israel increasingly came under attack by rockets fired from Gaza. In June, the Egyptians brokered a ceasefire, but this collapsed when rocket attacks resumed in December in response to Israeli raids on the tunnels that connected Gaza with Egypt. On 27 December, Israel launched air strikes, followed by major ground operations that lasted until 18 January. When Operation Cast Lead ended, it was believed, although estimates varied, that thirteen Israelis and over 1,100 Palestinians, including many civilians, had been killed. When Israel next held Knesset elections in February 2009, Kadima, now led by Tzipi Livni, did well to hold its own, but Likud's fortunes soared; with right-wing parties a majority in the Knesset, Netanyahu was able to form a coalition government.[27]

The Obama administration and the search for a settlement

Once again, the political cycles in Israel and the United States resulted in key changes of leadership. As the Israelis prepared for the Knesset elections that brought Netanyahu back to power, the Democrat Barack Obama was inaugurated president on 20 January 2009. Obama has recorded how he was able to understand both the Israeli and Palestinian positions.[28] His choice of secretary of state was Hillary Rodham Clinton, former first lady and senator from New York. Clinton was well versed in the dynamics of the Israeli–Palestinian conflict. An early priority for her was a visit to the Middle East and Europe from 28 February to 8 March, during which time she participated in the Gaza Reconstruction Conference at Sharm el-Sheikh, pledging $900 million for humanitarian and recovery work. This was a contribution towards the goal of peace and a two-state solution, a message that she repeated in Jerusalem and Ramallah. Financial support was also promised for Israel's Iron Dome anti-missile system, while Hamas was criticised for the rocket attacks from Gaza.[29]

Obama addressed the issues in a keynote speech before a large audience at Cairo University on 4 June 2009 in which he said that he had come in search of a new beginning. In a carefully balanced presentation, he asked his audience not to deny the Holocaust or advocate Israel's destruction, while recognising the sufferings of the Palestinians as they pursued a homeland. He criticised both Hamas and Israel's ongoing settlement policy, ending with a plea for two states that would meet the aspirations of both sides. Netanyahu's response soon came in a speech at Bar-Ilan University in which he indicated for the first time that he might accept a Palestinian state, albeit with certain conditions affecting Israel's security.[30]

In 2013, as his second term began, Obama's new secretary of state was Senator John Kerry, chair of the Senate Foreign Relations Committee. Israeli elections in January saw the virtual collapse of Kadima and the establishment of another Netanyahu-led coalition. This was immediately followed by a visit by Obama to Jerusalem and Ramallah in which he attempted to reassure the Israelis on security and asserted the right of the Palestinians to have their own land. His visit was the prelude to a major effort by Kerry to move the parties together, announcing in July the resumption of final-status negotiations so that at the end of nine months there would agreement on two states. The Israelis were to release 104 Palestinian prisoners, and the Palestinians were not to press ahead with bids to enhance their status at the United Nations and other bodies. But, by the spring of 2014, it was clear that failure was in sight. Claiming that Israel was failing to release the final tranche of prisoners, Abbas applied for membership of a group of international conventions. On 25 April 2014, Fatah and Hamas announced the resumption of relations with a view to a unity government, at which point Israel suspended the negotiations.

In June, three teenage Israelis were abducted and killed in the West Bank. As the situation worsened, a young Palestinian was murdered in East Jerusalem. On 8 July, Israel began Operation Protective Edge against Hamas targets in Gaza, triggering violent protests in the West Bank. Fighting only came to an end on 26 August, by which time an estimated 2,000 Palestinians and seventy-three Israelis had been killed.[31]

The Arab Spring in Egypt

While the Middle East was dominated by the events in Iraq and the ongoing crisis in Gaza, other important developments were in the making. What came to be known as the Arab Spring spurred street demonstrations and protests across the Middle East and North Africa, where it had started. The movement had its immediate origins in December 2010 in Tunisia when a young street trader, Muhammad Bouazizi, set himself on fire in protest against oppression, subsequently dying from his injuries. His action inspired protests that led to the overthrow of the regime. Street protests against the established governments spread to other countries. These were essentially youth movements, generated in large part by lack of economic progress and opportunity for rapidly growing populations. They were also protesting against the longevity of existing regimes that they felt were failing to provide for them.[32]

Hosni Mubarak had assumed the presidency of Egypt with Sadat's assassination in October 1981. Born in 1928, he represented a new generation from the original Free Officers. Domestically, his priority was the threat from the Islamists responsible for Sadat's assassination. Mubarak's relations with Israel survived the invasion of Lebanon in 1982, although for a period he withdrew his ambassador in protest. He ruled the country through his National Democratic Party, although rival parties, such as the New Wafd, were tolerated. Traditional sources of revenue were maintained. With its wealth of cultural sites, Egypt continued to attract visitors despite temporary setbacks after terrorist attacks, including 9/11 and, in 1997, a mass shooting at the world-famous tomb of Queen Hatshepsut near Luxor where fifty-eight tourists and a number of Egyptians were killed. The Suez Canal's importance was undiminished, and it was adapted to accommodate the supertankers and container ships on which so much of the world's maritime commerce had come to depend. The country's main problem was demographic, with the economy striving to keep pace with the expanding population.[33]

On 25 January 2011, the tensions simmering in society burst out in Cairo when thousands gathered in Tahrir Square, demanding an end to Mubarak's regime. As clashes broke out between protesters and the president's supporters, Mubarak announced that he would not seek re-election and would negotiate with opposition groups. But it was not enough, especially when he later confirmed that he would see out his term in office. On 11 February, however, Vice-President Omar Suleiman announced that Mubarak was resigning, power being transferred to the high command of the armed forces.

In June 2012, elections were held which saw a narrow win for the US-educated engineer Dr Mohamed Morsi's Freedom and Justice Party. Hailed as a victory for the democratic process, Morsi's government came under increasing opposition, in part because many believed that it was pursuing an Islamist agenda. As street protests broke out once again, the army deposed him in July 2013. In September, the Muslim Brotherhood was declared illegal. Morsi was put on trial and eventually collapsed in court and died on 17 June 2019. With the removal of the Freedom and Justice Party government, power passed to the defence minister, General (later Field Marshal) Abdel Fattah al-Sisi, who was elected president in May 2014.[34]

The Syrian Civil War

On the death of President Assad in 2000, power had passed seamlessly to his son, Bashar al-Assad. His designated successor had originally been his son Basil, but he had been killed in a car crash in 1994. Bashar al-Assad was then studying in London for his intended career as an ophthalmologist but was recalled home. When his father died in June 2000, the regime's elite ensured his succession to the presidency. His father had kept Syria on a tight rein, particularly ensuring that the military and security service were dominated by his fellow Alawite officers. While he had not allowed his people freedom in the Western sense, Hafez al-Assad had given them stability, no small matter when compared with what had been happening in neighbouring Lebanon and Iraq. Unlike his father, Bashar al-Assad was familiar with the West. Not only had he been studying in London but his Sunni wife, Asma, had been working in finance in the City of London. The essential problem facing Assad, in common with other Middle Eastern rulers, was how to meet the aspirations of a young and educated population, while retaining the support of the established elite.

Opposition to the regime surfaced not in the capital but in the southern city of Dera'a where a group of children who had daubed anti-government slogans were arrested. When demonstrators called for their release on 15 March 2011, four of them were killed. This action was followed by mass demonstrations that were not confined to Der'aa but spread to other provincial cities and even parts of Damascus. Attempts by Assad to calm the situation failed.

By the summer, demonstrations were giving way to violence, with the regime's forces facing the opposition Free Syrian Army, which attracted sympathy in the West. This military move was followed by the creation of an opposition Syrian National Council in Istanbul, which joined other groups to form the Syrian National Coalition. Much of the country fell to the rebel forces, although they lacked stability. By any reckoning, the country was in a state of civil war. There were the expected accusations and denials of atrocities. The opposition attracted support from the country's Sunni majority, but, although there were desertions, the government retained the loyalty of the armed forces, with the major asset of the air force. Support also remained strong in the minority communities, especially but by no means exclusively among the Alawite. It was also backed by Hezbollah members from Lebanon as well as Iraqi Shi'as. A critical intervention came in September 2015 with the involvement of Russia against Islamist extremists. Since there was little appetite in the West for a competition with Russia in the region or for any kind of repetition of Iraq, support for the opposition was muted. As a military solution seemed to elude either side, after ten years of war President al-Assad was still in power. An estimated 400,000 Syrians had been killed, while millions of men, women, and children became refugees, causing severe strain in Lebanon, Jordan, and Turkey.[35]

Islamic State

Despite the success of the United States' military surge in Iraq in 2007, discontent continued to fester amongst the Sunnis, who felt discriminated against by the predominantly Shi'a government. In 2012, trouble escalated between the two communities, foreshadowing what was to emerge. It seems that this sentiment was shared by the young Iraqi Sunni Abu Bakr al-Baghdadi, who had spent some time in US detention. This experience may well have helped radicalise him, as it did other young men. In 2010, he had been chosen as leader of a new Sunni group, Islamic State of Iraq, which was bitterly opposed to the Shi'as and was attracting some former officers of Saddam Hussein's army.

In 2013, having renamed itself Islamic State in Iraq and Syria (ISIS) and drawing support in both countries, the organisation began an armed campaign that enjoyed remarkable initial success. In June 2014, it proclaimed a caliphate, which attracted adherents from around the world. From its initial base in the strongly Sunni Anbar Province, its fighters defeated the Iraqi forces sent against them, capturing the key city of Mosul and positioning themselves to threaten Baghdad only forty miles distant. An offensive westward gained them territory in Syria, where the city of Raqqa became a major base. Their strong presence in Syria further complicated the ongoing tragedy there.

In the area they now controlled, ISIS members made it clear that the old Sykes–Picot border between Syria and Iraq no longer existed. Atrocities were committed against other religious communities, with the plight of the Yezidis attracting international attention. Foreign hostages – three American, two British, two Japanese, and a Jordanian pilot – were murdered. In their pursuit of a radical Islamic state, pre-Islamic monuments were destroyed, most notably at the UNESCO World Heritage Site of Palmyra in Syria after its capture in May 2015.

The actions perpetrated by ISIS members provoked an armed reaction. On 7 August 2014, President Obama authorised air attacks on ISIS targets in Iraq, which were later extended to Syria. Some Middle Eastern aircraft also took part. Britain's Royal Air Force and other Western countries flew operations against bases in Iraq and in Syria. On the ground, hostile Syrians, a reorganised Iraqi Army, and the Kurdish armed forces, the Peshmerga, joined the campaign. After a bitter siege in July 2017, the Iraqi Army avenged its earlier defeat by retaking Mosul. Their success was followed in Syria in October when Raqqa fell. With the loss of its two strongholds, the military defeat of ISIS was inevitable. On 26 October 2019, during the Republican presidency of Donald J. Trump, US special forces mounted an attack on al-Baghdadi's headquarters, which had been identified in north-west Syria, in the course of which the ISIS leader died. The movement's threat to Iraq and Syria had gone, but the power of its ideology remained intact.[36]

'Normalisation'

Trump's administration saw the launch of two new major initiatives. The template for an Israeli–Palestinian peace settlement entitled 'Peace to Prosperity', which was released on 28 January 2020, had both an economic and a political dimension.

What the economic element of the plan envisaged was an ambitious $50 billion investment over ten years, focused on both the public and private Palestinian sectors, as well as economic links with neighbouring economies. The political part was to involve the recognition of Israel as the nation-state of the Jewish people and the future state of Palestine as the nation-state of the Palestinian people, with Israel being responsible for security in the whole area west of the River Jordan. The plan was rejected by the Palestinians.

In the summer of 2020, negotiations for the normalisation of relations between the United Arab Emirates and Israel were concluded together with the Americans. Joining them was Bahrain. Termed the Abraham Accords, the agreements were signed at a ceremony in Washington on 15 September. The Accords were subsequently signed by Sudan and Morocco.[37]

Jerusalem and Gaza

The following year Jerusalem yet again provided the spark for another armed confrontation between Israel and Palestine, which served to remind the world of the intensity of their conflict. The crisis was provoked by a bitter property dispute in Sheikh Jarrah, a mainly Arab district of East Jerusalem whose normally bustling Salah al-Din Street leads directly to the Damascus Gate, one of the principal entrances into the Old City. Fearing property encroachments by Jewish Israelis, Palestinians assembled at the Damascus Gate and the Haram al-Sharif/Temple Mount area, where serious clashes with the security forces erupted. In an apparent response, on 10 May 2021, thousands of rockets were launched from Hamas-controlled Gaza into Tel Aviv and southern Israeli towns. Israel's Iron Dome anti-missile defensive system intercepted most of them, but some penetrated, inflicting casualties – thirteen of them fatal – and causing damage to property.

The IDF responded with a succession of air strikes on Gaza, their avowed purpose being to disrupt the intricate system of tunnels that Hamas had constructed. Given the highly congested nature of Gaza, buildings were destroyed and some 240 killed. Violent clashes also broke out between Arabs and Israelis in several Israeli towns. Egypt and the US, under the new administration of President Joseph R. Biden, actively pursued a ceasefire, which was implemented on 21 May. In announcing the ceasefire, Biden affirmed his belief that 'the Palestinians and Israelis equally deserve to live safely and securely and to enjoy equal measures of freedom, prosperity, and democracy'. A package of some $360 million was promised by Secretary of State Antony J. Blinken to help the West Bank and Gaza, while Israel was to be assisted with the rebuilding of its Iron Dome defensive system.[38]

A clear indication of the Middle East's role in the world's economy, not to mention its strategic dimension, came at the meeting of the G20 world leaders held in New Delhi in September 2023. The region was at the heart of the memorandum of understanding for an 'India–Middle East–Europe

Economic Corridor' announced by the leaders of a key grouping of world economies: the United States, India, Saudi Arabia, the United Arab Emirates, France, Germany, Italy, and the European Union. Its stated purpose was to link Europe, the Middle East, and Asia with a railway and ports to drive economic development.[39] On a separate track, there was speculation that other Arab countries might move towards a normalisation of relations with Israel similar to the Abraham Accords, as Morocco and Sudan had done. Some saw this process as being linked to progress for the Palestinians, however.

For a while Israeli politics seemed to be edging in new directions, prompted in part by the range of political parties, each with its own agenda. In March 2021, a new coalition government had taken office. Naftali Bennett of the Yamina party became prime minister in an alternating arrangement with Yair Lapid of Yesh Atid, with former IDF Chief of Staff Benny Gantz of Kahol Lavan, later the National Unity party, as defence minister. Mansour Abbas of the United Arab List was also included in the coalition. When the coalition collapsed in June 2022, Lapid assumed the resulting caretaker premiership. In the ensuing November election, Netanyahu once again became premier as head of a right-wing coalition with Otzma Yehudit and the Religious Zionist Party. The new government set in hand controversial proposals for judicial reforms, which provoked widespread protest demonstrations, but these were overtaken when the state was confronted by a crisis of unprecedented proportions.

The Israel–Hamas war

Ever since the fedayeen guerrilla raids of the early 1950s and Ben-Gurion's Operation Black Arrow in 1955, Gaza had never been far from an epicentre of the Israeli–Palestinian conflict, but the war that broke out in 2023 was both more prolonged, as well as far more destructive of lives and property, than anything that came before. On 7 October 2023, Israel came under a two-pronged attack mounted by Hamas and its Palestine Islamic Jihad allies from the Gaza Strip, which the organisation had controlled since ousting its Fatah rival in 2007. The assault came almost fifty years to the day after Egypt and Syria launched the 1973 war. Barrages of rockets were fired at targets in southern Israel while hundreds of heavily armed gunmen broke through the fortified border fence, some by paraglider. In the course of what was clearly a carefully planned operation, their targets involved military installations but also civilians and kibbutzim close to the border. In the latter, massacres, including of women and children, were perpetrated and atrocities committed. Amongst those attending the popular open-air Supernova music festival just inside Israel, several hundred were killed, while others were seized as hostages. In all, it is believed that some 1,200 were killed and around 252 taken hostage into the Gaza Strip, where they could be hidden throughout Hamas's tunnel network.

Faced with the nature and extent of this attack, the Israeli government declared war on Hamas, triggering various measures. A blockade of the Gaza Strip was put in place. Two crossings were affected – Erez and a commercial crossing at Keren Shalom in the south-east – while the Rafah Crossing in the south was controlled by Egypt. A war cabinet was established which included, alongside Netanyahu, Defence Minister Yoav Gallant, a Likud colleague and former general, and opposition politician Benny Gantz. Reservists were mobilised in preparation for what was termed Operation Swords of Iron, which began almost immediately with air strikes on Gaza in preparation for a ground assault – the objectives being the elimination of Hamas and the freeing of the hostages.[40]

On 18 October, speaking in Tel Aviv, Biden set out his response to the Hamas attacks in what became a template for his administration's subsequent policies. Castigating Hamas's actions as 'pure, unadulterated evil', he assured Israelis that the United States would never let them 'be alone'. Israel's qualitative military edge would be sustained, including its Iron Dome defence system. He also announced a humanitarian aid programme for Gaza and the West Bank. Israel and the Palestinians, he counselled, should 'both live safely, in security, in dignity, and in peace', which for him meant a 'two state solution', and stated that the US would work towards 'Israel's greater integration with its neighbors'.[41]

By 28 October the IDF was engaged in full-scale air and ground operations in the Gaza Strip. As in previous Gaza engagements, it was an asymmetrical conflict. With an estimated upwards of 20,000 armed fighters embedded in a complex and extensive tunnel network, Hamas held some military assets; but they could not match the IDF's heavy weaponry, much less its unassailable air power, which was able to mount regular strikes. With an estimated 2.1 million people living in the densely populated and highly urbanised areas of Gaza City, Khan Younis, and Rafah, along with the refugee camps, it was inevitable that civilian casualties would rapidly mount.[42]

Given the intensity of the fighting, there were fears of an escalation into a wider regional war. In the West Bank there were serious clashes between activist Israeli settlers and Palestinians, but despite the fact that there were fatalities, there was no repetition of the Intifadas of 1987 and 2000. Able to deploy an estimated fighting strength in excess of 40,000 and a formidable arsenal of rockets, Hezbollah's potential to mount attacks from its strongholds in southern Lebanon could never be discounted. Although there were repeated cross-border clashes which resulted in substantial evacuations, there were no immediate full-scale offensives.[43]

Active support for Hamas came from Yemen's Houthis, who mounted a series of attacks on shipping in the critical Bab al-Mandeb Strait at the entrance to the Red Sea, claiming that their targets had links with Israel. After a ship was sunk, shipping companies rerouted their voyages around southern Africa, with obvious implications for journey time and cost. On 22 and 23 January, American and British aircraft began strikes against Houthi targets, while several countries sent warships to the area.[44]

On 1 April 2024 a strike on an Iranian complex in Damascus killed thirteen people, including two senior Islamic Revolutionary Guard Corps officers. Assuming Israeli responsibility, Iran threatened retaliation, while Biden affirmed that American support for Israel was 'ironclad'. The Iranian response soon came on 13 April, with the launch of a barrage of over 300 missiles and drones targeted on Israeli territory. Almost all of them were successfully intercepted by Israel's Iron Dome anti-missile system, with the help of aircraft from the United States and several other countries. Even so, neither side seemed anxious to escalate the situation, Israel's apparent response being an attack on facilities in the central Iranian city of Isfahan. This tense and potentially dangerous situation did not, however, escalate into a regional war as many had feared.[45]

As the weeks became months with no immediate end to the conflict in sight, diplomatic efforts to resolve the crisis were led by a triumvirate of Qatar, Egypt, and the United States. On 21 November, Biden announced that they had secured an agreement for the release of hostages. As a result, over 100 hostages were freed in return for a number of Palestinian prisoners.[46]

The mounting humanitarian crisis was addressed by a range of countries and agencies, including *inter alia* those of the United Nations, the World Health Organization, the United Arab Emirates, Jordan, the European Union, and the United Kingdom, as well as major charities. The immediate challenges facing them were access, distribution, and the safety of staff. On 21 October 2023 an initial aid convoy of twenty lorries was permitted to enter Gaza, well short of daily requirements, followed in November by two fuel trucks. Since the IDF was determined that supplies should not reach Hamas, there were delays at checkpoints.

While the size of convoys subsequently increased, distribution of their aid in the face of ongoing hostilities remained problematic. The police were reluctant to help. At the end of February 2024, over 100 people were killed when trying to access an aid delivery in north Gaza. This was followed on 3

March by the use of air drops by American and Jordanian aircraft to parachute aid into Gaza amid warnings of famine. In his annual State of the Union Address to Congress on 7 March, Biden announced that the United States military would construct a temporary pier on the Gaza coast enabling ships to deliver aid, which was able to commence operations on 17 May. He also used the speech to reaffirm his view that 'the only solution to the situation is a two-state solution over time'.

On 1 April, seven aid workers from the charity World Central Kitchen were killed in an air strike. Confessing himself 'outraged and heartbroken', Biden stated that Israel had not done enough to protect aid workers or civilians. Referring to the tripartite negotiations in Cairo, he confirmed that the United States was 'pushing hard for an immediate ceasefire as part of a hostage deal'.[47]

Negotiations continued into May 2024 but the two protagonists could not be brought to an agreement on whether there should be a temporary pause in the fighting or a ceasefire, which Israel believed would favour the Hamas position. Such was the scale of the IDF's air and ground campaign, it was estimated that those killed numbered in the tens of thousands, many of them women and children, while much of Gaza's physical infrastructure had been devastated. As the number of casualties mounted, so too did the pressures on medical facilities, hit by medicine shortages and power interruptions, with Gaza's main hospital, Al-Shifa, particularly badly affected. With the IDF engaged in northern and central Gaza, people were told to move south to the Rafah area. As they did so, some 1.5 million were estimated to be in temporary shelters, many of them lacking clean water and sanitation.[48]

Negotiations in abeyance, the clear focus was directed on Rafah. Arguing that it was Hamas's remaining stronghold, the Israelis signalled their intention to mount a major operation there. It soon became apparent that there was clear water between them and the Biden administration, with Blinken confirming on 1 May during a visit to Israel that they would not support a major military operation there without a plan to ensure that civilians were not harmed, and that they had not seen one. Then, in what was a major *démarche*, a pause was initiated on a shipment of 2,000-pound and 500-pound bombs.[49] Although IDF forces entered eastern Rafah, ordering inhabitants to leave for a safer location, there was no immediate major offensive.

On 22 May, Norway, Ireland, and Spain announced their intention to recognise Palestine as a state, which they did a week later – a move welcomed by Palestinians but excoriated by Israelis. Slovenia soon joined them. Hostilities continued, with a Hamas rocket attack targeted at Tel Aviv followed by an Israeli air strike on an area of Rafah which reportedly killed senior Hamas figures, but also dozens of civilians who were sheltering there.

After months of negotiations, on 31 May Biden presented what he said was 'an update on my efforts to end the crisis in Gaza'. Noting that 'the past eight months have marked heartbreaking pain ... of those whose loved ones were slaughtered by Hamas terrorists on October 7th', and that the 'Palestinian people have endured sheer hell in this war ... Too many innocent people have been killed, including thousands of children', Biden said that Israel had offered a roadmap 'for an enduring ceasefire and the release of all hostages' and that the Qataris had transmitted this to Hamas.

The proposal, he said, fell into three phases. Phase one, to last for six weeks, would see a complete ceasefire and an IDF withdrawal from populated areas. A number of hostages, including women, the elderly, and the wounded, would be exchanged for the release of Palestinian prisoners. Humanitarian aid would be increased to 600 trucks a day. During this period, there would be negotiations for phase two, which would see a permanent end to hostilities, the release of remaining hostages, and an IDF withdrawal. Phase three would see a major reconstruction plan for Gaza'. Confirming that it was 'what we have been asking for', he said that 'we cannot lose this moment'. He also held out the possibility of a normalisation agreement with Saudi Arabia.

The following day, the United States, Egypt, and Qatar issued a joint statement urging Hamas and Israel to finalise the agreement along the principles that Biden had outlined, while the plan was immediately endorsed by the leaders of the G7 countries. Notwithstanding such influential endorsement for what Biden had announced, fighting continued. On 8 June, as the conflict passed the eighth-month mark, Israeli forces successfully freed four hostages, with one of the rescuers being killed. The operation reportedly cost scores of Palestinian lives. The following day, tensions simmering in Israeli politics surfaced when Benny Gantz announced his resignation from the war cabinet, resulting in its dissolution. As Blinken embarked on his eighth mission to the Middle East, the UN Security Council added its voice to those supporting the plan that Biden had announced.[50]

12

Conclusion

As the Middle East enters the second quarter of the new century, many of the legacies of the First World War remain to be resolved, and its effects can still be seen more than a century afterwards. This is especially true in Iraq, Lebanon, and Syria, the political borders of which reflect agreements that were made during the war and in its immediate aftermath, while Yemen has had its own distinctive problems. Meanwhile, the tragic intensity of the Israeli–Palestinian conflict has held the two protagonists in its bloody grip in 2024 – also, to some extent, a result of decisions made during and in the immediate aftermath of the war.

These were decisions reached by imperial statesmen in London and Paris and their local agents, and they were taken for imperial reasons without reference to the wishes of the inhabitants of the region, with one exception. Britain negotiated with the Hashemite Emir Hussein, helping to stimulate the Arab Revolt of 1916, but the Arabs and the British were later to dispute what the latter had promised. One champion of the Arab cause, T. E. Lawrence, keenly felt that the Arabs' participation in the war had been ill-rewarded.

The Zionist leader Dr Chaim Weizmann was closely consulted during the war and at the Paris Peace Conference over the evolution of the 1917 Balfour Declaration and its implementation as the subsequent British Mandate for Palestine. Otherwise, the boundaries of the Arab areas about to be freed from four centuries of Turkish rule were an Anglo-French *fiat* foreshadowed in the Sykes–Picot Agreement of 1916. Here was the seedbed for the subsequent instability of Iraq, Syria, and Lebanon, as well as the Israeli–Palestinian conflict that was to emerge as the region's most intractable dispute. All these problems remain evident a century later.

In the event, British and French rule under the mandate's system proved to be ephemeral. Britain's position in the Middle East was to be a vital Allied asset in the Second World War, but it could not be sustained for long. Undermined by the outcome of the 1956 Suez Crisis, the remaining British presence in the Gulf was terminated twelve years later.

Other parts of the Middle East were largely unaffected by the decisions made during the First World War. Egypt emerged ready to throw off the protectorate that Britain had unilaterally proclaimed in 1914. The year 1919 saw a revolution that began the process, albeit protractedly, towards full independence, which culminated in the humiliation of Britain and France in 1956. The real transformation of Egypt began with the revolution of 1952 and the subsequent presidency of Nasser, whose initial foreign policy successes were applauded not just at home but throughout the Arab world. Although Nasser has a claim to be remembered as the greatest Arab leader of the twentieth century, Nasserism as a political force did not survive him, partly because his successor, Anwar al-Sadat, had a different agenda.

Saudi Arabia only emerged in the 1920s, when Ibn Saud defeated his Hashemite rivals to forge a new kingdom. The Emirates of the Gulf and Muscat and Oman were part of the economic periphery of British India, barely touched by the world conflict. All of this was to change dramatically over the course of the century; with their relatively small populations and abundant oil and natural gas wealth, Saudi Arabia, Kuwait, Bahrain, Qatar, the United Arab Emirates, and Oman were to be transformed into major participants in the world economy. OPEC and OAPEC proved to be powerful vehicles for the petroleum industry.

The burgeoning skylines of the Arabian Peninsula's major cities told their own story. Based upon their formidable economic wealth, these countries sought to position themselves in new ways. One of them was to secure a leading position in international sport – golf, tennis, and motor and horse racing being obvious examples. Qatar's staging of the 2022 FIFA World Cup confirmed the Arab world's aspirations for a global sporting role. Tourism, too, was actively promoted, drawing on the region's rich heritage, the Louvre Abu Dhabi being an imaginative cultural collaboration with France. Airlines were major carriers, while airports such as Doha International Airport in Qatar became international hubs.

Despite their relatively small populations, their economic strength and strategic position meant that the Gulf states became key players in the region's affairs, as Qatar has demonstrated during the 2023–24 conflict. Positioned as a nodal point in Europe's maritime links with the economies of the

Middle East and the Indo-Pacific region, Yemen was very different.

Other Middle Eastern countries that lacked these advantages had to meet the economic, social, and political challenges of population increase, with that of Egypt rising tenfold since the early twentieth century.[1] Egypt could, of course, rely on its unique heritage to attract visitors, while Jordan featured the 'rose-red city' of Petra as a tourist attraction beyond compare. That said, the region's international dynamic turned, to a large extent, on the policies pursued by Egypt, Saudi Arabia, and Israel. For its part, based upon a well-developed third-level educational system and partly prompted by defence needs, Israel became a leading high-tech economy.

While Christianity retained a presence in the Middle East, most obviously so in Lebanon and Egypt, Arab society was overwhelmingly defined by Islam, in both its Sunni and Shi'a forms. Secular Arab nationalism was repeatedly challenged by Islamist movements, of which the Muslim Brotherhood spanned the decades despite official persecution. For some women, the shedding of the veil by Huda Shaarawi and her supporters was a sign of progress, while for many others wearing it is still a symbol of their Muslim faith and identity in a changing world a century later.

Fundamentalist, anti-Western Islamist belief found its most extreme expressions in al-Qaeda and ISIS. The elimination of the latter's territorial bases did not render it incapable of mounting attacks in the Middle East and elsewhere; in March 2024 one of its affiliates claimed responsibility for a massacre at a music venue in Moscow in which over 130 people were killed. Muslim, especially Shi'a, sentiment derived great encouragement from the success of the Iranian Revolution. In Israel, the secularism of early pioneers like Ben-Gurion was challenged by the emergence of ultra-Orthodox Jewish political parties. The Palestinians became split between the secular Fatah and the strongly religious Hamas. On the international front, the tensions between the two forms of Islam surfaced in the mutual suspicions between Saudi Arabia and the predominantly Sunni Arab states of the Gulf on the one hand and Shi'a Iran on the other.

With the Balfour Declaration and the adoption of the Palestine Mandate by Britain, the future of Palestine increasingly entered the political discourse, even more so as the extent of the Holocaust began to emerge during the course of the Second World War. With the Nazis' tragic genocide of the European Jews revealed in 1945, Palestine's future became a matter of intense debate, culminating in the independence of the State of Israel in 1948 and the Palestinian al-Nakba. The subsequent centrality of the Israeli–Palestinian conflict can be seen in the succession of five Middle Eastern wars involving Israel and its Arab neighbours and in two Palestinian Intifadas. The Israel–Hamas war that erupted in October 2023 consolidated the legacy of conflict between the protagonists.

The United States became intimately involved in Middle Eastern affairs, most obviously so in leading coalitions to end Saddam Hussein's invasion of Kuwait, and then again in 2003 in a campaign culminating in his overthrow. Kissinger engaged in intense diplomatic efforts to secure a ceasefire in the 1973 Arab–Israeli War and then to negotiate disengagement agreements. America's continuing engagement with the region was partly prompted by the Cold War, which formed a backdrop to events there – as did the invasion that Russia launched against Ukraine on 24 February 2022, igniting fears of renewed East–West tension. The widening gulf between Russia and three other permanent members of the United Nations Security Council, the United States, France and the United Kingdom – all strongly supportive of Ukraine – did not seem to augur well for the success of a binding resolution on prospects for peace in the Middle East (although one was passed in June 2024).

A series of Israeli–Palestinian peace initiatives, largely brokered by the Americans, had mixed results, partly as a result of the truism that in the American political cycle an incoming administration brings with it its own agenda. The 1969 Rogers peace plan really marked the start, while others followed: Carter secured the Egyptian–Israeli peace treaty in 1979, the 1982 Reagan plan never really survived the tragic events in Lebanon, George H. W. Bush brokered the Madrid conference, and under Clinton an Israeli peace treaty was agreed with Jordan. Clinton then came tantalisingly close to achieving an Israeli–Palestinian settlement at Camp David in 2000, when both he and Israeli Premier Barak made far-reaching concessions, but Arafat could not agree. George W. Bush launched his Road Map for Peace in the wake of the Iraq war and the Obama administration also pursued major initiatives. The Trump administration advanced the Peace to Prosperity plan while securing the Abraham Accords, and during the 2023–24 conflict Biden and Secretary of State Blinken were actively engaged from the very beginning in months of negotiations.

Negotiations on the Israeli–Palestinian conflict came to turn on the creation of a viable two-state solution that would reconcile Israel's security needs and concerns with Palestinian hopes of sovereignty. During the Israel–Hamas war this message was consistently driven home by the Biden administration, as well as by friends and allies in the Middle East and Europe.

In the West Bank and East Jerusalem Israeli settlements were extensive, with their combined populations numbering some 468,000 and 236,000 respectively.[2] The aspirations of the Palestinian refugees and the nature of the border were also points of issue. The future of Gaza seemed especially problematic, as it had been for decades, but was brought into sharp focus by the events of the war that broke out in 2023. But above all, there was the apparently intractable problem of Jerusalem, with its holy places sacred to Jews, Christians, and Muslims.

Neither Israelis nor Palestinians are ready to compromise on positions that go to the very core of who they are. A resolution of the gulf between them remains – like the Greek calends – elusive. Here, it may be thought, is the ultimate contested land.

Acknowledgements

I am grateful to the following people, who have provided their recollections and observations over many years: Sir Harold Beeley, Sir Francis Evans, Ambassador Loy W. Henderson, Albert Hourani, Dr Floresca Karanasou, Dr Paul Lalor, Sir John Martin, Secretary of State Dean Rusk, and Professor L. F. Rushbrook Williams. I am also grateful to Professor William V. Wallace, who first pointed me in the direction of the Middle East. Keith Kyle, my colleague as visiting professor of history, spent hours discussing the Middle East with me. None has been quoted directly, but their insights are there just the same.

Dr Barbara Schwepcke and Harry Hall of Haus Publishing encouraged me with this project from the start, while Alice Horne and Ed Doxey were model copyeditors. Much of the text of the original edition was written during the coronavirus lockdown in the spring of 2020, when my neighbours Alan, Lydia, and Callum Peters gave unstinting help. As ever, my friend and former colleague Professor Alan Sharp and my wife Grace read through the manuscript with care and perception. The latter gave unfailing support throughout, informed by her own experience of the Middle East. Any errors are, of course, my own.

In the transliteration of names, I have tried to standard-ise on the usage most familiar to English-speaking readers, hence, Feisal rather than Faysal and Hussein rather than Husayn. The notes to each chapter indicate the main sources on which the account is based and by no means reflect the enormous literature that the subject has generated or that has been consulted.

T. G. F., June 2024

Notes

Crown copyright material is reproduced by permission of the Controller of His Majesty's Stationery Office.

1. The Middle East on the Eve of War

1. D. G. Hogarth, *The Nearer East* (London, 1905).
2. 'Turkey' in *Encyclopaedia Britannica*, vol. 27 (11th edn., Cambridge, 1911), 426–7.
3. Ibid.
4. W. B. Fisher, *The Middle East: A Physical, Social and Regional Geography* (London, 1950).
5. S. H. Longrigg, *Oil in the Middle East: Its Discovery and Development* (London, 1954), 1–47.
6. S. McMeekin, *The Berlin–Baghdad Express: The Ottoman Empire and Germany's Bid for World Power 1898–1918* (London, 2010).
7. R. McNamara, *The Hashemites: The Dream of Arabia* (London, 2009), 7–26.
8. J. Jones & N. P. Ridout, *A History of Modern Oman* (Cambridge, 2015).
9. 'Egypt' in *Encyclopaedia Britannica*, vol. 9 (11th edn., Cambridge, 1911), 21–130.

10. J. Marlowe, *The Making of the Suez Canal* (London, 1964).

11. B. Meier, *Verdi*, tr. R. Smith (London, 2003), 103–9.

12. J. Thompson, *A History of Egypt: From Earliest Times to the Present* (Cairo; New York, 2009), 253–72.

13. W. Laqueur, *A History of Zionism* (New York, 1989); N. Sokolow, *History of Zionism 1600–1800*, two vols. (London; New York, 1919).

14. G. Antonius, *The Arab Awakening* (London, 1938); C. Ernest Dawn, *From Ottomanism to Arabism: Essays on the Origins of Arab Nationalism* (Urbana, IL, 1973).

2. The Remaking of the Middle East

1. H. Strachan, *The First World War, Volume I: To Arms* (Oxford, 2003), 644–93.

2. T. G. Fraser with A. Mango & R. McNamara, *The Makers of the Modern Middle East*, 2nd rev. and updated edn. (London, 2015), 50–1.

3. Strachan, *The First World War*, op. cit., 729–44.

4. L. Tarazi Fawaz, *A Land of Aching Hearts: The Middle East in the Great War* (Cambridge, MA; London, 2014), 233–74.

5. C. S. Sykes, *The Man Who Created the Middle East: A Story of Empire, Conflict and the Sykes–Picot Agreement* (London, 2017).

6. E. Rogan, *The Fall of the Ottomans: The Great War in the Middle East, 1914–1920* (London, 2015), 129–58, 185–215.

7. C. Townshend, *When God Made Hell: The British*

Invasion of Mesopotamia and the Creation of Iraq, 1914–1921 (London, 2010).

8. Sir Henry McMahon to Sherif Hussein, 24 October 1915, in T. G. Fraser, ed., *The Middle East 1914–1979* (London, 1980), 12–13. See also Sykes, *The Man Who Created the Middle East*, *op. cit.*; T. J. Paris, *In Defence of Britain's Middle Eastern Empire: A Life of Sir Gilbert Clayton* (Eastbourne, 2016).

9. T. G. Fraser, ed., *The Middle East*, *op. cit.*, 12–13.

10. E. Kedourie, *In the Anglo-Arab Labyrinth: The McMahon-Husayn Correspondence and its Interpretations 1914–1939* (Cambridge, 1976); T. J. Paris, *In Defence of Britain's Middle Eastern Empire*, *op. cit.*, 121–37.

11. C. S. Sykes, *The Man Who Created the Middle East*, *op. cit.*

12. T. E. Lawrence, *Seven Pillars of Wisdom: A Triumph* (London, 1935), 91, 126; J. Wilson, *Lawrence of Arabia: The Authorized Biography of T. E. Lawrence* (London, 1989).

13. T. G. Fraser, *Chaim Weizmann: The Zionist Dream* (London, 2009).

14. T. G. Fraser, *Chaim Weizmann*, *op. cit.*; L. Stein, *The Balfour Declaration* (London, 1961); J. Schneer, *The Balfour Declaration: The Origins of the Arab–Israeli Conflict* (London, 2010); British Cabinet discussions, 3 September, 4 October, 31 October 1917, in T. G. Fraser, ed., *The Middle East*, *op. cit.* 13–18.

15. C. Townshend, *When God Made Hell*, *op. cit.*

16. M. Hughes, ed., *Allenby in Palestine: The Middle East*

Correspondence of Field Marshal Viscount Allenby, June 1917–October 1919 (Stroud, 2004); E. Rogan, *The Fall of the Ottomans, op. cit.*, 326–83.

17. T. E. Lawrence, *Seven Pillars of Wisdom, op. cit.*, 643–60.

3. The New Imperialists Under Challenge

1. A. Sharp, *The Versailles Settlement: Peacemaking after the First World War, 1919–1923* (3rd edn., London, 2018).
2. T. G. Fraser with A. Mango & R. McNamara, *The Makers of the Modern Middle East, op. cit.*, 115–43.
3. *Ibid.*, 143–9.
4. *Ibid.*, 149–50.
5. S. S. Lanfranchi, *Casting off the Veil: The Life of Huda Shaarawi, Egypt's First Feminist* (London, 2015), 66–8.
6. T. G. Fraser, 'Egypt in 1919: Founding Year of the American University in Cairo' in A. Byrne, ed., *East-West Divan: In Memory of Werner Mark Linz* (London, 2014), 21–35; M. Hughes, *Allenby in Palestine, op. cit.*, 228–47; Field-Marshal Viscount Wavell, *Allenby in Egypt*, vol. 2 of *Allenby: A Study in Greatness* (London, 1943).
7. T. J. Paris, *In Defence of Britain's Middle Eastern Empire, op. cit.*, 325–45; H. Carter, *The Tomb of Tutankhamen, Discovered by the Late Earl of Carnarvon and Howard Carter* (London, 1972); J. Thompson, *A History of Egypt, op. cit.*, 278.

8. T. G. Fraser with A. Mango & R. McNamara, *The Makers of the Modern Middle East*, op. cit., 157–60.

9. *Ibid.*, 182–97.

10. R. McNamara, *The Hashemites*, op. cit., 120–3; J. McHugo, *Syria: From the Great War to Civil War* (London, 2014), 66–7.

11. C. Tripp, *A History of Iraq* (3rd edn., Cambridge, 2007), 30–44; J. Marlowe, *Late Victorian: The Life of Sir Arnold Wilson* (London, 1967), 212–31; A. T. Wilson, 'Preface' in *Loyalties: Mesopotamia, a personal and historical record*, vol. 2 (London, 1936).

12. T. G. Fraser with A. Mango & R. McNamara, *The Makers of the Modern Middle East*, op. cit., 237–9; M. Gilbert, *Winston S. Churchill: Volume 4, 1916–1922* (London, 1975), 544–99.

13. Viscount Samuel, *Memoirs* (London, 1945), 150–1; T. G. Fraser, *Chaim Weizmann*, op. cit., 107–118.

14. P. Mattar, *The Mufti of Jerusalem: Al-Hajj Amin Al-Husayni and the Palestinian National Movement* (New York, 1988).

15. *Statement of British Policy in Palestine*, 3 June 1922 (Cmd. 1700, 1922) in T. G. Fraser, *The Middle East*, op. cit.

16. P. Aarts & C. Roelants, *Saudi Arabia: A Kingdom in Peril* (London, 2015), 6–8.

4. The Middle East in Transition

1. Article 2, *Palestine Royal Commission Report* (Cmd. 5479, 1937), 34–7.

2. J. McHugo, *Syria, op. cit.*, 75–90; L. Parsons, *The Commander: Fawzi al-Qawuqji and the Fight for Arab Independence 1914–1948* (London, 2016).

3. W. W. Harris, *Lebanon: A History, 600–2011* (Oxford, 2015), 173–85.

4. Anon. (Chatham House research staff); Royal Institute of International Affairs. Information Dept., *Great Britain and Palestine 1915–1939* (London, 1939).

5. T. Segev, tr. H. Watzman, *A State at Any Cost: The Life of David Ben-Gurion* (London, 2019).

6. Anglo-American Committee of Inquiry on Jewish Problems in Palestine and Europe, *A Survey of Palestine,* vol. 2 (London, 1946), 956–62.

7. *Ibid.*, 945–55.

8. T. G. Fraser, *Chaim Weizmann, op. cit.*, 125–6.

9. *Ibid.*, 126–30.

10. C. Tripp, *A History of Iraq, op. cit.*, 44–74.

11. L. R. Murphy, *The American University in Cairo: 1919–1987* (Cairo, 1987).

12. S. S. Lanfranchi, *Casting off the Veil, op. cit.*

13. P. J. Vatikiotis, *Egypt: From Muhammad Ali to Sadat* (2nd edn., London, 1980), 327–30.

14. T. G. Fraser, 'The Middle East and the Coming of War' in F. McDonough, ed., *The Origins of the Second World War: An International Perspective* (London, 2011).

15. Anglo-American Committee of Inquiry on Jewish Problems in Palestine and Europe, *A Survey of Palestine,* vol. 1 (London, 1946), 35–45; T. Segev, *A State at Any Cost, op. cit.*, 276–7.

16. T. G. Fraser, 'Sir Reginald Coupland, the Round

Table, and the Problem of Divided Societies' in A. Bosco & A. May, eds., *The Round Table, the Empire/Commonwealth and British Foreign Policy* (London, 1997), 407–19; T. G. Fraser, Chapter 6 in *Partition in Ireland, India and Palestine: Theory and Practice* (London, 1984); *Palestine Royal Commission Report, op. cit.*

17. T. G. Fraser, 'A Crisis of Leadership: Weizmann and the Zionist Reactions to the Peel Commission's Proposals, 1937–8', *Journal of Contemporary History*, 23/4 (Oct. 1988), 657–80.

18. T. G. Fraser, 'The Middle East and the Coming of War', *op. cit.*

19. *Palestine Partition Commission Report, op. cit.* (Cmd. 5854: 1938).

20. T. G. Fraser, 'The Middle East and the Coming of War', *op. cit.*

21. T. Segev, *A State at Any Cost, op. cit.*, 284–8.

5. The Second World War and the Middle East

1. The military campaigns in Egypt of such commanders as Wavell, O'Connor, Auchinleck, Alexander, Montgomery, Graziani, and Rommel have attracted a library of their own. The references in this chapter have been confined to events directly bearing on the Middle East.

2. P. Longerich, tr. J. Noakes & L. Sharpe, *Heinrich Himmler: A Life* (Oxford, 2012), 427–36, 461.

3. H. R. Trevor-Roper, *Hitler's War Directives 1939–1945* (London, 1964), 39–43, 52–5.

4. G. E. Kirk, *The Middle East in the War* (London, 1952), 56–78; C. Tripp, *A History of Iraq, op. cit.*, 100–4.

5. G. E. Kirk, *The Middle East in the War, op. cit.*, 78–104.

6. W. W. Harris, *Lebanon, op. cit.*, 193–8.

7. J. McHugo, *Syria, op. cit.*, 108–10.

8. P. J. Vatikiotis, *Egypt, op. cit.*, 347–9.

9. The Holocaust has rightly generated a vast literature. A useful guide is P. Longerich, *Heinrich Himmler, op. cit.*, especially Chapters 20 and 21; see also D. Cesarani, *Eichmann: His Life and Crimes* (London, 2004).

10. T. Segev, *A State at Any Cost, op. cit.*, 310–11.

11. P. Mattar, *The Mufti of Jerusalem, op. cit.*, 99–107; P. Longerich, *Heinrich Himmler, op. cit.*, 675–7.

12. A. Shilon, tr. D. Zilberberg & Y. Sharett, *Menachem Begin: A Life* (New Haven, CT; London, 2012).

13. J. Bowyer Bell, *Terror Out of Zion: The Fight for Israeli Independence 1929–1949, Irgun Zvai Leumi, LEHI, and the Palestine Underground* (Dublin, 1979), 62–3.

14. *Ibid.*, 93–100.

15. I. Levitats, 'Pro-Palestine and Zionist Activities' in *American Jewish Year Book 1943–1944*, vol. 45 (Philadelphia, 1943), 208–9.

16. L. Benedict, 'Reactions to Events Overseas' in *American Jewish Year Book 1943–1944, op. cit.*, 191–2.

17. T. G. Fraser, *The USA and the Middle East Since World War 2* (Basingstoke, 1989), x–xi.

18. S. H. Longrigg, *Oil in the Middle East, op. cit.*, 132–5.

19. T. G. Fraser, *The USA and the Middle East, op. cit.*, x–xii.

6. The United States, the United Nations, and the Future of Palestine

1. *Report to the General Assembly by the United Nations Special Committee on Palestine*, 31 August 1947, Geneva Switzerland (London, 1947), 42. Hereafter *UNSCOP Report*.

2. *A Survey of Palestine*, vol. 1, *op. cit.*, 80.

3. G. E. Kirk, *The Middle East in the War*, *op. cit.*, 333–44.

4. M. Erdman, 'A Tale of Two Nationalists: Parallelisms in the Writings of Ziya Gökalp and Michel Aflaq' in T. G. Fraser, ed., *The First World War and its Aftermath: The Shaping of the Modern Middle East* (London, 2015), 225–42.

5. *A Survey of Palestine*, vol. 2, *op. cit.*, 945–55.

6. M. Jones, *Failure in Palestine: British and United States Policy after the Second World War* (London; New York, 1986), 48–57; W. R. Louis, *The British Empire in the Middle East 1945–1951: Arab Nationalism, The United States, and Postwar Imperialism* (Oxford, 1984), 3–5.

7. T. Segev, *A State at Any Cost*, *op. cit.*, 383–4.

8. G. E. Kirk, *The Middle East 1945–1950* (Oxford, 1954), 197–8.

9. J. Bower Bell, *Terror Out of Zion*, *op. cit.*, 169–74; A. Shilon, *Menachem Begin*, *op. cit.*, 90–3.

10. H. W. Brands, *Inside the Cold War: Loy Henderson and the Rise of the American Empire 1918–1961* (New York, 1991).

11. *A Survey of Palestine*, vols. 1 and 2, *op. cit.*

12. T. G. Fraser, *The USA and the Middle East*, op. cit., 12–20.

13. *Ibid.*, 20–1.

14. T. Segev, *A State at Any Cost*, op. cit., 386–92.

15. *UNSCOP Report*, op. cit.; T. G. Fraser, *Partition in Ireland, India and Palestine*, op. cit., 160–1.

16. J. Bower Bell, *Terror Out of Zion*, op. cit., 229–34.

17. *UNSCOP Report*, op. cit., 9–10.

18. A. Eban, *Personal Witness: Israel Through My Eyes* (London, 1993), 93–106.

19. T. G. Fraser, *Partition in Ireland, India and Palestine*, op. cit., 162–4.

20. *UNSCOP Report*, op. cit.

21. T. G. Fraser, *Partition in Ireland, India and Palestine*, op. cit., 169–70.

22. T. G. Fraser, *The USA and the Middle East*, op. cit., 27–31.

23. T. G. Fraser, *Partition in Ireland, India and Palestine*, op. cit., 173–5.

24. T. G. Fraser, *The USA and the Middle East*, op. cit., 32–4; Z. Ganin, *Truman, American Jewry and Israel, 1945–1948* (New York, 1979), 142–6.

25. L. Parsons, *The Commander*, op. cit.

26. J. & D. Kimche, *Both Sides of the Hill: Britain and the Palestine War* (London, 1960), 86–9.

27. J. Bower Bell, *Terror Out of Zion*, op. cit., 291–6.

28. T. G. Fraser, *The USA and the Middle East*, op. cit., 36–43.

29. G. Meir, *My Life* (London, 1976), 184–7.

30. T. G. Fraser, *Chaim Weizmann*, op. cit., 144.

7. War and Revolution

1. Secretary-General of the Arab League to the Secretary-General of the United Nations, 15 May 1948, in T. G. Fraser, *The Middle East 1914–1979*, op. cit., 68–70.

2. K. M. Pollack, *Arabs at War: Military Effectiveness, 1948–1991* (Lincoln, NE, 2004), 447–55; L. Parsons, *The Commander*, op. cit., 217–47.

3. K. M. Pollack, *Arabs at War*, op. cit., 149–54.

4. *Ibid.*, 15–16.

5. Lieutenant-General Sir J. B. Glubb, *A Soldier with the Arabs* (London, 1957), 89–91.

6. This question is fully examined in: A. Shlaim, *The Politics of Partition: King Abdullah, the Zionists and Palestine 1921–1951* (Oxford, 1990); G. Meir, *My Life*, op. cit., 176–81; F. Klagsburn, *Lioness: Golda Meir and the Nation of Israel* (New York, 2017), 316–19.

7. C. Herzog, *The Arab–Israeli Wars: War and Peace in the Middle East from the War of Independence Through Lebanon* (New York, 1984), 17–21.

8. P. Longerich, *Heinrich Himmler*, op. cit., 724–9.

9. E. Ben-Dror, tr. D. File & L. Schramm, *Ralph Bunche and the Arab–Israeli Conflict: Mediation and the UN, 1947–1949* (London; New York, 2019), 1–31.

10. J. B. Glubb, *A Soldier with the Arabs*, op. cit., 106–38.

11. J. & D. Kimche, *Both Sides of the Hill*, op. cit., 204–5.

12. T. Segev, *A State at Any Cost*, op. cit., 432–5; A. Shilon, *Menachem Begin*, op. cit., 117–31; Eric Silver, *Begin: A Biography* (London, 1984), 97–109.

13. T. Segev, *A State at Any Cost, op. cit.*, 438–41.
14. F. Bernadotte, tr. J. Bulman, *To Jerusalem* (London, 1951), 200.
15. J. B. Glubb, *A Soldier with the Arabs, op. cit.*, 157–72.
16. G. E. Kirk, *The Middle East 1945–1950, op. cit.*, 286.
17. Y. Shamir, *Summing Up: An Autobiography* (London, 1994), 74–5; F. Bernadotte, *To Jerusalem, op. cit.*
18. T. G. Fraser, *The USA and the Middle East, op. cit.*, 51–2.
19. T. Segev, *A State at Any Cost, op. cit.*, 435; A. Shilon, *Menachem Begin, op. cit.*, 131–4.
20. C. Herzog, *The Arab–Israeli Wars, op. cit.*, 99–104.
21. E. Ben-Dror, *Ralph Bunche and the Arab–Israeli Conflict, op. cit.*, 149–67.
22. A. Shlaim, *The Politics of Partition, op. cit.*, 390–98.
23. *Ibid.*, 417–18.
24. T. G. Fraser, *The Middle East 1914–1979, op. cit.*, 78–81; 'The World Factbook, Gaza Strip', *Central Intelligence Agency*, accessed online 7 Jun. 2024.
25. T. G. Fraser, *The Arab–Israeli Conflict* (4th edn., London; New York, 2015), 55–9.
26. E. M. Wilson, *Jerusalem, Key to Peace* (Washington, DC, 1970), 79–83; B. Wasserstein, *Divided Jerusalem: The Struggle for the Holy City* (London, 2001), 176–8.
27. J. Bulloch & A. Darwish, *Water Wars: Coming Conflicts in the Middle East* (London, 1993), 33–57.
28. G. Gillessen, 'Konrad Adenauer and Israel', The Konrad Adenauer Memorial Lecture (Oxford, n.d.).

29. R. Stephens, *Nasser: A Political Biography* (Harmondsworth, 1971), 21–84.
30. *Ibid.*, 85–108; J. Gordon, *Nasser's Blessed Movement: Egypt's Free Officers and the July Revolution* (Cairo; New York, 2016).
31. T. G. Fraser, *The USA and the Middle East, op. cit.*, 61–4.
32. A. Sharon with D. Chanoff, *Warrior: The Autobiography of Ariel Sharon* (2nd edn., New York, 2001), 9–82.
33. T. G. Fraser, *The Arab–Israeli Conflict, op. cit.*, 63.
34. D. Hopwood, *Egypt: Politics and Society 1945–1981* (London, 1982), 37–40.
35. F. A. Gerges, *Making the Arab World: Nasser, Qutb, and the Clash that Shaped the Middle East* (Princeton, NJ; Oxford, 2018), 236–83.
36. R. R. James, *Anthony Eden* (London, 1986), 379.
37. T. Segev, *A State at Any Cost, op. cit.*, 544–7; A. Sharon with D. Chanoff, *Warrior, op. cit.*, 102–9; S. Shamir, 'The Collapse of Project Alpha' in W. R. Louis & R. Owen, eds., *Suez 1956: The Crisis and its Consequences* (Oxford, 1989), 75–100.
38. T. G. Fraser, *The Arab–Israeli Conflict, op. cit.*, 66–7.
39. J. B. Glubb, *A Soldier with the Arabs, op. cit.*, 419–28.

8. From War to War

1. R. Stephens, *Nasser, op. cit.*, 170–2.
2. The Suez Crisis may be followed in: K. Kyle, *Suez* (London, 1991, 2003); K. Love, *Suez: The Twice-Fought*

War (New York; Toronto, 1969); W. S. Lucas, *Divided We Stand: Britain, the US and the Suez Crisis* (London, 1991); M. H. Heikal, *Cutting the Lion's Tail: Suez Through Egyptian Eyes* (London, 1988); W. R. Louis & R. Owen, eds., *Suez 1956, op. cit.*

3. M. Dayan, *Story of My Life* (London, 1976).

4. C. Herzog, *The Arab–Israeli Wars, op. cit.*, 111–40; A. Sharon with D. Chanoff, *Warrior, op. cit.*, 133–53.

5. T. G. Fraser, *The Arab–Israeli Conflict, op. cit.*, 73.

6. *Ibid.*, 74.

7. J. McHugo, *Syria, op. cit.*, 135–42.

8. T. G. Fraser, 'Lebanese Civil Wars (1958, 1975–90)', in G. Martel, ed., *The Encyclopaedia of Diplomacy*, vol. 3 (Chichester, 2018), 1117–24.

9. C. Tripp, *A History of Iraq, op. cit.*, 139–42.

10. G. Barraclough, *Survey of International Affairs 1956–1958* (London, 1962), 373–7.

11. A. Gowers & T. Walker, *Behind the Myth: Yasser Arafat and the Palestinian Revolution* (London, 1991), 9–39; H. Cobban, *The Palestinian Liberation Organisation: People, Power and Politics* (Cambridge, 1984).

12. J. McHugo, *Syria, op. cit.*, 141–3.

13. F. A. Gerges, *Making the Arab World, op. cit.*, 243–83.

14. C. Tripp, *A History of Iraq, op. cit.*, 157–78.

15. T. Segev, *A State at Any Cost, op. cit.*, 652.

16. A. Gowers & T. Walker, *Behind the Myth, op. cit.*, 49–50.

17. The war may be followed in: M. B. Oren, *Six Days of War: June 1967 and the Making of the Modern Middle*

East (Oxford, 2002); T. Segev, tr. J. Cohen, *1967: Israel, the War and the Year that Transformed the Middle East* (London, 2007).

18. J. M. Ennes, Jr., *Assault on the Liberty: The True Story of the Israeli Attack on an American Intelligence Ship* (New York, 1980).

9. The Middle East Transformed

1. 'Principles for Peace in the Middle East', President Johnson, 19 June 1967, Department of State Bulletin, 57/1463, in T. G. Fraser, ed., *The Middle East 1914–1979, op. cit.*, 113–15.

2. Lord Caradon, A. J. Goldberg, M. El-Zayyat & A. Eban, 'U.N. Security Council Resolution 242: A Case Study in Diplomatic Ambiguity' (Washington, DC, 1981).

3. A. Gowers & T. Walker, *Behind the Myth, op. cit.*, 65–91; H. Cobban, *The Palestinian Liberation Organisation, op. cit.*, 43–4.

4. A. Shlaim, *Lion of Jordan: The Life of King Hussein in War and Peace* (London, 2008), 311–40.

5. R. Stephens, *Nasser, op. cit.*, 554–7.

6. T. G. Fraser, ed., *The Middle East 1914–1979, op. cit.*, 184–96.

7. E. Monroe, *Britain's Moment in the Middle East 1914–1971* (2nd edn., London, 1981), 207–19; J. Jones & N. P. Ridout, *A History of Modern Oman, op. cit.*, 132–60; I. Gardiner, *In the Service of the Sultan: A First Hand Account of the Dhofar Insurgency* (Barnsley, 2006); V. Clark, *Yemen: Dancing on the Heads of*

Snakes (New Haven, CT; London, 2010) 78–80; H. Lackner, *Yemen in Crisis: Devastating Conflict, Fragile Hope* (London, 2023); 'Houthi Attacks in the Red Sea: Issues for Congress' (*Congressional Research Service*, Washington, updated 26 Feb. 2024), crsreports. congress.gov, accessed online 28 Feb. 2024.

8. I. L. Kenen, *Israel's Defense Line: Her Friends and Foes in Washington* (Buffalo, NY, 1981), 218–19; E. Tivnan, *The Lobby: Jewish Political Power and American Foreign Policy* (New York, 1987), 66–8.

9. A. Shilon, *Menachem Begin, op. cit.*, 237–40.

10. T. G. Fraser, *The USA and the Middle East, op. cit.*, 92–5; I. L. Kenen, *Israel's Defense Line, op. cit.*, 237–9.

11. K. M. Pollack, *Arabs at War, op. cit.*, 98–105, 478–82.

12. C. Herzog, with a new introduction by Colonel M. Herzog, *The War of Atonement: The Inside Story of the Yom Kippur War, 1973* (London, 1998), 1–12.

13. G. Meir, *My Life, op. cit.*, 356–9; F. Klagsburn, *Lioness, op. cit.*, 620–1.

14. The military side of the 1973 war is covered in: C. Herzog, *The War of Atonement, op. cit.*; K. M. Pollack, *Arabs at War, op. cit.*; A. Rabinovich, *The Yom Kippur War: The Epic Encounter that Transformed the Middle East* (New York, 2004).

15. T. G. Fraser, *The USA and the Middle East, op. cit.*, 103–5.

16. A. Sharon with D. Chanoff, *Warrior, op. cit.*, 306–33.

17. Essential sources for diplomacy in the war are: H. Kissinger, *Years of Upheaval* (London, 1982); H.

Kissinger, *Crisis: The Anatomy of Two Major Foreign Policy Crises* (New York, 2004).

18. H. Kissinger's *Years of Upheaval, op. cit.* and *Years of Renewal* (London, 1999), are the indispensable sources for his diplomacy. See also T. G. Fraser, *The USA and the Middle East, op. cit.*, 113–40; M. Golan, tr. R. G. Stern & S. Stern, *The Secret Conversations of Henry Kissinger: Step-by-Step Diplomacy in the Middle East* (New York, 1976); for the political consequences in Israel, see F. Klagsburn, *Lioness, op. cit.*, 657–61.

19. H. Cobban, *The Palestinian Liberation Organisation, op. cit.*, 58–63.

20. T. G. Fraser, 'Lebanese Civil Wars', *op. cit.*, 1117–24.

10. The Search for Stability

1. J. Carter, *Keeping Faith: Memoirs of a President* (New York, 1982), 277.

2. T. G. Fraser, *The USA and the Middle East, op. cit.*, 141–2.

3. W. B. Quandt, *Camp David: Peacemaking and Politics* (Washington, D.C., 1986), 48.

4. Y. Rabin, *The Rabin Memoirs* (Boston; Toronto, 1979), 308–14.

5. Y. Harkabi, tr. L. Schramm, *Israel's Fateful Decisions* (London, 1988), 80–3.

6. A. Sharon with D. Chanoff, *Warrior, op. cit.*, 355–72, 395.

7. M. Dayan, *Break-Through: A Personal Account of the Egypt-Israel Peace Negotiations* (London, 1981), 1–16.

8. *Ibid.*, 38–54.
9. W. B. Quandt, *Camp David*, *op. cit.*, 146–8, 345–55.
10. J. Carter, *Keeping Faith*, *op. cit.*, 311–13.
11. *Ibid.*, 319–403; W. B. Quandt, *Camp David*, *op. cit.*, 206–58; M. Dayan, *Break-Through*, *op. cit.*, 321–31; for the texts see, *Department of State Bulletin*, 78/2019 (October 1978), in T. G. Fraser, ed., *The Middle East 1914–1979*, *op. cit.*, 170–6.
12. M. Dayan, *Break-Through*, *op. cit.*, 332–55.
13. K. Ghattas, *Black Wave: Saudi Arabia, Iran and the Rivalry that Unravelled the Middle East* (London, 2020).
14. D. Murray, *US Foreign Policy and Iran: American–Iranian Relations since the Islamic Revolution* (London and New York, 2010), 13–37.
15. C. Tripp, *A History of Iraq*, *op. cit.*, 186–214.
16. T. G. Fraser, *The USA and the Middle East*, *op. cit.*, 159–61.
17. A. Sharon with D. Chanoff, *Warrior*, *op. cit.*, 395–402.
18. J. Bulloch & H. Morris, *Saddam's War: The Origins of the Kuwait Conflict and the International Response* (London, 1991); C. Tripp, *A History of Iraq*, *op. cit.*, 215–39.
19. For an overview, see Z. Schiff & E. Ya'ari, ed. and tr. I. Friedmann, *Israel's Lebanon War* (London, 1985); R. Fisk, *Pity the Nation: Lebanon at War* (3rd edn., Oxford, 2001); S. Feldman & H. Rechnitz-Kijner, *Deception, Consensus and War: Israel in Lebanon* (Tel Aviv, 1984).

20. A. Sharon with D. Chanoff, *Warrior*, *op. cit.*, 437–42.

21. R. Fisk, *Pity the Nation*, *op. cit.*, 359–400.

22. A. Shilon, *Menachem Begin*, *op. cit.*, 410–12; A. Bregman, *A History of Israel* (Basingstoke, 2003), 201–2.

23. T. G. Fraser, *The USA and the Middle East*, *op. cit.*, 182–3.

24. T. G. Fraser, 'Lebanese Civil Wars', *op. cit.*, 1117–24.

25. A. Arsan, *Lebanon: A Country in Fragments* (London, 2020).

26. Z. Schiff & E. Ya'ari, ed. & tr. I. Friedman, *Intifada: The Palestinian Uprising – Israel's Third Front* (New York, 1990); D. Peretz, *Intifada: The Palestinian Uprising* (Boulder, CO, 1990).

27. B. Milton-Edwards & S. Farrell, *Hamas: The Islamic Resistance Movement* (Cambridge, 2010).

28. T. G. Fraser, *The Arab–Israeli Conflict*, *op. cit.*, 140.

29. C. Tripp, *A History of Iraq*, *op. cit.*, 244–50; A. H. Cordesman, 'Persian Gulf War' in J. Whiteclay Chambers II, ed., *The Oxford Companion to American Military History* (Oxford, 1999); Y. Shamir, *Summing Up*, *op. cit.*, 217–25.

30. T. G. Fraser, *The Arab–Israeli Conflict*, *op. cit.*, 143–6.

11. The Middle East in Turmoil

1. B. Milton-Edwards & S. Farrell, *Hamas*, *op. cit.*, 78–9; T. G. Fraser, *The Arab–Israeli Conflict*, *op. cit.*, 147–8.

2. A. Shlaim, *Lion of Jordan*, *op. cit.*, 532–46.

3. L. Benedikt, *Yitzhak Rabin: The Battle for Peace* (London, 2005), 163–5.

4. T. G. Fraser, *The Arab–Israeli Conflict, op. cit.*, 153–4.

5. B. Netanyahu, *A Place Among the Nations: Israel and the World* (London, 1993); B. Netanyahu, *Fighting Terrorism: How Democracies Can Defeat the International Terrorist Network* (New York, 1995, 2001); A. Bregman, *A History of Israel, op. cit.*, 254.

6. D. Ross, *The Missing Peace: The Inside Story of the Fight for Middle East Peace* (New York, 2004), 415–59.

7. B. Clinton, *My Life* (London, 2004), 832; D. Ross, *The Missing Peace, op. cit.*, 483–90.

8. E. Barak, *My Country, My Life: Fighting for Israel, Searching for Peace* (London, 2018); A. Bregman, *A History of Israel, op. cit.*, 261.

9. J. McHugo, *Syria, op. cit.*, 174; E. Barak, *My Country, My Life, op. cit.*, 336–42.

10. See B. Clinton, *My Life*, 911–16; E. Barak, *My Country, My Life, op. cit.*, 357–81; D. Ross, *The Missing Peace, op. cit.*, 650–711; A. Qurie ('Aba Ala'), *Beyond Oslo, The Struggle for Palestine: Inside the Middle East Peace Process from Rabin's Death to Camp David* (London, 2008).

11. E. Barak, *My Country, My Life, op. cit.*, 387–8; G. Sharon, tr. M. Ginsburg, *Sharon: The Life of a Leader* (New York, 2011), 345–6.

12. T. G. Fraser, *The Arab–Israeli Conflict, op. cit.*, 162–3.

13. M. Indyk, *Innocent Abroad: An Intimate Account of*

American Peace Diplomacy in the Middle East (New York, 2009), 366–76.

14. G. W. Bush, *Decision Points* (London, 2010), 400–1.
15. T. G. Fraser, *The Arab–Israeli Conflict, op. cit.*, 171–5.
16. T. H. Kean, chair, & L. H. Hamilton, vice-chair, with reporting and analysis by *The New York Times, Final Report of the National Commission on Terrorist Attacks Upon the United States* (New York, 2004).
17. G. W. Bush, *Decision Points, op. cit.*, 226–9.
18. C. Tripp, *A History of Iraq, op. cit.*, 270–6.
19. *Ibid.*, 313–14.
20. Ambassador L. P. Bremer III with M. McConnell, *My Year in Iraq: The Struggle to Build a Future of Hope* (New York, 2006), 40–2, 54–9.
21. G. W. Bush, *Decision Points, op. cit.*, 355–94; C. Tripp, *A History of Iraq, op. cit.*, 277–316.
22. *Ibid.*, 403–6; T. G. Fraser, *The Arab–Israeli Conflict, op. cit.*, 180–2.
23. G. Sharon, *Sharon, op. cit.*, 543–59.
24. T. G. Fraser, *The Arab–Israeli Conflict, op. cit.*, 188–9.
25. *Ibid.*, 191.
26. G. W. Bush, *Decision Points, op. cit.*, 407–10.
27. T. G. Fraser, *The Arab–Israeli Conflict, op. cit.*, 201–2.
28. B. Obama, *A Promised Land* (London, 2020), 625–9.
29. H. R. Clinton, *Hard Choices* (London, 2014), 304–6.
30. B. Obama, *A Promised Land, op. cit.*, 364–6, 633;

H. R. Clinton, *Hard Choices, op. cit.,* 317; T. G. Fraser, *The Arab–Israeli Conflict, op. cit.,* 205–6.

31. T. G. Fraser, *The Arab–Israeli Conflict, op. cit.,* 210–17.

32. J. Bowen, *The Arab Uprisings: The People Want the Fall of the Regime* (London, 2013), 1–10.

33. J. Thompson, *A History of Egypt, op. cit.,* 341–8.

34. T. G. Fraser with A. Mango & R. McNamara, *The Makers of the Modern Middle East, op. cit.,* 261–2.

35. J. McHugo, *Syria, op. cit.,* 203–36; N. van Dam, *Destroying a Nation: The Civil War in Syria* (London, 2020).

36. F. A. Gerges, *ISIS: A History* (Princeton; London, 2016); P. Cockburn, *The Rise of Islamic State: ISIS and the New Sunni Revolution* (London; New York, 2015.

37. 'Peace to Prosperity', *Trump White House Archives* (2020), accessed online 20 Apr. 2021; 'The Abraham Accords Declaration', *US Department of State,* accessed online, 10 Apr. 2021; 'Remarks by President Trump on the Death of ISIS Leader Abu Bakr al-Baghdadi', *Trump White House Archives* (2019), accessed online 20 Apr. 2021.

38. 'Remarks by President Biden on the Middle East', *The White House* (2021), accessed online 23 May 2021; 'Secretary Antony J. Blinken and Israeli Prime Minister Benjamin Netanyahu Statements to the Press', *U.S. Department of State* (2021), accessed online 8 Jun. 2021; 'U.S. Assistance for the Palestinian People', *U.S. Department of State* (2021), accessed online 27 May 2021.

39. 'Fact Sheet: World Leaders Launch a Landmark India–Middle East–Europe Economic Corridor', *The White House* (2023), accessed online 8 Mar. 2024.

40. J. Zanotti and J. M. Sharp, 'Israel and Hamas Conflict in Brief: Overview, U.S. Policy, and Options for Congress', updated 3 Jun. 2024, *Congressional Research Service*, accessed online 16 Jun. 2024.

41. 'Remarks by President Biden on the October 7th Terrorist Attacks and the Resilience of the State of Israel and its People', Tel Aviv, Israel, 18 Oct. 2023, *The White House*, accessed online 30 May 2024.

42. As 40 above; J. Zanotti, 'Hamas: Background, Current Status, and U.S. Policy', 14 Dec. 2023, *Congressional Research Service*, accessed online 27 Jan. 2024; 'The World Factbook, Gaza Strip', *Central Intelligence Agency*, accessed online 17 Jun. 2024.

43. C. Thomas, 'Iran-Supported Groups in the Middle East and U.S. Policy', *Congressional Research Service*, 7 Feb. 2024, accessed online 6 Mar. 2024.

44. C. M. Blanchard, 'Houthi Attacks in the Red Sea: Issues for Congress', updated 26 Feb. 2024, *Congressional Research Service*, accessed online 28 Feb. 2024.

45. 'Statement from President Biden on Passover', 21 Apr. 2024, *The White House*, accessed online 31 May 2024.

46. 'Statement from President Joe Biden on the Hostage Release in Gaza', 21 Nov. 2023, *The White House*, accessed online 30 May 2024.

47. 'Background Press Call on the Humanitarian

Assistance Airdrop into Gaza', 2 Mar. 2024, National Security Council, *The White House*, accessed online 4 Mar. 2024; 'Remarks by President Biden in State of the Union Address', 8 Mar. 2024, *The White House,* accessed online 30 May 2024; 'Statement from President Biden on the Death of World Central Kitchen Workers in Gaza', 2 Apr. 2024, *The White House,* accessed online 10 Apr. 2024.

48. As 40 above.

49. 'Secretary Antony J. Blinken at a Press Availability', 1 May 2024, Ashdod, *Department of State*, accessed online 30 May 2024; 'Press Gaggle by Press Secretary Karine Jean-Pierre En Route Mountain View CA', 9 May 2024, *The White House*, accessed online 1 Jun. 2024.

50. 'Remarks by President Biden on the Middle East', 31 May 2024, *The White House*, accessed online 1 Jun. 2024; 'Joint Statement of the United States, Egypt, and Qatar', *Department of State*, 1 Jun. 2024, accessed online 3 Jun. 2024; 'G7 Leaders Statement on Gaza', 3 Jun. 2024, *The White House*, accessed online 5 Jun. 2024.

12. Conclusion

1. 'The World Factbook, Egypt', *Central Intelligence Agency*, accessed online, 3 Dec. 2020.

2. 'The World Factbook, West Bank', *Central Intelligence Agency*, accessed online 5 June 2024.

Index